The Vicar Calls

*For my father, mother and family, and
for all who heard and read, or will read
the words of the Vicar*

The Vicar Calls

...from the *Parish Notes*, 1968–1982

Rev. Oliver Willmott (1910–1996)

Edited by Michael Willmott
Illustrations by Andy James

Robin John
Willmott

BSP

Michael
Willmott

Acknowledgements

Family and friends	–	for information, and inspiration
Julian Pandya	–	for research
Choir Press	–	for the guiding mind of Clive Dickinson
	–	for the professionalism of Miles Bailey and Rachel Woodman and staff
	–	for typographical care from Fiona Thornton
Readers	–	for their interest
Reviewers	–	for their recognition

First published by Bishop Street Press 2001

ISBN 0-9531802-8-X

Produced by Action Publishing Technology Limited, Gloucester
Printed in Great Britain

Contents

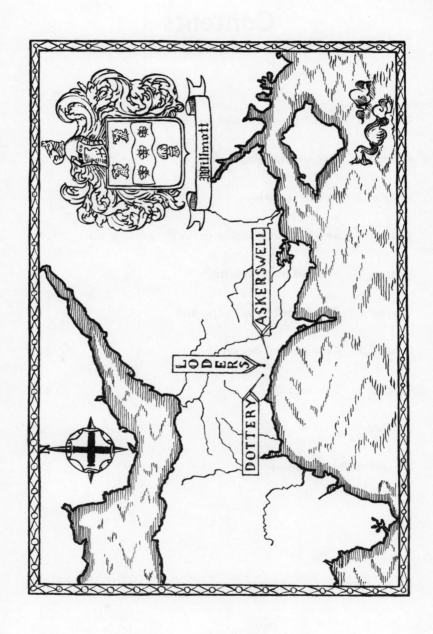

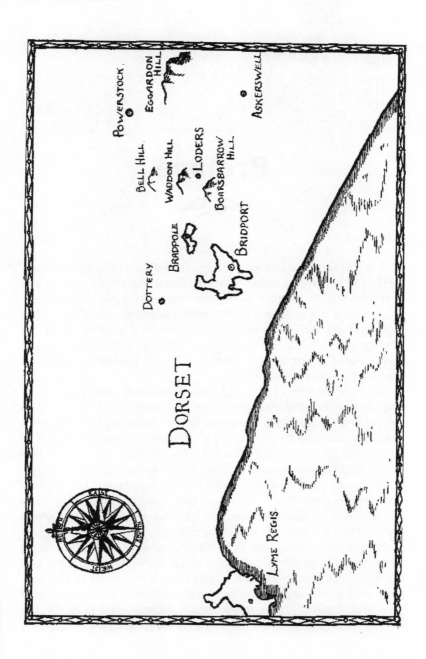

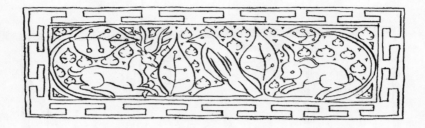

Preface

This is the final volume of a trilogy based upon the *Parish Notes* 1948–1982 of Rev. Oliver Willmott. Since the publication of the first two volumes there have been some changes of emphasis made in the organisation of the eight chapters, though the core material and the style remain very much the same. (Damian Thompson – *The Daily Telegraph* – 'What is amazing about the *Parish Notes* is not their quantity – 750,000 words – but their amazingly consistent quality.')

Yours Reverently 1948–1953 was filled with detail about an English countryside recovering its old ways after the Second World War. It was as if the Vicar in particular, and the parishes generally, wanted to return to a traditional rural stability. The Christmas gift from the Lord of the Manor to all his tenants had been scaled down to two shillings and sixpence plus an orange, as against an order for the family from Harrods, but the custom was maintained. The climax of this settling phase was the Coronation of Queen Elizabeth the Second in 1953, which encouraged a welter of rustic patriotism.

At the same time the signs of the emergent Welfare State were to be seen. After rationing came form-filling, queuing and the National Health Service. Other services, including the railways and buses, water and sewage, changed the patchwork of the countryside. There were teams of men working on the railway-lines, and clearing the hedgerows in the lanes.

Private spending on cars and television meant the hardly perceptible but very real end of a tight-knit rural community. Bingo took over from whist, washing-machines and spin-dryers from fetching and carrying in tubs, and the Vicar inherited a car to replace his bicycle.

Nevertheless, the first phase of the *Parish Notes* had a glow of optimism and stability that continued well into the period of *The Parson Knows* 1953–1968. It was as if the Vicar were getting to know his extended family, and enjoying the process. There was an excitement about sputniks and the Beatles, and life on the move: the Vicar had fallen into his stride, and was enjoying being the centre of his universe. Most of all, he enjoyed his lifelong hobby of collecting information, and sharing it wittily from his editor's chair.

So, what is new about *The Vicar Calls* 1968–1982? The Coronation has mellowed into the Silver Jubilee, and Prince Charles marries Lady Diana. Some readers of the first two books commented on the absence of more personal notes about the Vicar and his family. His own daughter Juliet's marriage nearly coincides with the Prince and his Lady's: it gets equal coverage here. Chapter Five is devoted entirely to such family references – *Vic and his quiverful*.

At first, Mrs. Willmott got scant attention. Then she came in for the same jocularity that greeted the Women's Institute. In the unwritten parts of this book there would be mention of the Christian tenderness that united the Vicar and his wife in his last years.

Then, certain matters of parish organisation began to assume a heavy significance. There was the responsibility for the church-yard maintenance, the planning for new school locations, pastoral reorganisation into team ministries, the closing down of West Milton Church and the selling off of Loders Vicarage. Some of the articles in *The Parish Notes* were lengthy extensions of on-going debates. There has been a ruthless cutting back to the essentials.

The countryside and nature and the weather continued unchanged – *The Diurnal Round*, of *Yours Reverently*, turned into *Of birds, bees, beasts and flowers* in *The Parson Knows*, and now, in the words of Arthur Fallowfield, from the BBC's *Beyond our Ken: The Answer lies in the soil.*

The illustrations by Andy James have changed significantly. At first the endeavour was to establish an artistic mode that corresponded with the style of the writing and the spirit of the content. This led to linedrawings and motifs with a mediaeval/Saxon feel. In *The Parson Knows* the same decorative patterns appear (as they do in *The Vicar Calls*), but there were many more portraits of village characters. In the last book we have concentrated on key features in the Vicar's life – St. John's Church, Frome, Kelham College, the Tudor fireplace at the Vicarage, and so on.

An impression that might emerge is that he was an impressive character, but awkward to live with (see p. 00 the Ayatollah Willmott). Sometimes, all of that was true. He was only human, after all.

He had some strange habits – as we all do. He didn't need nut-crackers for hazel-nuts, and he ate the skin of pineapple, despite, or perhaps because of the quinine, and the prickles. Having been an Army chaplain, he was 'not squeamish', and could deal with non-believers, outsiders and critics. He sometimes met such, on the doorstep, with their rebuff, "Not today, thank you." He still spoke on.

St. John's, Frome, Somerset

Editorial notes

1. The words of the Vicar are in normal type. Any editorial comment is as typed on this page in square brackets [   ].

2. The Vicar's headings have been used where possible: where not, the Editor has endeavoured to make up an appropriate introduction.

3. On pages 270–274 there are some background facts about the period covered by the book, with cross-references to the text where possible.

4. The typing customs of the 1950s and 1960s were not the same as the typing customs of 2001. If there are any anomalies, we apologise. (Whether to add a full-stop after Mr. or a hyphen in a hybrid word was difficult to regularise.)

5. Chapters Four and Five were a nightmare of compression and extraction. Any interested persons may apply to *Bishop Street Press* for the full versions, at 8 Bishop Street, Shrewsbury SY2 5HA. Tel: 01743 343718 with a £5 cheque towards photocopying and postage.

6. The photocopied two volume set of the complete Parish Notes are available at the same address, for £50.

CHAPTER I
Last lap – little and large
~⊙~

As a Christian, Rev. Willmott was staunchly Anglican, with a strong ecumenical bias – Uploders Chapel, and the works of any good people, including non-believers, were important to him. January 1979: 'The Bridport and District week of prayers for Christian unity will include a service at Uploders Chapel ... all who believe in prayer and a united Christian witness are warmly invited to attend.'

As a reporter, he had a voracious appetite for any local scoops, and an eye for matters of national significance. He enjoyed putting Loders on the map. If he had moved on from the *Somerset Standard* to a national paper, he would have been hard put to decide where to apply. His political instincts started with the flavour of *The Daily Telegraph*. He raked it daily for leads for his proliferation of sermons. He enjoyed the literary stability of *The Times*. He never bought a *Guardian*, associating it with strangely-bearded gentlemen in minor posts at Polytechnics, and wild women protesting at Aldermaston. He still quoted from it when it suited his purpose (p. 238 The English pub). He always wrote in sympathy with a strong, outside viewpoint, so long as it coincided with his own.

He might accept the description 'radical Tory'. His icons might have included the unpopular cerebral clarity of an Enoch Powell (p. 19), and the persistent nagging conscience of a Wedgwood Benn. If he were not put off by his accent and his demeanour (in his funny way, he was a snob, and would probably admit it), he might be a Ken Livingstone fan, very quietly. In later years he turned for support to scientists who were still with God – John Polkinghorne (p. 265).

He was naturally punctilious about proper English usage, on paper, and then became broader and broader Dorset in speech: it seeped into him. In life he was an independent, and knew his own voice. He was a permanent, self-determined, backbencher. He had an inner confidence, which may have come from his meditations on the vegetable patch, or his drawings from the udder, or his walks in the Dorset lanes, or whilst slaying an oak. He was always thinking.

In fact, he had no icons. Except the One. (And Savanorola – p. xii *The Parson Knows*). Whether he had studied him or not, he was nearest in spirit to the practical Christian spirit to be found in George Herbert's *A Priest to the Temple* 1652. The latter advised humour as one of the best avenues to God:

'The Countrey Parson is generally sad, because hee knows nothing but the Crosse of Christ, his minde being defixed on it with those nailes wherewith his Master was: or if he have any leisure to look off from thence, he meets continually with two most sad spectacles, Sin, and Misery; God dishonoured every day, and man afflicted.

Neverthelesse, he sometimes refresheth himselfe, as knowing that nature will not bear everlasting droopings, and that pleasantnesse of disposition is a great key to do good; not onely because all men shun the company of perpetuall severity, but also for that when they are in company, instructions seasoned with pleasantnesse, both enter sooner, and roote deeper. Wherefore, he condescends to humane frailties both in himselfe and others; and intermingles some mirth in his discourses occasionally, according to the pulse of the hearer.

Sometimes he tells them stories, and sayings of others, according as his text invites him; for them also men heed, and remember better then exhortations; which though earnest, yet often dy with the Sermon, especially with Countrey people; which are thick, and heavy, and hard to raise to a poynt of Zeal, and fervency, and need a mountaine of fire to kindle them; but stories and sayings they will well remember.'

Twenty-first

The Parish Notes enter their twenty-first year this month. When they began, they were the only parish magazine in the Deanery to be duplicated. Now, thanks to the high cost of printing, most of the magazines are duplicated. We have achieved about the maximum circulation for villages the size of ours – 240 – the number of readers must remain conjectural. Many copies are borrowed, and some circulate all over the world. It is an awesome thought that more copies of this poor little sheet are read in these villages than any other publication, which encourages in us a seemly sense of responsibility.

How true is the saying that editors divide the wheat from the chaff – and print the chaff. The best parish news cannot be published. Yet that which we purvey is sufficiently interesting to cause a stir if the *Notes* do not appear on time. Well, many thanks to all our readers for their unflagging support, to Mrs. Olive Legg, Mrs. Jack Osborne, Mrs. Savage and Mrs. Rhennish for doing the monthly chore of distributing with the zest of sellers of hot cakes; and not the least to the one who does our duplicating, often under domestic difficulty and at a price whose resting quality will be restful indeed, if it can withstand the urge of all prices to escalate.

July 1968

Outposts of Empire

It is very pleasant to get letters from former parishioners of Loders now in far-flung outposts of empire, especially when they contain a cheque for the Church Restoration Fund, as did Mrs. Robin Chater's, from Khartoum. She says: 'I was so very sad to read in the *Notes* of the deaths of Mr. Thomas, Mr. Gale and Mr. Wells. I shall miss dear Mr. Thomas dreadfully, and will never forget his welcoming smile at the door whenever we came back to Loders Church. One can only be thankful his long illness, with all its pain and discomfort, is over.

Charlie Gale was always such a help with Rocket (her horse) and a very good blacksmith, and Mr. Wells always so cheerful

on his rounds. They will all be sadly missed. I am glad you
did so well at the fête. We are in the throes of the Cathedral
Bazaar, which goes on for a year! It is triennial, and I have the
second-hand clothes stall, called 'The Bishop's Boutique'. So
far, since March, we have made £500 and nothing has been
over £4, mostly cotton frocks at 5/-.

I am having such an interesting time with the lepers at the
Church Missionary Society Hospital. They now have 100 inpa-
tients and 500 outpatients, all from the streets of Khartoum.
Some have walked up from the south. None have any money
and just the clothes they are wearing. They have never had
physiotherapy before and we are getting wonderful results at
straightening out hands and feet. They all need special sandals
which protect their toes and Bata factory have given the insoles
free. The Sudanese are terrified of the disease and do nothing
to help.'

Presumably, Mrs. Chater as a qualified physiotherapist is
herself helping with that.

November 1968

The Archbishop in Jerusalem

'When will there be a Confirmation service in Loders?' is a
question that has often been asked in the past few months. It
can now be answered – on Sunday, 26th October, at 11 a.m.
There are frequent Confirmations in the Bridport Deanery to
which our candidates could have been taken, but we like to
save them up to make it worth the Bishop's while to come
here, which works out at once in four years.

The service is listed to be taken by the former Archbishop
in Jerusalem and Metropolitan, Dr. A.C. MacInnes, who is
now living in semi-retirement in The Close, Salisbury. The
Vicar met the Archbishop during the former's short stay in
Jerusalem, and can promise that the candidates will take to
him. St. George's Cathedral and Close is a bit of England
close to the walls of old Jerusalem. Multitudes of visitors
have enjoyed there the spirit of hospitality that the Archbishop
fostered. He was much loved all over the Middle East, and
not least by the Arabs, with whom he could converse
fluently.

Incidentally, his father was Bishop in Jerusalem. That was before Jerusalem acquired the oversight of the other Middle East bishoprics.

February 1969

New Parish Hall at Askerswell

Anybody with any knowledge of the frustrations and delays inherent in any dealings with officialdom will marvel at Askerswell's achievement in getting its hall from planning to completion in eighteen months. One suspects that it needed an ex-submarine commander like Captain Lumby to do it. He was chairman of the building committee and this probably took more out of him than the war at sea.

Here is one instance of what he had to contend with:- When the building was finished and he was in urgent need of the government grant to pay bills and had written and phoned all over the place, and been assured that the matter was receiving attention, he got an official letter containing a postcard, which said, 'Fill in and dispatch postcard the day site work begins'.

One also suspects, if one is knowledgeable about building costs, that the village owes more to Mr. Savage and his family (which helped with the painting) than it will ever know. The price he did it for was obviously his family's contribution to the common cause. Major Evan's public spirit was again shown in his making available the ground for a car park. His decision to lease it for a nominal rent instead of to give it outright to the hall is a wise one, for in the latter event the ground would have passed to the ultimate control of the Charity Commission, and Loders has found to its cost what this can mean. The playing field is not included in the trust deed of the hall, and is likewise free of the Commission.

October 1969

Joseph Fison

The Bishop of Salisbury has sent a donation of £150 from his discretionary fund to the new village hall at Askerswell. This will be appreciated, not for its usefulness alone, but as a mark of the sympathy shown all along by the Bishop for the parish in its struggle to get justice over the old school. The struggle was worthwhile. Without it the new hall would have had nothing from the old school, whereas it has now had £500, doubled by government grant to £1,000. Doubtless the Parish Church Council will now offer an olive branch to the Diocesan Board of Finance – a resumed payment of quota.

November 1969

On the air

Southern Television informed us a few hours before the event that they were proposing to include shots of Loders Good Friday morning service in a religious feature to be shown after the news the same evening. The cameramen were here early on Good Friday and not lacking in energy. They took pictures from Boarsbarrow and the church tower. They caught the congregation filtering into church and gushing out of it. In the service itself, for the sake of the evangelistic element in the broadcast, we endured the distraction of camera eyeing us over as we sang, and even repeated verses for its convenience.

In the afternoon our policeman summoned us to the telephone where a cameraman told us that the pictures were perfection, and what channel they could be seen on. *Southern Television* is not readily available in this region, but many locals saw themselves on the screen that evening, and excited friends from further afield let us know they had seen us. Incidentally, television editors are like newspaper ones: they have a genius for leaving out the really interesting pictures, like that of little Rachel Price hiding from the camera behind her hymn book.

April 1970

Sunday School Festival in Salisbury

The 2,000 children who attended the Sunday School Festival in Salisbury Cathedral included Askerswell Sunday School. They went in a minibus kindly provided by Mr. Garrard and stopped on the way for an appetising picnic lunch prepared by Mrs. Garrard. In the cathedral they added to the diocesan collection the record of their own activities since their formation in 1967. They greatly enjoyed the pageant, whose theme was the

Kelham College, Nottinghamshire

excellence of the Bible and the work of the British and Foreign
Bible Society. What the boys will remember of the service will
be a scholar dressed as an Indian pedlar cycling down the nave
of the Cathedral with a supply of bibles.

August 1970

Adge Cutler and the Wurzels

Askerswell people have their fête safely 'in the bag', and their
Village Hall fund the richer by about £100. The setting of the
Village Hall lacks the attractions of a private garden, but it was
magnet enough to draw almost the entire local population and
not a few neighbours. Bales of golden straw dotted about the
arena made appropriate seats.

Adge Cutler and his Wurzels blared rustic songs out of the
loud-speaker and two lovely nurses on short leave from Bart's
dosed the company with just the medicine for so hot an after-

noon: ice-creams. Providence was at work in other ways as well, for half-bottles of whisky were won by two convalescents who said it was exactly what the doctor had ordered – better than all the sleeping pills. Let it not be thought that the general concern was for stomachs only. A fair pedlar of immaculately typed histories of Askerswell fed the minds, and soon sold out.

August 1970

The strike bug

Loders bells will not be rung for two Sundays. Let nobody think that our devoted ringers have caught the strike bug. The clappers and pulleys of the bells have been taken away for repair.

September 1970

The last of the village policemen

The police station at Well Plot, although a newish building is now officially described as *The Old Police Station*, because Loders comes under an area police service operated from Beaminster and no longer has a police officer of its own. Having had good reason in the past to value its policemen, Loders is pleased that one of the team policemen is occupying the old police station. He is Constable Brian Tufnail, from Poole, and he has a wife and two young children.

February 1971

A coincidence

The sermon in Loders Church on the Sunday before Lent was on the theme of the day, the New Testament idea of love. To show that the idea was not impracticable, the preacher reminisced over the life of Edward King, Bishop of Lincoln, who died in 1910, and yet is still remembered and revered all over that vast agricultural diocese as a saint. After the service a visitor, an elderly lady of great charm, whispered to the Vicar as she went out, 'I was intensely interested in what you said about Bishop King. It was all so true. He confirmed me'.

March 1971

Enemies in Northern Ireland

After the harvests of October, and the fêtes of the summer months, November looks dull. By the time these *Notes* are in readers' hands, All Saints will be past, and a Guy Fawkes Eve social in aid of Loders Village Hall will be but a vivid and pleasant memory. But the great solemnity which two World Wars have given to November is yet to come.

Remembrance Sunday is November 14th. Besides the dead of the World Wars, we shall be honouring those gallant young soldiers and policemen who have been murdered in trying to save Ulster from hit-and-run terrorists. Unfortunately the terrorists are not the only enemies soldiers and police have to contend with. The latter must be finding the terrorists less exasperating than our own knights of the camera and the microphone, who strain out the gnat of a soldier's slightest incorrectitude, and swallow the camel of terrorist perfidy.

November 1971

The miners' strike

A gratifying number of Dottery people attended a Sunday evensong last month and stayed behind afterwards to discuss how to make it easier for the sexton to keep the churchyard tidier now that a considerable part of it is covered thickly with mounds. A general levelling to make it amenable in the growing season to bi-monthly cutting by rotoscythe was considered too expensive. It will continue to be scythed by hand, and the sexton will grapple with the present situation until the end of this season. People who want to keep their mounds will have to trim them, or make some financial arrangement with the sexton to do it. At the end of the season the mounds which have not been tended will be levelled.

The sexton was thanked for his good work in the church-yard; the meeting congratulated itself on having a sexton at all, and voted him an increase in pay of 80%. Somebody piped up that the organist deserved an increase, too and she was promptly awarded 50%. This makes the miners' recent victory look like defeat. Anybody inclined to report the matter to Ted Heath had better tell him, before he gets a coronary, that the increases bring the sexton's pay to £18 and the organist's to £12, both per annum.

March 1972

The Morley Report

The Dean of Salisbury [the Very Reverend Fenton Morley] has agreed at short notice to preach at the Askerswell Festival of Flowers. This is specially good of him. He will have addressed a morning conference at Salisbury and officiated at the cathedral evensong before driving the fifty-five miles to Askerswell.

After the service there will be the fifty-five miles return, for he must be back that night. The Dean is so nice on personal acquaintance that one can almost forgive him for being the author of the *Morley Report*, which townspeople would dub 'famous', and countrypeople 'notorious'. Like Pascall's, the Dean's heart may have reasons that his reason knows not of.

April 1972

Demos

English people once had a reputation for being phlegmatic and undemonstrative. Surely this has been demolished by the present passion for 'demos', of which there seems to be at least one a week. It does not do religion any harm for Christians to 'show the flag' occasionally, and what better time than Easter?

If all who bear the baptismal cross of Christ on their foreheads were to spare their Leader one hour on his triumph day, and attend a service in their parish church, then the churches of England could nowhere near hold them. A simple act like that, costing nothing much in effort, could hit the world harder than a Belfast bomb explosion, and for good.

April 1972

Retiring *Parish Notes* deliverer

Advancing years and indifferent health have prompted Mrs. Olive Legg of Well Plot, to resign from Loders Church Council, and to give up the distribution of the *Parish Notes*,

which she has done since they were first published. The sad
news was conveyed in a letter to the Easter Vestry. She began
attending Loders Church at the age of three. Her whole life
has been bound up with it, and nobody can have served it more
faithfully. She has got the better of so many illnesses in the
past that we do not despair of seeing her in her familiar pew
yet again. Meanwhile, Mrs. Martin Thornton has kindly
offered to take round the *Notes* in Loders. To walk worthily in
Mrs. Legg's footsteps, she will need to do the job leisurely,
having a homely little 'tell' with each customer.

May 1972

Drug addicts

Mr. Sidney Fry of Askerswell found himself in a medical ward
at Weymouth General Hospital after moving a fowl-house.
When the effects of the fowl-house had worn off, he was
disposed to enjoy the enforced rest, and to be confirmed in his
long-held opinion that nurses are the salt of the earth. He
deplored the wasting of their time by the likes of a raving drug-
addict, who was suddenly foisted on the ward, and treated by
the nurses as considerately as though he had been laid low by
a fowl-house.

November 1972

From Loders to the U.S.A.

The Reverend Doctor Martin Thornton of Loders, has been in
the United States, at the invitation of the Bishop of Georgia,
addressing the area conferences of that diocese on 'The spiritual life'. The Bishop's newspaper describes him as 'the noted
English author, teacher and spiritual director, a priest of the
Oratory of the Good Shepherd'. Dr. Thornton is no stranger to
the U.S.A. He has twice been St. Mark's Lecturer at the
General Theological Seminary in New York. He was also
Bohlen Lecturer at the Philadelphia Divinity School.

November 1972

Missionary from South Africa

For your diary: One of the Cowley Fathers, the Rev. James Naters, will be staying a few days in Uploders this month, and has kindly agreed to preach at matins in Loders on Sunday, February 25th, at 11 a.m. In a letter, he says, 'I shall look forward to paying my first visit to your part of the world. If it is acceptable to you, I should rather like to preach a missionary sermon arising from my experience in South Africa.' It is acceptable.

February 1973

The Common Market and Whitsun

A spring holiday separate from Whitsuntide seemed to have no ill effect on Whitsuntide as far as church was concerned. Indeed, church stood to benefit. People came to church for the spring holiday in good numbers, and again for Whitsuntide. At Loders two schoolboys, Alan Read and Kevin Tiffin, braved the treble solo in the Whitsun anthem with pleasing effect.

How long Whitsuntide and the spring holiday will remain separate now that we are in the Common Market remains to be seen. When we were on the spring holiday the continentals were at work, and possibly cursing our perverse ways: when they were on holiday for Whitsun we were at work and cursing them; that is, if we had business dealings with them.

July 1973

Getting the collywobbles

Preachers in churches in holiday areas like ours are apt to get the collywobbles when they discover to whom they have been holding forth, although it is undoubtedly better that the collywobbles should come after and not before the holding forth. The ancient clergyman attending Loders matins the other Sunday was none other than the famous Adam Fox, one time Canon, Archdeacon, Subdean and Treasurer of Westminster Abbey, Doctor of Divinity of St. Andrews, Dean of Divinity and Fellow of Magdalen College Oxford, Warden of Radley College, and Professor of Poetry at Oxford. In his chat with the Vicar after church he said he hoped to come again – if he survived preaching in St. Margaret's Westminster on his ninetieth birthday, which was two weeks ahead.

August 1973

Elizabeth Taylor of Matravers

Miss Elizabeth Taylor of Matravers, died at the age of 79 in Weymouth General Hospital on August 17th, and was buried in Loders cemetery after a service in Church. Unlike the film star with the same name, the circle of those who knew her was small, but their admiration was just as fervent, for it was her achievement to have borne years of physical disability with fortitude and good humour. For one of her healthy and energetic temperament to be so crippled must have been more than irksome. It did not sour her, but made her more concerned for the troubles of others. Her secluded home at Matravers was a place where several learned to re-charge their spiritual batteries.

September 1973

Nationwide

Miss Muriel Smelt put Loders on the map when she appeared in the B.B.C. Television programme *Nationwide*. Few parishioners are aware that she nobly sits in an upper room for hours on end translating books into Braille for the blind. She also has the gift of languages. It is a pity that the television appearance came on without notification in the *Radio Times*, and some of us missed it. Miss Smelt herself was told only about an hour before.

Another connection of Loders, the poet and educationalist Mr. Leonard Clark, appeared recently in a Sunday night religious discussion on B.B.C. television. He had been called as a witness by Cardinal Heenan in defence of the R.C. church's educational record. Mr. Clark is a convinced and convincing Anglican. We trust it is not 'spilling the beans' to say that part of the small fee paid him by the B.B.C. got into the till of the Loders mission sale at Christmas.

February 1974

From Loders to Uppsala

The fact that February is usually a month lacking in church news braces us to brave the possible displeasure of Loders' shy theologian-writer, Dr. Martin Thornton, in mentioning a compliment he has lately had bestowed on him. That great divine of international stature, Archbishop Anthony Bloom, was unable to fulfil an engagement to address a conference of the Church of Sweden in Uppsala in August, and Dr. Thornton has been asked to take his place. He has accepted and will be accompanied by his wife and daughter. Not so very long ago he deputised for another eminent theologian, Dr. William Barclay, in the pulpit of Christchurch Cathedral, Oxford. We must be the envy of many seekers after wisdom in having him on our doorstep.

February 1974

Break-ins

The intruders who broke into Loders Court on April Fools' Day also broke into the church. They broke a small panel of the coloured east window, as if they intended to get through there; then they burst open the doors in the south porch. They prised an alms box, which was empty, off the wall, opened drawers, and bundled all the brass pots and dishes they could find with the brass cross and candlesticks on the altar. The safe, which only contains the modern registers, was untouched. Nothing seems to have been taken. The church was tidied up in time for the Communion service for the clergy of the Deanery at 8.30 a.m.

May 1974

Littery Loders

Loders is getting littery in the region of the church, and it is not the Sunday worshippers who are the culprits, but people with a passion for crisps and Benson and Hedges cigarettes, who throw the empty packets about during the week. In the sylvan glade at the top of Yellow Lane two abandoned mattresses are in an advanced state of decay. Tramps are not likely depositors of these, nor of fish and chip wrappings.

May 1974

Trendier brethren

If variety is indeed the spice of life, then Askerswell's substitute for a fête this year should make exceptionally pleasant the raising of money for the church. Mr. and Mrs. Derek Newall are issuing a general invitation to a summer supper at South Eggardon House. It will be on Friday, July 19th, at 8 p.m., admission by ticket only at £1 a piece. The ticket promises buffet, fruit and cream, and a glass of wine, and shows a benign evening sun dipping behind the Iron Age fortress of Eggardon as the guests regale themselves in the house nestling beneath. Surprising, perhaps, that the guests are not invited to come looking like Iron Agers. Or is that because our trendier brethren look that way already?

June 1974

V.A.T. and *The Notes*

The subscription of some of our readers for these *Notes* falls due in June. We regret that with V.A.T. and rising costs the price from now onwards will have to be twenty pence per annum. If it is any consolation, the price of most parish magazines today is around sixty pence per annum. These are always bulkier than ours but not, we submit, meatier.

June 1974

The Maiden Newton Line

By a happy coincidence another Loders-inspired book by Mr. Leonard Clark on the Bridport–Maiden Newton railway theme, will be reaching the bookshops just as the question of closing the line or turning it into a private railway is hotting up. We have had a preview of the cover, which is most attractive. The illustrations are again by Miss Toffee Sanders, well-known for her portraits in oil and pastel of children and dogs. This book's predecessor, *Mr. Pettigrew's Harvest Festival* was a godsend for those trying to find presents with a local flavour at a reasonable price. *Mr. Pettigrew's Train* could be a further godsend.

March 1975

End of the line

A sad side-effect of the closing of the Bridport–Maiden
Newton railway is that those of us who told the time by the
passing to and fro of the little train now have to look more
closely at our clocks.

Vegetation is already restoring the track to Nature. It was
such a personable little train. It would stop to render assistance
if it saw a sheep on its back. Less prudently it would sometimes stop to let a passenger alight at Loders, where the
absence of a platform and the precipitous step down could
splay him for ever.

June 1975

Tailpiece

Undertakers, or morticians as they like to be called nowadays,
are required by the nature of their profession to meet all situ-
ations with solemn inscrutable faces. We gather, however, that
a local mortician did indulge in the flicker of an eyelid when
he found that the corpse he had been summoned to make a
coffin for and inter was a dog, a St. Bernard, who weighed
fifteen stone.

May 1975

Maragoli to Hong Kong

The reason for the refurbishing of the former Gillespie cottage
in Uploders, now in progress, is that is has been acquired by
two natives of Lancashire, Mr. and Mrs. Clifford Hughes, in
the hope that they may be living in it in eighteen months time.
At present Mr. Hughes is a lecturer in mathematics at a
teacher training college in Maragoli, Kenya. A well-known
hazard of family life in the Services has befallen Major Martin
Burnham, his wife Georgina and their two sons. He took the
late Miss Taylor's cottage in Matravers, and began to do it up,
becoming quite enchanted with West Dorset in the process,
when he was posted to Hong Kong.

June 1975

A village vignette

There was nothing in Yondover to make the passerby think about the mysterious ways of the local planning authority until a magnificent stone shelter, standing on a concrete lay-by, and set like a jewel in a half bracelet of stone walling, appeared, as if by magic, to form the portico of our sorry-looking village hall, which at present is a discoloured hut of wood and corrugated iron, with a moss-infested roof, awaiting a facelift.

When the hut is facelifted, it and its portico will cease to illustrate so vividly what the Sermon on the Mount says about putting a new patch on an old garment. The glazed stone shelter is quite a suntrap. The other day it was truly heart warming to see that devoted servant of the parish, Mr. Harold Brown, working at his papers in it, and conserving energy. The miniature in the jewel!

June 1975

A kingly heart

The new Mayor of Bridport, Mrs. 'Kit' Shirley, is now thoroughly immersed in the multitudinous duties of her office. She does not let them encroach, however, on what she considers her duty as a member of the Loders congregation. By awkward mischance, Melplash Fête falls on the same afternoon as Loders Fête. More surprising, Mrs. Shirley will be opening Melplash Fête and running – in person – her usual stall at Loders! A confession from her, though, that in her woman's body 'does not beat the kingly heart' claimed by the first Queen Elizabeth. This year she feels unequal to making doughnuts all night for her stall. The stall has surprises in store.

August 1975

St. Albans Remembrance

The discontinuing of Remembrance Sunday observance at St. Albans will not tempt any right-minded church to follow suit.

November 1975

Mr. Wykes

Since Mr. Nigel Wykes, of Uploders House, lectured an open meeting of Loders Women's Institute on the River Asker, it is being apprehended by the many, what was known to the few, that we have genius in our midst. The Dorset County Museum is staging an exhibition of his pictures and collection of flowers and insects until March 28th. He is a retired master of Eton College and probably working harder in Uploders than he did at Eton.

March 1976

Up the ladder

The sight of a young lady up a ladder working at the windows of the south chapel of Loders Church might have made an intelligent observer think that the building trade was taking seriously the Sex Discrimination Act. In fact, she was an agent of the British Academy, photographing for the record the five panels of fifteenth century glass, and preparing a report on their condition.

She says they need re-fixing. The panels depict a mitred abbot, St. Barbara holding a tower, St. Dorothy with a basket of flowers, St. Leonard with a manacle in his right hand, and a man with a bag and staff. Lovers of the Victorian stained glass over the high altar will like to know that this agent of the British Academy is not one of those whose artistic sense is offended by it. She thinks it functions well, and is pleasing. And she is an expert.

April 1976

Women's Lib.

Weddings at Askerswell average one in two years. It was a happy coincidence that that of Miss Doreen Miller and Mr. Richard Stephens should herald the spring equinox, on a sunny day, after a long winter of sickness and dying. Miss Miller is one of the family who used to live at Spyway, and, like the Normans, enjoy coming back to Askerswell to services. Her bridegroom is a company director living at North Perrott. The church was well filled with friends, the bells pealed, and Mr. Christopher Miles deputised for the organist. A bocage of exuberant spring flowers marked the place of plighting of troth.

Probably this wedding made history in Askerswell, Women's Lib. is not only in the air. It was in the church. The bride came up the nave on the arm of her mother, who gave her away. Her father is long deceased. Up till now it has been the custom for a male relative to perform the part of the deceased father. But Mrs. Miller was clearly the right person.

April 1976

The Enoch Powell of water conservation

A good muster of the annual parish assembly of Askerswell re-elected Group Captain Derek Newall to the chair. The invited presence of Major Golding, who is the Enoch Powell of the world of water conservation, showed where the interest of the meeting was focussed. Because it was he and nobody else saying that the sustained drought and the failure of other sources made it imperative to take water from Askerswell, the meeting acquiesced, and he was emphatic that the water would be taken from a depth that would not affect the present streams and wells, which were all that some houses had to rely on. The meeting learnt with dismay that the eruption of a new spring which had been hailed with such rapture was actually a leak in the mains.

Mrs. Bellis informed the meeting in a crescendo of indignation that the Women's Institute had protested to the County Council that juggernauts were defiling Parson's Lane and Gipsy Hill, and the Clerk had not the decency even to acknowledge receipt of the letter. Mrs. Bellis quickly subsided when her sense of audience told her she expected of County Council clerks what nobody else did. The meeting agreed that the increased traffic in The Square made halt lines necessary on the four roads converging there if accidents were to be prevented. Somebody complained that the bus was in the habit of leaving a nasty mess of oil where it stabled in The Square. The chairman ruled that it was natural for a bus to do this sort of thing and might suffer if impeded. A churchwarden who knows the transport world inside out said it was the responsi-

bility of the bus company to clean up the mess even if the bus
could not help it.

And so with a chuckle the annual parish assembly dispersed,
having lacked none of its annual entertainment value.

June 1976

The devolution of Scotland, and the delicatessen stall

'As I contemplate the thirtieth of the Loders church fêtes for
which I shall have been responsible, I take it for granted that
the weather will be kind, that the grounds of Loders Court and
the house itself will be as big a draw as ever, and that the devo-
lution of Scotland will not have happened soon enough to
prevent the Bridport Scottish dancers from entertaining us.'

August 1976

Our supersonic lady

On Sunday the eleventh of July the senior member of Loders
congregation, Mrs. Dora Boyd, was in her place as usual at the
early Communion. On Sunday the eighteenth of July she was
there again, looking her same imperturbable and charming self.
But in between, two mighty things had happened. The fourteenth
was her ninety-second birthday and she received the homage of
family and friends. On the fifteenth she flew in *Concorde*, alone,
to Washington, spent four hours there seeing the sights, and
returned to Heathrow in a Boeing. In the air she had covered ten
thousand miles in twelve hours, and some of this had been done
in *Concorde* at twenty-three miles a minute. *Concorde* was
rightly sensible of the compliment she had paid it, and accorded
her V.I.P. treatment from start to finish. At Heathrow she was
taken aboard ten minutes before anybody else.

When they were in the stratosphere, Captain Morley invited
her to the flight deck, where passenger had never trod before,
and she sat with him for ten minutes at the controls. After a
luncheon quite fittingly 'out of this world,' the Captain sent
her down his menu, signed by himself and the whole crew. At
Washington, *Concorde* produced a chauffeur-driven Cadillac
which took her to the White House and everything else she
chose to see. The chauffeur seemed a little too proud of

American achievement, but Mrs. Boyd cured him of that. When he had shown her the Arlington cemetery, etcetera, he asked, 'And what can I show you now?' 'Watergate,' came the swift answer, and Watergate it was.

Conscious of the publicity value of her trip, Concorde had offered a free ticket if they might use it. This she refused. All the blandishments of T.V. and Press also fell on stony ground. It says something for the *Parish Notes* that she did not refuse us permission to print. She might have, dear soul, but she was not asked.

August 1976

Of modern hymns, and sign language

Askerswell Sunday School took part in the archdeaconry Sunday School Festival in St. Mary's Church Dorchester. Mr. Barrow kindly augmented the Garrard transport with his car. The conductor of the service succeeded in keeping all age groups from three upwards, alert and interested. Our children had practised the new hymns, which were sung boisterously with much clapping. Paradoxically, the choir that led the singing did it silently by sign language, for they were deaf and dumb, and the whole service was oriented towards the work done for these unfortunate people.

In his address the Bishop of Sherborne, [Victor Joseph Pike], who heads the diocesan organisation, was at his best. He was fatherly, and dead on target. His retirement, which comes before he expected it, will be felt by none more keenly than by the deaf and dumb. The congregation dispersed feeling that the service had made the effort of attending worth while even on an ultra hot day, and Askerswell were extra glad to have brought purses towards the work among the deaf and dumb.

The usual Open Day at *Orchards* in August had for various reasons to be abandoned. This was regrettable, if only because the off-stage effects in the bible play are usually supremely good, and this year the engineers had devised an electrifying Voice of God to have boomed from an adjacent bedroom window.

September 1976

Of jungle music at Askerswell, and the pound

Why the attendance at the latest gathering of the Askerswell
Parish Assembly should be so large was not apparent until the
chairman, Group Captain Newall, asked, 'Any other business?'
A parishioner rose and made a complaint. That he would be
the last person to sound a discordant note in so harmonious a
village caused the meeting immediately to sense the gravity of
the matter.

Disharmony turned out to be the subject of the complaint.
He had been entertaining friends to dinner against a background of civilised music, when electronic beats and blasts of
jungle music stormed out of the village hall for two to three
hours, and spoilt the dinner. His misfortune had been to
choose the practice night of a dance band who hire the hall for
that purpose. Other parishioners living near the hall said they
too found the practices hard to endure. The husband of an
invalid wife said she dreaded the practices. But not everybody
agreed, including the gentleman occupying the former school
house, adjoining the hall. The chairman of the Village Hall
mollified a sore subject with a reminder that the band practices
brought the hall a useful revenue. It was left to him and his
committee to solve the problem.

The subject of The Pound – not that poor thing whose
decline agitates the media every day, nor that green thing that
makes the farmer see red, but the village receptacle for stray
cattle – was 'brought up' again, as it usually is. Everybody
agreed that in its overgrown state it was no credit to the village.
Somebody urged in the good name of the parish that the board
proclaiming it *The Pound* be taken away, and then visitors
would not know what it was.

The meeting dissolved, leaving The Pound in the suspense
it is so used to, but we have since noted signs there of a cleaning up operation. Actionwise, parish assemblies may be
sluggish things, but they leave their trail occasionally on somebody's better nature.

October 1976

Burglaries

Burglars broke into four Askerswell garages and the Village Hall on a Saturday night, abstracting batteries and wirelesses from the cars, and money from the Hall electricity meter. The stolen objects may be recovered, but it will take the parish a long time to recover its pride. As one lady said, it was the vulgarity of the occurrence that hurt. When she chose to settle in the parish she assumed it was above that kind of thing.

October 1976

The Lebanon

Before she started on a fortnight's tour of the Middle East, Miss Mona Edwards, a pillar of Loders Church, whispered that although she would not be returning to England until the second Sunday in October, which is Loders Harvest Festival, she hoped to be in time for the festival evensong at 6.30 p.m. and might the service end with her favorite hymn, 'The day thou gavest Lord is ended,' to which, of course, the answer was affirmative, although when once we sang, 'The darkness falls at Thy behest' the lights went out.

At the moment Jerusalem is tolerably quiet, but the Lebanon is erupting again, and we hope the hotel in Damascus that was hijacked was not Miss Edwards'. If it was, then perhaps she had the satisfaction, of seeing the hijackers hanged in front of the hotel. She is all for a firm hand with terrorists. Anybody inclined to bet on her being at Loders Harvest Evensong need have no qualms about his money. She is not a subscriber to the view that it is better to travel hopefully than to arrive.

October 1976

Accident at sea

Mr. and Mrs. Reginald Brill, of the Loders Arms, braced themselves wonderfully to the shocking news that their twenty-eight-year-old son Robert had died in an accident at sea. Mr. Brill had just finished a letter to him when the news came.

Robert was chief officer of the motor ship *Temple Inn*, and on
the company's short list for promotion to captain. He had a fall
in the cargo hold and died on 19th Oct. The ship was diverted
to Accapolco in Mexico to land the body, which was later
cremated in Mexico City. The ashes are to be scattered in the
sea off Plymouth Sound. He leaves a widow, Valerie, in
Plymouth, but no children.

* * * * *

The late Robert Brill, First Officer of the motor ship *Temple
Inn*, was virtually a stranger to Loders, but this could not have
been inferred from the memorial service held by the wish of his
family in Loders church. As he died in an accident at sea off
Mexico, and was to be cremated there, the coffin-stool on the
chancel step supported only a posy of flowers from his mother.
There was a sizeable congregation, including the father of his
young widow, who had flown with his wife from Rome, where
he is medical attache to the Australian Embassy.

The Chief Engineer of the *Temple Inn*, and most of the
cadets of Robert's apprentice class, were also present. The
service was a deeply moving one. It began with *Eternal Father
strong to save*, continued with the Crimond setting of the
twenty-third psalm, and concluded with *The day Thou gavest
Lord is ended*.

November–December 1976

The Queen's Silver Jubilee

Loders has beaten Askerswell to it in having a meeting about
the Queen's Silver Jubilee. Mr. Ronald Price, chairman of the
parish council, presided over a meeting of twenty parishioners,
which for Loders is a large number.

There is to be, of course, a special religious service, a
competition for the best decorated house, and souvenirs for
couples married in the parish in Coronation Year (1952) and
still living in it, most of the events to be paid for by a house-
to-house collection and money-raising functions, although the
main financial object will be the Queen's Jubilee Fund.

A perusal of the church marriage register for 1952 has

shown that there were five – Chater–Scott; Churchill–Read;
Jones–Tucker; Gill–Greening; and Hansford-Peckham. But
none of these couples lives in the parish now.

February 1977

World Wildlife

Some of our small boys are members of the Bridport Cub
Scouts, which are led by our Mrs. Diana Wrixon, of
Boarsbarrow. They have lately won a shield for raising £101 in
two years for the World Wildlife Fund. Their moneymaking
schemes included a nature-trail at Loders, and a 'sponsored
silence,' which sounds a good thing in this noisy world.

Farmers' wives generally are renowned for their thriftiness,
and Diana is no exception. She has her twenty-four boys
collecting ring-tops of cans towards a kidney-machine for
Bridport Hospital, and selling jam-jars at a penny each for
their own funds.

February 1977

Miss Bowyer and Jacques Cousteau

The regular Sunday morning congregation at a village church
may, and certainly does at Loders, contain members distinguished in their various vocations. But, oddly, it is sometimes
a dear little old lady exuding the air of Cranford's Miss Matty
who has done the valorous things and had the hair-raising
adventures.

Miss Mary Bowyer, who has long attended Loders church
with her friend Miss Hannah Hancock, is one such. The Great
War impelled her to do what we thought only boys did: she put
up her age, and became a nurse on the hospital ship *Britannic*.
On its way through the mine-infested waters of the Aegean to
pick up wounded from the beaches of Gallipoli, the *Britannic*
was sunk with the loss of 21 lives. Miss Bowyer was fished out
of the sea by a destroyer.

In Athens some benign British official gave her £1 for a refit,
and she spent the rest of her war helping with the appalling
casualties at a base hospital in France. But she had not finished
with the *Britannic*. Last summer the French underwater

explorer Commander Jacques Cousteau examined the *Britannic* and found that it had been torpedoed in the hull. He made a film of it.

Later he advertised in the *Times* for any survivors of the Britannic to contact him. Sixty years had elapsed since the ship sank, but the former Miss Shiela Macbeth, now the 84-year old Mrs. Mitchell (whose husband is 91) responded, and was taken down to the *Britannic* by Cousteau in his famous diving-bell.

It turned out that there are now only nine survivors of a crew and nursing staff of 1000. Cousteau laid on a dinner for them the other day at the Russell Hotel, Bloomsbury, and our Miss Bowyer was one of the nine. The dinner was sumptuous, she said, but she could not satisfy Miss Hannah's curiosity as to what exactly it consisted of. Carlyle should be turning in his grave and repenting his reference to 'ancient virginity tripping lightly to matins'.

March 1977

Country footpaths

Our Yoga enthusiasts may like to know of a less strenuous and more Christian way of keeping fit. Our Footpath Liaison Officer for Loders, Mrs. Jessica Dunn, is, to quote her, 'very anxious that everyone should appreciate the considerable network of attractive public footpaths and bridleways within the parish boundaries'. She is arranging a series of walks during the summer to which everyone is invited. The first is on May Day, beginning at *The Crown*, Uploders, and covering about 4 miles.

April 1977

The Queen's Silver Jubilee

The stump of the dead Victorian jubilee elm was a magnet that drew the patriots of Askerswell on a March Saturday morning to the point where the road from Dorchester divides towards the church and The Square. Beside the stump was a young horse chestnut to commemorate the jubilee of the second Queen Elizabeth, which Mr. Geoffrey Bellis had begun the planting of, and the youngest members of the oldest family in the parish, Linda and Diana Marsh, were to complete. The chairman of the parish assembly, Group Captain Newall, told the company what they were there for, and then gently directed the filling in of the hole with a silvery spade, and the trowelling-in of daffodil bulbs by the little girls, who were given the trowels as a memorial of the occasion.

A proud beholder of the spectacle was Mrs. Monica Bartlett, the senior of the Marsh family. The Group Captain invited the company to consider beautifying with shrubs and flowers the triangle of ground which the spreading chestnut tree will be gracing. The company then slowly filtered into the welcome warmth of the drawing-room of Court Farm, where they were plied with coffee and cakes at twenty-five pence a cup, which was prodigiously cheap, with coffee nearing £4 a pound. Grateful thoughts focussed on Mr. and Mrs. George Bryan for their hospitality, and for giving the jubilee tree.

* * * * *

We celebrated the Queen's Silver Jubilee happily and fervently without breaking any heads or windows, though Mr. Horace Read thought a Union Jack had been stolen from the exuberant exhibition of patriotism on his front lawn. The line of young people who lay across the road not a mile from the *Loders Arms*, ready to die for the Queen, quickly resurrected when Dennis Gibbs got out his car to see if there was a fish-and-chip shop open anywhere.

The Askerswell Jubilee Cricket Match up on the Dorchester road amused two eighteen-a-side teams representing all the seven ages of man, and women of course, in the lawful fashion one would expect on a field kindly lent by Mr. and Mrs. George Bryan. The old coconut matting from the church enjoyed its promotion to service between the wickets, and tripped more players than it had worshippers. A horse-box functioned as a pavilion, only, and tea and shelter from the occasional shower was to be had there.

On the playing-field down in Loders the cricket was between ladies and gents, whose appearance and antics, being characteristic of neither, amused the crowd even more than the

preceding sports had done. The daughter of a retired diplomat
was thrown into the nearby river: she got out, and threw in the
nearest naval officer she could lay hands on, which is not at
all unladylike these days.

By contrast, the Village Hall, the domain of the Women's
Institute for the afternoon, was a model of old-world decorum.
Madam President bade the Vicar invoke a blessing on the children's tea, which looked enough for the parents as well, and
it finished with a distribution of Jubilee mugs, and prizes for
the sports and fancy-dress winners.

The heights of Eggardon on that chilly evening could not
compete for the Askerswell barbecue with the comfort of
Major & Mrs. Gordon Hall's great barn near the church, so it
was held there. Sitting on bales of straw, the company did
justice to chicken and sausages being fried by a bunch of rosy
wenches without. Cider and beer washed it down, and outsize
cream meringues, and cheese, kept it down. Jubilee Crowns
were given to the children. The Loders barbecue was a sober
affair of hot dogs and beefburgers under a tree in the park.

Our Jubilee Church Services were well attended, and the
Guides camping at Boarsbarrow lent colour to the Loders
service by parading to it. Sir Denis Laskey held the attention
of young and old from his diplomat's viewpoint of the Royal
Family. We must have been a safe-looking lot, for he thought
fit to give us an anecdote of the Suez crisis, and there were no
international repercussions afterwards.

A shadow was cast over the Jubilee of the older inhabitants
of Dottery by the sudden death at 56 of Mr. Charles Barnes,
who was farming at Melplash. He was the eldest son of the late
Mr. Charles Barnes and Mrs. Frances Barnes, of Bilshay. The
later, who is 87, and only lately downstairs from a severe
illness, insisted on attending the funeral at Melplash. Although
'his sun had gone down while it was yet day', the theme of the
service was very properly thankfulness for his sterling qualities and cheerful nature. One hymn was *When all thy mercies
O my God my wondering soul surveys* and the other the harvest
hymn *Come ye thankful people, come*.

Melplash has been turned into a dual purpose church. A third
of it is partitioned off for worship, and the rest used for secular
gatherings. There were about two hundred mourners at this

service, so the whole building was in use. It was odd to look up from the hymn book and see 'No smoking' on the wall.

April–July 1977

Modern communications

Loders bells were heard in Woking as they rang for the Queen's Jubilee. If you find this hard to believe, consult Mr. Jack McDowall. He held his telephone to the open window while talking to his sisters in Woking.

July 1977

Mindless bingo

The newly formed Loders Entertainment Committee must be well pleased with the first-fruits of their labours. Despite unhelpful weather, the old-time dancing has been attended fort-nightly at the Village Hall by a nucleus of some twenty enthusiasts, and there was hope that the end of February might show a preference for whist over the mindless bingo.

The jumble sale was a great success. Not much to sell had come in beforehand, and the promoters were worried, but on the morning of the sale, table after table had to be set up to cope with the incoming goods. Customers were lined up at the hall door an hour before the sale began, and it took £63 for the Committee Fund.

Mr. Plows is proving an efficient Publicity Officer. He discovered that one of his neighbours at High Acres, Mr. Sidney Nash, makes a hobby of landscape painting, and is possibly better still at painting posters. These, posted strategically about the village are attractive and even enticing. The striking reds and blues of the lettering would seem to indicate that politically Mr. Nash is neutral. But note the white background.

March 1979

Hope deferred

No sooner had Authority decreed that our dustbin-emptying was to be stepped up from one a fortnight to one a week than our dustmen showed who were the real authority by striking and doing no emptying at all. Our response was more civilised than that of the cities, whose name is the root meaning of 'civilisation'. No heaps of festering garbage in our streets. Like the antennae of snails, the dustbins appeared in the hope that the dustmen might appear also, and when the latter did not, the former mostly withdrew, leaving the streets unsullied. But not the air. The ungodly stinks issuing from some chimneys showed what was happening to some of the garbage.

The only strike that could upset the countryside would be one of the ice-cream men. The times of their arrival at the appointed halting places are engraved on some hearts like Calais on Mary Tudor's. Come wind, come weather, they failed not. Their ice-cream was deliciously warm in the sub-zero air. And their progress reminiscent of the game of musical chairs. Nice tunes like *Greensleeves* or *Brahms Cradle Song* are the modern version of the Pied Piper's pipe. They stop abruptly when a customer is being served, and resume where they left off.

Hats off to the ice-cream men!

March 1979

Of snowdrops and Egon Ronay

A lovely spring morning brought a crowd of friends to Mrs. Doris Rudd's bungalow at Mangerton Green for coffee and bring-and-buy to help the Diabetic Children's Association, which received the gratifying sum of £48.30. The snowdrops were even more stimulating than the coffee, and that was a remarkably good brew.

It will interest friends of Mrs. Rudd's younger daughter, Alison, to know that *The Salad House*, which she took over at Chichester, has made its mark. Egon Ronay dined twice there, unknown to the management, and put it in his latest *Good Food Guide*. The launching of the Guide is to be at the London Savoy. Alison is one of the five chosen to present their own specialities for this occasion.

April 1979

Of white weddings and zimmers

The wedding at Loders Church on May 5th of Miss Valerie Johnston, of Lower Ash Farm, Dottery, and Mr. Peter House, of Lower Beerlands Farm, Whitchurch Canonicorum, was white in more than one respect. As the bridal party emerged from church, they were confettied by a swirl of snowflakes, and the photography which is usual there had to be done in an interlude of repentent sunshine outside *West Mead*, where the reception took place. This did not dim the jollity of the occasion: after last winter, snow on midsummer day would surprise nobody, farmers least of all.

At church there was a very homely touch: as the bells paused in their pealing, and the organ trumpeted *Here comes the bride*, and the great congregation rose with one accord, there came instead down the central alleyway the maternal grandfather of the bride, Mr. John Huxter, aged 87, straight from sick bay at Lower Ash, and propelling himself along with a zimmer.

If zoom were to be the root of zimmer, it would be surprising, for the zimmer is not suggestive of aerobatics or motor racing. Willing hands accelerated him to the front pew. With grandfather comfortably installed, the ceremony could proceed.

June 1979

Barbara Hepworth

The weather just managed to be kind for the Diocesan pilgrimage to Salisbury Cathedral. Mr. Sidney Barrow's little Sunday School from Askerswell found themselves part of a mighty army at the children's service on the Saturday. The children formed a crocodile that moved round the exterior of the cathedral twice – the advancing head almost catching up with the retreating tail.

On the Sunday, Powerstock and Loders filled a sumptuous forty-seater coach. After lunch on the green near the Chapter House, they inspected the exhibition in the Cathedral, with special attention to John Whyte's great picture, and then found themselves engulfed in the congregation of six thousand for the pilgrim service. This was terrific, with great blasts of organ and trumpets. It was also a test of endurance: an hour and a half of standing, with barely room to breathe.

At the age of 82, Mrs. Monica Bartlett of Matravers emerged fresher than most. So did Mrs. Beryl Bell. Outside, to the south of the west front, the Army, for so long a part of Salisbury Plain, had staged an exhibition. Their theodolites enabled the youngsters to get a very close view of the top of the 404-foot spire.

Unwittingly the Army also did much to improve Barbara Hepworth's piece of surrealist statuary, which normally has this plot to itself. In military company it now looked like a piece of advanced military equipment. On its own it is apt to strike the beholder as a new kind of railway signalling apparatus. It is Barbara's idea of the Crucifixion.

July 1979

The pollen count

Mr. Michael Savage, elder son of Mr. & Mrs. Tony Savage of Askerswell, has been in the press and on television in connection with the 'pollen count', which helps Britain's three million sufferers from hay fever and asthma. He is chief medical laboratory scientist at St. Mary's Hospital, Paddington. He operates an ingenious air trap on the hospital roof and takes the daily reading under a high powered microscope. Paddington would seem the unlikeliest place to fish in for pollen, but it is caught there all right – on sticky slides.

September 1979

Epitaph

The late Canon Adam Fox was one of those giants of learning that once made the Anglican clergy the wonder of the world. For five years he was also Professor of Poetry in the University of Oxford. When he stayed with his niece Eleanor in Bridport he liked to attend matins at Loders. She recently attended the unveiling of a memorial to Canon Fox in Poets' Corner, Westminster Abbey. She was sorry that the Dean of Westminster had declined to put on the memorial the epitaph her uncle himself had suggested. And what was that? 'Gone to earth'.

November 1979

The Vicar and Karl his cousin, Longleat

Catching!

By the time an observant visitor has got from Matravers in Uploders to the railway bridge in Loders he will have concluded that the inhabitants are a thrifty lot. Offers for sale pepper the route – Mikkimugs, surplus garden produce, dried cow dung, beds and breakfasts. The other day two small boys sat near the railway bridge, a jar beside them and a notice, 'Water creatures for sale'. It seems that either water creatures are not in demand, or sold out. The notice now reads, 'Cat for sale'.

* * * * *

One of the two small boys mentioned in our last issue as sitting beside the road with a jar and a notice saying, 'Water creatures for sale', stopped the Vicar as he was passing the other day and said, 'I hear you have been writing about me: maybe one day I'll write about you'. An embryonic fisher of men we hope, thinking of his own parish magazine!

November–December 1979

Cambodian Famine Relief

The *Blue Peter* programme on television inspired a sudden effort in the Bridport area to help Oxfam's work of relieving famine in Cambodia. Mrs. Sally Miles, whose home is not yet clear of the effects of the Loders flood, put on a bring and buy sale at short notice in Loders Village Hall, with the help of Dionne Aubrey of Askerswell, and raised a very creditable £200. When emergencies arise it is fitting that free-lance parishioners like Mrs. Miles should emerge from the pool of public compassion to grapple with them.

December 1979

Retirement

The Lord Bishop George Reindorp of Salisbury retires next year. It is fitting that his dynamic ministry should end with a bang, not a whimper. His operation IMPACT, reaching its climax in 1981, is aimed at confronting non-committed Christians in every parish of the diocese with the need to be committed, and the first salvo was his letter, read in every church on the first Sunday in Lent.

March 1980

The Man from the Ministry

Askerswell Village Hall is in good shape. The minutes recorded the tribute paid to Captain Michael Lumby on relinquishing his ten years as chairman. He had raised £750 by running the football competition and had lent money interest free for the building of the hall. (He was just the chairman for the building of the hall: when the Man from the Ministry came to inspect the proposed site, it was already up, and legitimately).

July 1980

Ripping Yarns

Loders Women's Institute gave their neighbours a pleasant evening of a different kind and in the process added £70 to their Village Hall Improvement Fund. The main item was a play in a relaxed Victorian atmosphere so well done that it might have come straight from the BBC's *Ripping Yarns*. The theme was the attempted murder in an old ladies' home of the oldest inmate by another inmate. We saw our Nan Balfour, the ninety-seven-year-old victim, making a speech after a severe throttling by Valerie Nash, the would-be murderess. All the speeches were clearly spoken and near word-perfect. We could do with more of this sort of entertainment.

September 1980

An end to hot meals

Meals at Loders School, like those of other Dorset Primaries, have ceased to be hot, and to be dispensed by Mrs. Ernest Crabb, the officiant in this capacity for sixteen years. While the children munched sandwiches and looked on, one of the managers, Mrs. Nick Prideaux, presented Mrs. Crabb with a handsome battery-operated clock, on behalf of the school, and flowers. The children cheered. The headmaster said Mrs. Crabb had served the school for longer than either he or his staff, and was held in affection and respect by several generations of pupils.

October 1980

State visit to Tunisia

On her triumphant state visit to Tunisia, her majesty the Queen did not forget the cemetery where many heroes of the North African campaign were buried, including two VC's. The Last Post was sounded and Binyon's ode recited:

> *They shall grow not old as we that are left grow old;*
> *Age shall not weary them, nor the years condemn.*
> *At the going down of the sun and in the morning,*
> *We will remember them.*

November 1980

Home at last

St. Candida's, the house of that name in Askerswell so christened by a former owner from Whitchurch Canonicorum and credited with a history going back to the Domesday Book, is now the home of Colonel Reg Edwards, his wife Ann, and their son Richard who is at Loders school. They took over from Miss Harrison, who moved some months ago. Colonel Edwards is still serving in Germany. His lady says she has had eighteen homes in her twenty-five years as an Army wife, and is glad to be settled, especially in so friendly a village.

November 1980

Tradition

Askerswell Church was full for its Carol Service. A full moon and a fine night following much rain seemed to bring every-body out, and many of them had not forgotten to bring torches to help them read the carol sheets in the candle light.

The rector remembered to thank the Women's Institute for their solo carols, and their accompanists, but clean forgot to read out a message of remembrance and goodwill from Frank, husband of the late and much lamented Faith Garrard, which would certainly have been reciprocated by the congregation. A copy of the new English bible inscribed to her memory, has been given to the Sunday School. This would doubtless be approved by the BBC religious affairs correspondent, Gerald Priestland, who said, 'I would vote for the alternative services book; I would read the New English Bible: but I would use the Book of Common Prayer, and the King James Bible.'

January 1981

Prince Charles and Princess Diana

The wedding of the Prince and Princess of Wales showed little sign of having 'caught-on' in our locality until the eve of the great day, and then the flags and bunting relegated to cupboards and attics after the last royal occasion came blinking into the light of a glorious day. The splendid royal insignia that appeared on doors which considered flags 'non-U' looked as if they had come from the Jewel House in the Tower of London. Their owners derived extra delight from telling admirers they were Woolworth's.

The bells of Askerswell made the welkin ring quite early. A

full team of six ringers raised them, rung them in rounds only, and lowered them, in a twenty-five minute serenade which was most effective. In the afternoon the village hall was the focus of attention, which transferred to the *Spyway* barbecue in the evening. Grown-ups waited on the children at tea outside the hall, and then tried to demolish, without success, all the delicacies spread out for them within. Commemorative mugs were given to the children.

Loders ringers aligned their activities with the arrangements of the not-too-distant *Loders Arms*. Having rung an afternoon fanfare, they adjourned to the bounteous tea organised by the hostess of that hostelry on the car park that conveniently adjoins the highway. The concluding fanfare in the evening fitted in with the period of half price drinks at the same hostelry, which was a magnet to the bibulous for miles around.

Meanwhile Uploders was not asleep. There the barbecue at *The Crown* was the magnet. That hostelry was so crowded within and without that those living nearby went home and fetched their own chairs. *The Travellers' Rest* are too respective of reverend ears to be specific about what went on there, but it was their way of expressing loyalty to The Throne. We note with pleasure that the ingenuity which went into the *Loders Arms* float in the Bridport Carnival won a prize.

September 1981

Of allergies, and parsons

Reginald Loveless, of Dottery died in Bridport Hospital, aged 80, and was buried in his mother's grave in Bridport cemetery. He seemed to be allergic to parsons. When the Vicar called, his answer was, 'Not today, thank you,' as to the milkman or the baker. He was a bachelor, abrupt in manner, but esteemed by his workmates at Brit Engineering as an upright, reliable character.

To the Vicar's surprise, he left instructions for a funeral service with hymns in Dottery church. To the Vicar's greater and happy surprise, the good neighbour who took him meals said he was a daily reader of the Bible. He was on safer ground with the Bible than with some of today's clerics.

February 1982

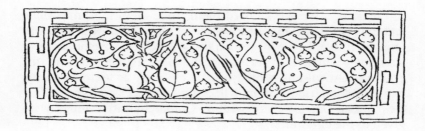

CHAPTER 2

The unchanging year

Like Francis Kilvert and Parson Woodforde before him, Rev. Willmott seemed to have infinite time to compose the most beautifully honed statements about the commonplace. *Yours Reverently* (p. 126) claims he had 'the rhythm of the year'. In September 1974 he wrote, 'the evenings are getting in, and autumn is gently ousting summer'.

In this chapter the extracts have been selected from the months of the year over the whole period. Really, the *Parish Notes* are a celebration of years lived communally, where everyone counted. The social whirl may have needed more deep spiritual input. It was on offer – but, in the English way, accepted spasmodically. At least, it was a community living in broad harmony.

Loders Midnight

Last year's experiment of beginning the Loders Midnight Service at a quarter to twelve on Christmas Eve was quite successful, and will be repeated this year. In some respects 'The Midnight' has more appeal even than harvest. Fifteen minutes before 'The Midnight' begins, the church may be empty. Then from the outer darkness people begin to troop in, to the light and warmth, sometimes whole families, united from the corners of the kingdom, and back in the church of their childhood. The lights go out, leaving only the flicker of the altar candles, and the little coloured lights on the Christmas tree.

In spirit we are at the cave of Bethlehem, with the Babe whose birthday it is, and every time the lights go up we sing him the songs of Christmas.

December 1968

Christmas

The dark days before Christmas go on getting darker until December the twenty-first. Then, imperceptibly, light takes over, and the days go on lengthening till June the twenty-first. For centuries before Christ, men celebrated the winter equinox with feasting. The early Christians were good psychologists. They did not try to abolish the feasting. They made December the twenty-fifth the official birthday of Jesus Christ (when light had triumphed over darkness) and focussed the equinoctial feasting on that.

To think only of feasting ourselves at Christmas would be pagan. In this corner of Dorset we have long practised a means of giving Him His present first. The children of Loders School will be giving a Christmas concert on Friday, Dec. 10th at 5.45 p.m., and this will be followed immediately by the mission sale, whose proceeds go to that work which Jesus obliges all disciples of His to support.

On the following Tuesday the school will be joined in church at 2.45 p.m. by parents and friends for the annual carol service. Here the collection will be for the children of soldiers killed on duty in Ulster. Finally, the choir will be carolling in Uploders on Monday the 20th, and in Loders on Wednesday the 22nd, and collecting for the Children's Society. The carol service at Askerswell will be on the Sunday before Christmas at 6.30 p.m. A carol will be sung by the Women's Institute choir, at their own kind suggestion.

December 1976

Carol-singing

Doing good is not invariably pleasant. But Loders Choir seems to find their annual carol-singing in aid of the orphan children increasingly so, which may be due in some measure to the general welcome they receive and the hospitality of those kind souls who entertain them.

On the Uploders expedition the Choir sang at the cottage of the oldest inhabitant, Mrs. Beatty Clark, whose ninety-first birthday it was. Coming in, as she bade them, was easier said than done, and coming to terms with the ceiling was difficult for the taller members of the party. But get in they all did, and the grand old lady regaled them with birthday cake and sherry, with the help of Mrs. Taylor and Mrs. Dennett. At Uploders House the hostesses, Mrs. Rust and Mrs. Sanctuary, had gathered their neighbours to hear the carols. They then plied the whole company with hot sausages and mincepies, and the homemade wine for which that corner of the Lord's vineyard is justly famed. As the carollers passed Upton Peep they recalled, with a pang, the hospitality of its former occupant, Mrs. Lenthall (now at West Mead Hotel); but some of them were to have the pleasure of meeting her and her family at the midnight service.

The Loders expedition got off to an excellent start at the Court. They were invited to a firework display postponed from Guy Fawkes Day. Fortified by mulled claret and hot dogs, they moved into the hall. The children's party with them made a pretty picture sitting all up the grand staircase. The party and the choir sang the carols together. At Miss Mona Edwards' the choir sang to the hostess, and to the neighbours she had asked in, while the punch was aheating. She was naughty in her own adorable way, for she liked the carols, and kept the choir at them by the simple expedient of making the punch take a long time to heat. They, knowing that she is a perfectionist, were unaware of the compliment in the reluctant punch.

Tired, but very happy, the choir at last reached the Vicarage. Here it was their turn to make a pretty picture, the youngsters sitting on the floor in the warmth of a volcano of logs in the Tudor fireplace, with the elders radiating benevolence on them from the settle. And the collecting boxes yielded a useful £15.1s.3d. for the less fortunate children.

January 1970

Sinners or saints

This lengthy report of Christmas now ends with the perambulations of Loders Church Choir. The Uploders tour ended pleasantly, first with soup in the courtyard at Uploders House, then with solid nourishment in Mrs. Rust's drawing room. There it was told how nervous some of the senior citizens are in opening their doors in these days of muggery and violence. One lady who had got her door unbolted in fear and trembling said, with relief, 'Ah, it's only the sinners'. Well, the sinners collected nearly £26 for the Children's Society.

January 1975

Christmas services

Falling on a Sunday, Christmas Eve had a Sabbath calm about it that was conducive to worship. The appeal of the carol service at Askerswell surprised everybody. By 6.30 every seat in the church was occupied and the congregation must have numbered more than the entire population of the village. It was good to have new residents, and their families – home-for-Christmas – blending with the old. Members of the congregation read the lessons. The organist, Miss Thelma Record, was in sparkling form for the carols and the congregation responded. By a lucky coincidence Mr. Michael Savage had staying with him a New Zealander, Mr. Maurice Connell, a professional singer, who gave two delightful solo items. A collection of over £20 cheered the churchwardens.

The scene now moves to Loders. By a quarter to midnight rain was teeming down and half a gale was blowing on Boarsbarrow. But the church filled as usual, and in the candle-lit calm the old carols were sung, and one hundred and twenty six of the congregation made their communion. The collection topped £21.

How versatile is our English weather. By nine o'clock on Christmas morning the air had a springlike quality, and the family of the faithful, drawn from far and near, were at Dottery in the little 'iron church' (as Vicar Edersheim called it) to greet the heavenly birth. Back at Askerswell the communicant congregation was undiminished by the mammoth attendance of the night before, and derived an appropriate family flavour from the presence of the Sunday School, two of whom, at the end of 'O Come all ye Faithful', presented a visitors' book for use in the church.

By eleven o'clock the sun was shining so strongly through the windows of Loders Church that the east end petitioned the west end to turn off the heating. The church had filled a second time within twelve hours, this time for the family service. Instead of a sermon, the Sunday School sang carols by the Christmas tree on the chancel step. One was the Loders carol to the accompaniment of recorders. As the children left the chancel they took with them packets of sweets given by the Mothers' Union and wrapped by Mrs. Olive Legg. Some of them were called back for prizes for good attendance.

January 1973

Christmas at school

None of the blackouts that we half expected in the lead-up to Christmas came to pass, and even the petrol situation did not prevent the remotest members of the Loders congregation, Mr. and Mrs. Parham, getting to church from their home in Weymouth. The festivities began as usual at school, with the children's concert and mission sale. The old building seemed to be bursting at the seams, with performers and audience on top of each other. When somebody remarked to one of the new mothers that conditions would be better if the new school building materialised she answered surprisingly that she adored the school as it is. This seemed to be the general feeling, for when Mrs. Willmott began her speech with a reference to Loders School as 'the best school in Dorset' she was loudly applauded.

The children's concert was a version of Ancient and Modern, with the modern coming first in the form of *The Charleston* and ditties such as *When you took a penny single you could hear the bell push jingle*. The ancient was of course the Christmas story, beautifully done, in clothes devised by Mrs. Price. She, the headmaster and staff, the performers and donors, were thanked by Mrs. Willmott. Within two hours of starting, concert and sale had made £60 for the church overseas.

January 1974

Ringing in the year

The blizzard that hustled the old year out did not prevent our ringers getting to Askerswell and Loders towers to perform the campanological ceremonies associated with the changing of the year. New Year's Eve was also the Sunday after Christmas. Four people managed to get to Loders Church for early Communion, and a dozen for matins, when they sang carols unaccompanied, and even managed a descant for *The first Nowell*.

January 1979

Counter-attractions

Lieutenant and Mrs. Christopher Hill are arranging a hockey match for the morning of Boxing Day on Loders Playing Field.

It will be ladies versus gents. It is not officially described as
comic, but may well be. The story that the Cattistock Hunt
fear it as a counter-attraction to their Meet, and want to buy
it off, is not well founded.

December 1977

Comic hockey

The Comic Hockey Match on the morning of Boxing Day
came up to the best expectations of the promoters. At the time
appointed to begin, two sets of beansticks suggesting goal-
posts, and an odd assembly of people seemingly sleepwalking
the morning after the night before, were the only indications
of the fun and fury that were shortly to splash all the water out
of the playing field at Well Plot, and bring the law-abiding
residents of the council estate to the chinks in their bedroom
curtains.

As the morning wore on, more and more players arrived and
took up the game, but the signal for it to become riotous was
the arrival of the three Miss Laskeys, in football shorts,
bearing a jeroboam or two of cider with a petrol flavour. One
of the more respectable of the male players (known to his
admirers as 'Cuddles') said that until then he had thought the
Girls of St. Trinian's were a figment of somebody's hyperten-
sion. On the business principle that what you cannot beat you
join, he switched to the female side. He had his own whistle,
with which he deftly countermanded the blasts of the referee's.
The females say they won five four, but nobody else does.

As the tattered remnants of the battle moved off to *The
Crown*, to the steaming hot punch of their imaginations, the
Cattistock Hunt came into view, making for Hillway Copse
nearby. The laudable object of the Hockey Match, the incen-
tive to get the players out of bed before sundown on Boxing
Day, had been to raise money for the Village Hall. But collecting boxes were not much in evidence, and had they been, most
of the spectators were keeping out of reach behind curtained
windows.

January 1979

The Ringers' New Year's Eve Supper

Loders and Askerswell Ringers have revived the tradition of a supper together which began at Mrs. Harry Legg's years ago. On New Year's Eve, having rung at Askerswell and then at Loders, they repaired to the parlour of the *Farmers Arms*, where Mrs. Maddison and a few lady helpers kept up an unfailing flow of roast pork and other delicacies from kitchen to dining-table. The merit of this kind of celebration is that it appealed to the young lady ringers, which the old 'Out In' did not.

Captain Harry Crabb in his post-prandial speech reviewed the activities of the year, and told everybody what he thought of them (his views on this occasion being somewhat mellowed by the refreshment taken). He thanked the ladies who had waited on them, and commended Mrs. Maddison on undertaking such a thing as this when she was waiting to go into hospital.

By this time it was nearing midnight, so the company went again to Loders tower to ring in the new year. They were the first to sing, *Happy Birthday* to Cynthia Newberry, one of their number, who was born on January 1st.

January 1979

New Year frolics

A new team, namely Mr. Stevens and Mr. Bellis, took over the running of Askerswell's New Year Party, to give Mr. George Bryan, Mr. Donald Marsh, and other hard-worked veterans, a rest. The new boys excelled with so little apparent effort that it could well be they have had previous experience. There was a good turn-out of parishioners of all ages. Dances to the music of Mr. Hirst's band, expanded now to three performers, were relieved by games, and lavish refreshments.

As so often happens in life generally, an item that fell into the programme accidentally is the thing everybody recalls most pleasurably now. The band struck up a seductive Spanish air. Askerswell people are not notably cosmopolitan, or given to fandangos and tarantellas, but Mrs. Bellis is. She took the floor. It was a blessing nobody was up to joining her. She whirled and strutted and pirouetted with authentic Latin abandon. The audience gasped in awe, and felt fortunate indeed to have her as president of their Women's Institute.

Thanks to a kind donation of £10 from Mr. Alexander, the hire of the band did not figure in the expenses. Mr. Alexander is not an active member of the church, but he seems well versed in the principle of tithing. His kind of offering was a tenth of the £100 he had lately won on the football draw which helps to finance the Hall.

February 1975

Relaxing leather-workers

The only snag in Mr. Derek Tiffin's prosperous leather business in Uploders is that it is too sedentary. To give him and his lady more exercise, he has presented a table-tennis table to the village hall, which they use when they can spare the time. Mr. Tiffin says that anybody caring to join them is welcome. Good to have the hall put thus to another use.

February 1975

Taking life as it comes

Snow, ice and gales were the background of last month's *Notes*, and so it stays as these are being written. Farmers are famous for grumbling, but those who had to get their milk to the collecting point through snowbound lanes had good reason. Nobody envied them their job. Some of them even grumbled cheerfully and resourcefully.

Take Raymond Crabb for instance. Smishops Lane in Loders was the main artery for his milk and Steve Newberry's as well. It was like a skating rink. In the dusk of a nasty day he and his man were gritting it with sand they had got from somewhere. The tiniest of his four daughters, and the next up, were augmenting this with soil they were digging out of the bank on either side. 'We must take life as it comes,' was Raymond's remark to a sympathetic passer-by.

February 1979

Brownies' Outing

The Loders Brownies celebrated the new year exactly to their own taste by going to a pantomime at Weymouth. They went in a coach with any of their parents and friends who were able to accompany them. There are pantomimes and pantomimes, some not at all fit for children. This one, *Snow White and the Seven Dwarfs*, was so exactly what they wanted that Brown Owl might have vetted it for the occasion.

February 1976

Winter Wedding

'Black Janiveer' in Loders was lighted and cheered by a joyous wedding. The bride was Linda Newberry, of Post Farm, and the bridegroom Martin Legg, of Loders End, which is the new name for Court Cottages. He is a net machinist, but like his late father has a flair for farm work and is high in the esteem of those farmers who have found him a ready help in trouble. Linda is a hairdresser, in personal appearance an inducement to the ill-favoured to make her their beautician. She is also a blessing to Loders church in being a skilled and dependable ringer. Her fellow-ringers heralded her procession to, and recession from, the service with campanological fanfares. Choir and organ led a large congregation in the singing, some of whom could only find seats under the painters' scaffolding in the Lady Chapel.

The wedding-feast laid on at *West Mead* by Harry, the bride's father, was a model of ungrudging hospitality, enjoyed by everybody except perhaps himself, who was off his oats and drank only two glasses of Guinness, looking as if he needed Oxo. All former fathers of brides in the company felt for him. The greatest tribute to his generosity issued from that other Harry, the ringer. Full of his favourite 'gin and pep', he could only say, 'Caw lummee'. Bride and groom will not be obliged to leave the parish, as most young couples are. They are housed in one of the Boarsbarrow cottages, near the Vicarage.

February 1980

The Shrove Tuesday Social

The Pancake Day Social at Loders Hut was a financial and a
social success, and was lucky in the weather, for it was on the
evening before the blizzard. The Hut was filled to capacity. As
guests arrived they were cheered by an unwonted gust of warm
air, and the sight of a buffet up to the ceiling. They knew,
without asking, that Mrs. Charlie Wilkins was ministering to
the inner man. She lived up to her reputation.

The schoolmaster, Mr. Ron Price, made his debut as M.C.,
and with the aid of the Burton accordionist, Mr. Hirst, soon
had the games and dancing going with a swing. Every age
group except the tiny tots was represented. Grandparents and
parents were as happy as the youngsters. In the pancake race
it looked as if the ringers would win, but they fell foul of the
female asbestos throat. Ringer Harry Crabb's throat does not
take kindly to hot potions. He was left gaping while Mrs.
Willmott swallowed a red hot pancake, and won for the choir.

March 1969

Golden Weddings

The proverbial 'little bird' whispered to the Vicar that Robert
and Adelaide Twyman, of Bradpole, have their Golden
Wedding coming up on 28th March. Genealogy is not one of
his hobbies. For years he had been content to know 'Addie' as
a delightful little woman with a great love of Loders church
who walked up from Bradpole week by week to put flowers in
the Ladye Chapel until deterioration in health stopped her.

She was a doer-of-good by stealth, and he reverenced her
shyness by never asking her questions. Neither did he ask
anybody questions about her – until now. There was no reason
to suspect that she had a husband, and his excursions into the
Loders marriage register had never registered her entry with
him, although it is there. He suspected that she might be a
member of the Paul family, because she showed some of their
endearing characteristics. This has been confirmed. In
congratulating Addie and her spouse on the joyful coming
event he prays he may not have fallen from grace in her sight.

March 1982

Lent

At the weekly divinity class in Loders school the Vicar was talking about the season of Lent now upon us, and lasting till Easter. He asked what fasting was, and to his surprise a forest of hands shot up. 'Yes?' said he to one boy. 'Going on hunger strike' was the answer. This was not what he expected, but it showed how strikes can become a way of life, even with small children.

Some hands remained up, so this time he asked a girl what fasting was. 'Slimming', came the answer, and the remaining hands dropped. So to this sample of contemporary youth fasting meant either going on hunger strike or slimming. But deep down they knew the Christian meaning. 'What would it be if you gave your ice-cream money to help feed a starving boy or clothe an old woman in India?' 'Fasting' came the answer in chorus.

And there is the difference. The hunger-striking of the fanatical I.R.A. prisoner, and the slimming, are self-centred. Fasting is self-denying, something given up for others. The naked and the starving are not the only ones in need. What about God, starved of our love, and even our attention? All the time we have is His gift to us, and how little of it we are ready to give Him! Lent is a time to put this right.

March 1979

Mothering Sunday

Our three churches kept Mothering Sunday in their own characteristic way. In Askerswell the Sunday School brought offerings of flowers to the altar at the beginning of family service, and distributed them to the congregation at the end of it. In Dottery little Angela Johnston waylaid the congregation as they left church, and gave them paper baskets of primroses.

In Loders Mrs. Willmott's congregation were happily surprised to be joined by old friends from Weymouth, the Noblets and their friends, who filled two pews. After service the children went through the village leaving their bunches of flowers at the homes of senior citizens. They did it to a background of thunder and lightning, and dodged the heavy showers.

April 1979

Spring drama

The dramatic talent lying dormant in some of the house-wives of Loders was awakened by Mrs. Latta to an entertaining purpose when she produced a comedy at the group meeting of local Women's Institutes at Loders Hut. The Hut was filled to capacity, the 'eats' were edible in a high degree, and such was the warmth that W.I. members from neighbouring villages who had come muffled to the chin against the legendary cold of Loders Hut were soon peeling off their mink and sealskin.

The Loders ladies who took part in the play were Mesdames Taylor, Wilkins, C. Newberry, Wells, Read and Osborne. *Her best foot forward* was the title of the comedy. Is it too much to hope that gentlemen may also be allowed to feel its tonic effect while it is still potent?

April 1969

Good Friday and Easter

The outlook for Easter is not promising at the time of writing. We are in the grip of unseasonal cold. Some of us are still afflicted by winter ailments. All of which does not mean that Easter Day cannot, therefore, dawn in a manner becoming the Queen of Seasons.

Our climate is full of surprises. And anyhow the real joy of Easter, the Resurrection of Jesus Christ, is nothing to do with the weather. Easter should be of special comfort to us this year. Death has severed so many precious friendships, and Easter is the guarantee of their knitting up again on Canaan's happy shore.

If we bear this in mind, the duty of communicants to make their communion, and of all Christians to join in the family worship of the risen Christ, will turn out to be more of a plea-sure than a duty. But before the crown, the cross. We shall not feel the triumph of Easter if we do not enter into the shame and seeming defeat of Good Friday.

April 1969

May Fair

The event of last month was the May Fair in Loders School. It brought together both young and old and was a pleasant way of raising over £72 for the school fund. It also entailed a game of hide and seek with the weather. For the crowning of the May Queen and for the maypole dancing, all in the playground, a thunderous black cloud skulked around, but did not drop any rain. When the assembly moved indoors to the stalls, down came the rain. When a return was made to the playground for the fancy dress, out came the sun.

The May Queen is elected by the children. This year she was Jane Crabb. Her attendants were Rosalind Crabb and Tessa Hyde, and her page was John Wrixon. Mr. George Bryan, of Askerswell was archbishop, and did the crowning. The May Queen got something her Majesty Queen Elizabeth the Second did not get from Dr. Fisher at her crowning – a paternal kiss. George knew he was better at this than at speechmaking, which he left to his wife, who did it to perfection. All present enjoyed themselves except, perhaps, Mrs. Olive Legg, who looked ill as she watched the dancing and later collapsed and was rushed from school to hospital. To the general relief, it was only a severe fainting fit and she was home an hour later.

One had only to look at the American with the camera who was filming the crowning and the dancing with huge zest to discover who was enjoying himself most. He is Dr. Bennett, Professor of English at the University of New England, who with his wife and five daughters, is here on a sabbatical leave, and staying awhile at Uploders House.

June 1969

May Fair – ten years on

The bad weather on the day after the Loders May Fair, getting worse on each succeeding day, made the sunshine and warmth of the day itself look miraculous, having regard also to the nasty weather that preceded it. A large crowd lined the school field, and watched with the awe that only child-play can inspire as the May Queen and her retinue processed to the throne, where Mrs.

Kathleen Shirley crowned her with the grace and eloquence of a good archbishop. Sophie Kennedy-Martin was the Queen, Lucy Kinchin, Susan Cousins and Penelope Scadden her ladies-in-waiting, and William Anderson her page.

Thereafter, the interest switched to the maypole-dancing, and finally to the fancy-dress parade. In a community where blood relationship is reckoned down to cousins three or four times removed, it is imperative for the headmaster to secure judges who cannot be accused of nepotism. Sometimes this is a headache. But not this year. Opposite the school is a cottage belonging to the Vicar of the Bray of the famous song. And the two churchwardens of Bray happened to be there on holiday. They might not have enjoyed the maypole dancing had they know that they were to pick the winners of the highly competitive fancy-dress. Their choice was not disputed. But they are kindly men, and they were relieved to know, that all the competitors got a prize, the head also being a kindly man and a diplomat. The stalls did a roaring trade. This year there was an extra one run by our Women's Institute as their offering to the Year of the Child.

June 1979

The coffee morning

The coffee morning at *The Croft*, Uploders, gave the curious the opportunity to see the new home of Mr. and Mrs. Shaw (which they entirely approved of), and raised the highly satisfactory sum of £80, with possibly more to come, for the chapel re-decoration fund. The cooler weather confined most of the happy chattering folk to the house, where the Brownies beguiled them with competitions. Mr. J.F. Morris rightly guessed, How many lentils ? and Mrs. Chainey, The length of the string ? Mr. Revett of Maiden Newton found the answer to Where did the puppy bury his bone ? One stallholder was heard to day: 'Isn't this a typically English scene – everybody talking, and nobody listening?'

May 1976

Youth Clubs

A youth club is meeting in Loders Village Hall on Monday nights with Mr. Price, Mr. Prideaux, Mr. Morris and Mrs. Dunn as its leaders. Mr. Price collected them by the simple expedient of writing to Loders children who attend Colfox School. Thirty children attended each of the first two sessions and amused themselves at table tennis, chess, darts and records. A County youth organiser looked in on them, was impressed by their good behaviour and murmured something about grants for equipment.

Meanwhile the local Brownie pack under Mrs. Price and helpers caters for the girls of primary age. They have just had their Easter-egg race down Boarsbarrow Hill. The eggs are hard-boiled in coloured water and painted. Little survives the rough road to the bottom, but as the egg decreases the fun increases. This year's winner was Tessa Hyde, and Mrs. Willmott rewarded the competitors with chocolate eggs.

April 1975

Youth and Age

Waking up to the realisation that they had not had an annual meeting for three years, Loders Ringers suddenly decided to have one and Captain Harry Crabb decreed that it should be in the playroom of his hostelry, *The Crown*, with the landlord thereof kindly acquiescing. He was re-elected captain, and nominated Tower Warden by the Vicar, who remarked on the good fortune of both Loders and Askerswell in having their bells fully operational every Sunday with teams of young and old of both sexes.

April 1976

Easter Joy

Twin notices outside the Bridport United Reformed Church proclaimed, one, 'Jesus lives', and the other, 'Coffee 10p today'.

May 1979

Happy Easter

Everything conspired to make this Easter one of the happiest
we remember. The Confirmation service on Palm Sunday had
created thirty-four new communicants, and most of these were
making their first communion on Easter Day. Our three
churches, lovingly and skilfully decorated, looked their very
best in the morning sun, and most of the new communicants
had parents and godparents kneeling beside them. Several
whole families were present, giving a family feeling to the
whole service. In all there were two hundred and nine communicants.

May 1974

Easter bells

A band of ringers collected by the Master Ringer of the
Diocese, the Rev. Roger Keeley, rang a peal of 'Kirkstall
Delight Minor' on Loders bells on April 20th. It was
conducted by Mr. Brian Woodroffe, consisted of five thousand
and forty changes, and took three hours and eight minutes to
ring. The time was a Saturday morning, and the flag of St.
George proclaimed Easter from the tower top. The church
ladies were giving the floral decorations a face lift for Low
Sunday, tennis was in play at the Court, and several other
people were about. It is safe to say they all enjoyed the music
of our deep-throated bells dancing a measured tread with six
expert campanologists.

May 1974

Good causes

Our contribution to Christian Aid was £83.40. The Lent boxes
from Loders produced £16.31 for the church overseas. The
nature trail in Loders run by the 1st Bridport Cub Scouts
raised £16 for the World Wildlife Fund. The coffee morning
held in the Bridport United Church schoolroom made, with
donations, £91.41 for the interior decoration of the Uploders
chapel. What was raised for Help the Aged is well known;
what for the mentally handicapped, the Scouts' minibus, and

the Loders Ringers we do not know, but seldom in local history can it have seemed that so much was owing to so many by so few.

Our Loders friend Mr. Aldridge is a spontaneous and cheerful giver to good causes, but even he seemed to have lost his sprightliness of step on his dogwalk after a fortnights' bombardment by good causes. It should not be beyond the wit of man to stagger the good causes. Like manure, they are tolerable when well spread, but offensive in a heap.

June 1976

Male preserves

Congratulations to Mr. and Mrs. Peter Foot, of Purbecke Close, Uploders, on a son, Jonathan, born in Bridport Hospital on 10th May. They have preserved the Close's character as a men-only sort of place. This is their fourth boy, and the Close's eleventh. It has no girls. But it bids well to become a girl's paradise when the boys grow up.

June 1976

Morris dancers

A pretty sight brought bank holiday traffic to a halt and customers streaming out of *The Crown* where New Road meets Old Road in Uploders (the Uploders of Mr. Kenneth Allsop). With a fine disregard for the modern world, a band of Morris dancers, in gay hats, black breeches, with knees gartered with jingling bells, were performing the ritual of the old Teutonic sword dancers – only with staves instead of swords – to the lilting music of fiddle and accordion. They had come all the way from Sussex, performing wherever they sensed a welcome, seeking alms for their sustenance, and conceding that third class riding, in a minibus, is better than first class walking.

Their next stop was to be *Spyway*. The traditional green dragon collected the alms. You had to brave his champing teeth to put your piece down a neat hole in his gullet. He ate so much that he fell down dead. The burly Master of the Dance besought the fairest damsel among the spectators to give the

Mothers' Union

dragon the kiss of life. She obliged. While he was reviving, all
the other dancers hopefully fell down dead. When they
revived, it was to find that they had received the kiss-of-life
vicariously, through the good offices of the Master of the
Dance, who had not been dead.

June 1975

Tea on the Vicarage lawn

A sunny afternoon sandwiched between two dull ones brought
a crowd of Mothers' Union members to Loders Church for the
Deanery Festival. The church was gay with flowers in the
Mothers' Union colours. Yellow seemed to predominate. It
being General Election time, an intelligent visitor could have
inferred that the sympathy of the church was with the Liberals.

The Vicar of Bradpole took the service, the Vicar of Loders preached, and the Vicars of Burton, Allington and Bothenhampton were in attendance. Mrs. Tiltman was at the organ.

Tea was a colourful affair on the Vicarage lawn. Loders is famed for its teas. The justice that had been done to these was later apparent in the chairs, some of whose feet had sunk well into the lawn, hard though the lawn was, and took some pulling out.

July 1970

Eyes on Wimbledon

The first of the bungalows to be built on the site near Mr. Jack Ellis in Uploders is now the home of Mr. William Stratton and his wife Rhoda. They were watching the Wimbledon tennis when the Vicar called and had the grace to turn it off without appearing too anxious to turn it on again.

July 1975

Treasure at Piddletrenthide

The evening chosen by Mrs. Shirley Foot for the Askerswell treasure hunt was the first dull and wet one after a long sunny sequence. The hunters thoroughly enjoyed themselves despite this. Mr. and Mrs. Holloway won the first prize, and Mr. and Mrs. Hemmings the second. A good supper at *The Poachers*, Piddletrenthide, ended the hunt. The journey home was less eventful than might have been expected.

July 1978

'The Loders Loonies'

'The Loders Loonies' made their first appearance in the Loders firmament at the Women's Institute birthday party in the Village Hall, and left such a trail of glory that we hope it may not be their last. They were Mrs. Dunn (Director), Mrs. Morris, Mrs. Bell and Mrs. Hampson. Mrs. Taylor, famous in the past for her Dorset monologues, was in orbit again, this time with an absorbing collection of her own reminiscences.

Miss Smelt, the senior member, cut the cake made and presented by Mrs. Wells, the president, and it was washed down with sherry. An odd thing is that we ourselves are intent on modernising our Village Hall when the guests on this occasion from neighbouring W.I.'s were saying how refreshing it was to be in an unsophisticated, countryfied, Village Hall.

July 1974

Summer wedding

Loders Church was the setting for another delightful 'village wedding' on June 8th. This time the bride was Paula, daughter of Mr. and Mrs. Basil Leigh, of New Road Farm, Uploders, and the bridegroom Dr. Sureshchandr Keetarat. Incidentally, they got to know each other when they were on the staff of Yeovil Hospital. Dr. Keetarat is now at a hospital near Peterborough.

The weather was kind and sunny after a bout of uncertainty, and the lupins bordering both sides of the churchyard path, in all their glory, made a floral guard of honour. Flowers inside the church, deftly set in a few strategic places by a friend of the bride, were highly effective. The bride entered the church to the pealing of bells and Purcell's *Trumpet Voluntary*, and left to *The sound of music*. A marquee at New Road Farm housed the reception, which was notable for friendliness and informality.

July 1974

Open gardens

This year is turning out to be one of the driest of the century. Our gardens were like powder until the thunderstorms of late June turned it back into soil. Things are growing again, and the people of Askerswell are hoping that their gardens may be at the peak of perfection for the open afternoon on Sunday, July 14th. This year the proceeds will go to the Women's Institute. The rain will also be filling out the raspberries and late strawberries for the summer supper at South Eggardon House on July 19th. We hear that the tickets for this are selling well. There is to be no entertainment other than that of eating a delicious meal in congenial surroundings on a balmy summer evening. Practitioners of the art of table-talk may be able to show that this is all the entertainment a good dinner needs. Ordinary mortals will relish what Mr. Sidney Fry calls a 'a darned good natter'.

July 1974

One church, one faith, one Lord

There is a hymn whose every verse ends with the line, 'One church, one faith, one Lord'. Naughty theological students have been known to parody this and sing instead 'One church, one fête, one lawn'. Gift days and even football pools are more up-to-date methods of raising money for church repairs, but the old fête still merits the mild ridicule of Punch; and given a fine day, a pleasanter way of making money for a good cause has yet to be devised.

July 1971

Tug-o'-war

On Saturday, July 1st, at 7.15 p.m., at the Well Plot Playing field, Loders, the party that staged the hilarious hockey match on Boxing Day will do a tug-o'-war across the river. Lieutenant Christopher Hill R.N., will be down from Northolt to captain the gentlemen, and Michelle Laskey, the Boodikka of Loders, will captain the ladies, who are fortunate to have as their anchor Kuddills (the husband of Kozey). The staying power of the said Kuddills is at its finest in a feminine context. The Mayor of Bridport will be on a stool in mid-stream umpiring – if he remembers his promise.

July 1978

An organ crawl

'Crawls' of one kind and another are common. Last month produced one we had never heard of – an 'organ crawl'. Organs may not strike the community in general as being the crawl most beneficial to a hot day, but the crowd of organists participating in this one were deriving very apparent satisfaction from it.

They were members of the South Dorset Organists' Association, and this was their third annual crawl. Having amused themselves with the organs of Langton Herring and Portisham, they came to Askerswell, where our organist, Mr. Bill Tiltman, awaited them. Before they tried the organ for themselves, Mr. Tiltman, expounded its characteristics, notably the sensitivity which almost makes looking at it causing it to play.

At Loders they had the former supplementary organ of Exeter Cathedral to absorb them. This was the kind of organ they would like transplanted to their own churches. Mr. Tiltman expounded not only the organ but the anatomy of the parish. An eavesdropper deemed it a masterly performance and wished he·had had shorthand.

August 1970

Mothers' Union Prayer Group

The Prayer Group which emerged from our branch of the Mothers' Union will resume meetings, after its summer recess, at the Vicarage, on the third Thursday in September.

August 1974

Summer supper

The summer supper at South Eggardon House might have better pleased the hostess, Mrs. Derek Newall, had it been held the evening following that on which it was, because that evening was sunny, but it could not have much better pleased the guests, who one and all declared it perfect. The greyness of the evening seemed somehow appropriate to a place with a background of pre-history, and what mattered the lack of sunshine as long as the evening was warm and dry?

As the guests were sipping their pre-prandial drinks, a bell summoned them to the lawn where the bride of the morrow, Miss Thelma Record, and her groom, stood shyly holding hands. Miss Record is the church organist. Group Captain Newall presented her with an electric clock given by the parishioners, and made a felicitous speech. The clock, being battery-operated, is proof against power-cuts.

The guests were a representative cross-section of the village, leavened by a few choice spirits from Loders. When they had viewed and approved the garden, they went into the house for supper. And such a supper. The old rooms, with their beamed ceilings, or minstrel gallery, or oak-panelling, or great stone fireplaces, conveniently lead into each other, so that birds of a feather could flock together with their platters in many a secluded corner. The flowers were lovely. How such a spread at a pound a head could produce any profit for church funds is a mystery, but it did – around £40.

August 1974

The day of the year

Saturday, August 2nd, is Loders Fête, of many happy memories and of much assistance to the church repair fund. Most of our readers will have planned to attend. This is not likely to be the business for them that it will be for Mr. J.G. Romanes, the Dorchester eye surgeon, who has kindly agreed to bring his veteran steam-engine, to give rides.

As the engine only moves at three miles an hour, and will have to make use of water points en route, it will take him a good five hours to reach the fête and, we presume, another five to get home again. But Mr. Romanes is proud of his rare and splendid beast and thinks any effort to display it to the public is worth while. It was one of the features of the Hardy Festival, and won a prize. It was made in 1902. Like veteran cars, it has appreciated in value. Models like it have lately changed hands at Christies for £4,000. But they need to, for new parts are expensive. A fire box, for example, costs £400 and does not last long. Like other road vehicles, it has to pass an M.O.T. Test, so would-be passengers at the fête are not putting their lives greatly at risk.

The Weymouth Flying Club had the kind intention of helping the fête with a display of aerobatics by their model aircraft. But an inspection of the fête site decided them reluctantly against it: there are too many trees. However, the children's sports are still on the programme! Past experience has proved that fête goers are not avid for overmuch entertainment. They are content to stroll about, listen to the band, meet friends, take copious cups of tea and imbibe the beauty of the setting – Loders Court.

August 1969

Underneath Eggardon

The late Mr. Fred Samways, who died in Bridport Hospital within a few days of his ninety-second birthday, was the first of the three Askerswell parishioners who are over ninety to shake off this mortal coil. (The remaining two are Mrs. Martha Marsh and Miss Tuck.) His was a character so colourful and so instinct with the Dorset countryside that it needs the pen of a Thomas Hardy to delineate it. Mr. William Graves, a former landlord of *The Crown* in Uploders, could mimic him to perfection, but has long since been domiciled in Frampton, denying us that entertainment.

Mr. Samways was born at Chilcombe, where his father and grandfather had been lords of the manor. He remembered in his boyhood racing across two fields at the call of another boy to see one of the first motor cars negotiating the Dorchester road. He also remembered how the driver of the Royal Mail, for some reason known to himself, used to whip his six horses into a gallop to go down Stony Head, which was then somewhat stonier than it is now. (Perhaps he liked to enter Bridport with a flourish.)

When Mr. Samways moved over the hill into Askerswell he became sexton. The only enemy he ever made was the unruly drystone wall dividing the churchyard from Parson's Lane, which was always falling about and which he vowed to reduce to order and never quite did, though he used to have a jab at it when in extreme old age he would come from Litton to cut the churchyard grass. At the death of his wife his son and daughter-in-law shared their home with him. He deeply appreciated this and was happy there. He must also have appreciated it that one of his old friends, Mr. George Rendall, a martyr to ills of various sorts, managed to attend his funeral, which was in Askerswell Church.

August 1968

Bells from St. Barts

The country weekend spent here by the ringers of St. Bartholomew the Great in the City of London would appear to have been a success, seeing that their clerical leader, the Reverend Brooke Lunn, sent a letter of thanks on behalf of them all, and then they all wrote individually. Kindly July weather filled their cup of joy to the brim as they nosed through the Dorset lanes to sample the bells of Netherbury, Stoke Abbott, Powerstock, Askerswell and Abbotsbury. At Powerstock they were welcomed by the Dean Rural. Dropping into *The Crown* in Uploders they savoured the royal hospitality of landlord, Reg Small and his Lady, and were loth to leave. They would have been unable to leave *Rose Cottage* had not their self-control been equal to the flow of Mrs. Harry Crabb's dandelion wine.

On each of the two evenings the day ended pleasantly round the capacious dining-table of Loders vicarage. The ringers were too full and too tired to be aware of the deficiencies of their makeshift beds, some of them in Chuck Willmott's attic workshop. At Loders their ringing began on the Saturday morning, and at Loders it ended with a farewell flourish to the congregation as they were streaming out of matins on Sunday. The ringers had a good journey back to London. That evening they were ringing for evensong, finding perhaps that the powerful numinous atmosphere of the Norman apse of the priory church of St. Bartholomew the Great was all the more wonderful for comparison with the light and graceful chancel of the priory church of St. Mary Magdalene.

August 1974

Sunday School Party One

Wet weather reduced the attendance at Askerswell Sunday School party at Mrs. Garrard's, but the programme was carried out as far as possible in the house and the playlet was postponed to an afternoon which turned out to be delightfully fine. The play proved that morality can be a highly entertaining subject. It enacted *The Good Samaritan*. The thieves, in Arab kafiyahs and dishdashes, had the faces of cherubs; the

Spirit of Evil, who deflected Priest and Levite from their duty, was indeed a spirited fellow that one could not help liking as much as the Good Samaritan, and the discomfiture of the racialist innkeeper was funny to behold as he stood by his notice 'Jews only – Samaritans not served', confronted by a Samaritan asking service for a half dead Jew. The thieves took up a collection for Oxfam, but were seen to pass it intact to Mrs. Garrard.

September 1968

Sunday School Party Two

Another happy August memory was the mini-fête staged by Askerswell Sunday School at the home of their superintendent, Mrs. Frank Garrard. The Lord could not have been loving Askerswell very much on this occasion, for the weather was uncharacteristically fine, and the fullest use was made of the lawns lying wait behind unlikely hedges to accommodate hidden treasure and tantalising trials of skill. Unexpected talent was exposed in some of the more respectable members of the congregation.

For instance, there was a big tin bath of water with a crowd of sherry and claret corks bobbing about on it, and Mrs. Savage had us sore amazed at her skill in spearing them. We were assured that other households had contributed corks. The master of the house gave the bath a wide berth. He was in the lounge giving shows of his colour slides of local events. These shows are always popular, for Mr. Garrard is a tip top photographer, and we all like to see ourselves on the screen.

The main event of the afternoon was the acting of Bible stories by the children. What was so engaging about the performance was the way in which former members of the Sunday School, now young men and women, took part with the infants without any apparent selfconsciousness, and because the actors were getting so much fun out of it without themselves being funny the audience enjoyed it too.

A piece of gymnastic equipment made an admirable prop for Jacob's dream at Bethel. We saw Leonard Vicary looking like Lawrence of Arabia and dreaming on a jagged stone pillow, while behind him a gang of very athletic angels hoisted themselves up one side of an n-shaped ladder and lowered themselves down the other, and the voice of the Lord God, rather resembling that of Mr. Paul Clark, issued from behind a curtain.

September 1972

The Fête

Loders Fête was on the last day of what the weather man said was the wettest week of the wettest summer for ten years. But its good fortune survived. There was only one shower, a short and heavy one that came at an awkward time, 2.30 p.m., as if to give us a taste of what we were being spared. The electronically-controlled aeroplane was able to perform, to everybody's delight, but the breeze might have driven the helicopter into the trees, so it was grounded. The sun shone for the dog-handling display, the *Punch and Judy* and the children's sports. A little old lady in period dress did a brisk trade in lavender sachets. Some of her customers seemed wary of her, as if she were the ghost of a former fête-helper now reposing in the churchyard just over the wall. The temperature was lower than usual (this always goes with a supernatural visitation) but what was bad for the ice-cream was good for the refreshment tent, whose wares were greatly relished.

September 1978

Wine into water

Askerswell Sunday School triumphantly turned its annual summer party into a miniature fête aimed at raising nine hundred fivepences for Salisbury Cathedral to mark the ninth centenary of the diocese. It made £65 in all – £45 for the Cathedral and £20 for the Sunday School. The weather caused some anxiety beforehand. The tropical sequence of bright hot days seemed to be broken, but the organisers had faith enough not to make alternative arrangements. A gorgeous day rewarded them, and a crowd big enough to overtax the capacity of Orchards.

The highlight of the afternoon was an enactment of the Book of Ruth to the pre-recorded voices of the children. Our

Askerswell correspondent remarks that actions and words did not always synchronise, but nobody minded. The clothes and scenery were really charming. For the harvest scene straw was strewn around, there was a stook of real sheaves, and a real sack of corn, and the gleaners in their gay costumes looked so pretty. But the skill of the organiser at adaptation really shone when the winner of the bottle of wine was found to be an ardent tee-totaller. The bottle obligingly turned into a writing compendium!

September 1975

Village outing

Loders entertainment committee have hired a 41-seater coach for Brympton D'Evercy, near Yeovil, on 17th September. Seats are free, but limited, and obtainable from the committee, or by phoning Powerstock 356. The coach will leave the *Crown* car park at 2.00 p.m. It will cost 80p to view the house and cider museum, grounds and vineyard. Cream teas will be available.

* * * * *

Good weather blest the Loders Village Outing to Brympton D'Evercy. It was meant first for the housebound and aged, but spare seats in the large plush coach were gratefully taken by motorist parishioners who enjoyed the view over hedges that a car denies them. The kindness of the Entertainment Committee in laying on this free trip was much appreciated.

September–October 1980

Askerswell's cast-offs

The Jumble Sale that Askerswell Church recently staged in the Bridport United Church Hall proved for the second time (the Women's Institute having proved it for the first) that Askerswell's cast-offs are a prize to be pushed, shoved, wrestled and paid for by the burgesses of Bridport. It made a profit of £167.97. A man issuing laden from the hall, and seemingly a judge of jumble sales, was saying to a woman similarly laden, 'That's the best organised jumble sale I've ever been to.' Askerswell is lucky to have several retired managerial types in its congregation.

October 1978

Daily bread

On a lovely summer evening in late September it seemed as if the Uploders Chapel had become the hub of the universe. Cars from both directions were trying to park outside. Cheerful pedestrians were braving a barrage of welcoming handshakes to get inside, where the flower bedecked windows, and groceries both natural and processed, piled against the rostrum, left no room for doubt that the occasion was harvest festival. The chapel stewards, Mr. and Mrs. Morris, who have done so much to keep the little place alive, beamed on a congregation packed upstairs and downstairs. It included the Mayor of Bridport, who was there as a member of Loders church, and a full parade of the Bridport branch of the Loyal Order of Moose. High and lifted up above the babble of conversation, the veteran Miss Daisy Boxall and her harmonium seemed lost in the tunes of harvest past.

The Reverend Norman Skinner welcomed the company. They and the harmonium were soon at one in *We plough the fields*, and he and the children in the front row were thereafter absorbed in the variety of God's handiwork as illustrated by the Island of Shells in Wales, and a cucumber from the manse garden that looked like an anaemic apple, whose identity nobody could guess. Mr. Skinner's address to the adults was about man's continuing dependence on God for daily bread. But what everybody likes most about Mr. Skinner is his talent for moving among a congregation with his Rolls-Royce of an accordion, and getting them really to sing. When the company streamed out of the chapel into the twilight they wore the fulfilled look of the thoroughly entertained.

October 1975

Harvest

Four vocalists of the Bridport Operatic Society, led by Mrs. Daphne Stebbings, sang *Linden Lea* at the Uploders Chapel

Harvest Festival. The congregation showed that they too were possessed of voices in the hymns, which filled the little building with about as much joyful sound as it could take. Members of the Loyal Order of Moose helped to swell the congregation, as they have been doing for some time now. Mr. Parker, a Minister from Bridport, took the service in a refreshing old-fashioned way, and inspired us all with his harvest vision of the glory of the Lord.

His manner had a maturity that seemed not quite in accord with his head of youthful black hair, which was obviously his own. His mention in the sermon of his being upwards of three score years and ten accounted for the maturity. The chapel steward, giving out the notices, observed with thankfulness that the outside of the chapel had been repaired and painted, and appealed for help to do the inside. His computation that this was about the hundred and fortieth harvest festival to be celebrated in the Uploders chapel made two at least of the congregation wonder whether he had taken into account the date of Parson Hawker, the Cornish vicar who started the religious harvest festival in this country.

The Harvest 'tell' at Dottery

An old world picture was to be seen at Dottery on the evening of the last Thursday in September. In the twilight of a perfect autumn day the bell was ringing and from up and down the road whole families of the hamlet were converging on the little 'iron church'. There was nothing metallic about its interior, which seemed, when one crossed the threshold, to be like the Chelsea Flower Show. Fine samples of local produce were relieved by the occasional orange and banana. Macaroni and gelatine reinforced the lesson that England is not sustained by the local harvest alone, and a packet of tea in a place of high honour by the altar acknowledged the debt church unity owes to that benign beverage.

On the south wall hung a whole branch of apples clustered as tightly as the grapes on the altar cross. When a comfortably full church had silently given top marks to the decorators, the business began of thanking the Lord for one of the best all-round harvests in memory. Under the firm hand of Mrs. Sylvia

Johnston the harmonium played no tricks and was in tuneful accord with the rustic voices. At the end of the service the congregation seemed reluctant to part with each other. Whoever extinguished the outside light quickly put it on again when he found the 'tell' was not finished.

October 1970

Come ye thankful people, come

Bad weather has made this year's harvest one of the worst in living memory. But still we decorate our churches and sing, *Come, ye thankful people*. And rightly so: we have not received all we would have liked, but what we have received is all from God and we cannot exist without it.

October 1968

Village Hall Anniversary Party

The stamina of Askerswell people became apparent on Fête Day. Having toiled all day at the fête (and taken much), they turned up fresh as daisies at the Village Hall in the evening to celebrate the second anniversary of its opening. About half of the village were present, comfortably filling the hall, and presenting a cross section of young and not so young. Three young ladies from Bridport, calling themselves SAM (Susan, Alexandra and Maureen) delighted everybody by their folk songs to the guitar and banjo and in the process disclosed unpublished information about heaven.

Another lady from Bridport charmed even the wallflowers into folkdancing, but she underestimated the soporific effects of an Askerswell supper when she tried to get the dance going again after that. The cutting of a splendid birthday cake by the hall caretaker, Mrs. Prior was the climax of a merry evening, little Miss Foot having first blown out the two candles.

October 1971

Of cough lozenges and lobsters

The scene outside the Uploders chapel was an animated one as car after car pulled up and disgorged passengers who had come for harvest festival. As the time for the service approached, the vicar, who was in the congregation, wondered what had become of dear old George Lee, our retired Sunday paperman, who never misses this service, and puts an offering of Parma violet cachous on the rostrum. But George made it. He came hurrying in and up to the rostrum, where he deposited a bottle of milk, a packet of tea and a bag of sugar – and a packet of those brown, oblong cough lozenges that make you cry if you bite one.

To the question why the cough lozenges instead of the violet cachous, George replied that the firm had given up making them, a sure instance of divine foreknowledge, for he had no West Bay lobster to bring with them this year. It appears that the purpose of the violet cachous was not to sweeten anybody's breath but to neutralise the presence of the lobster. But why did the lobster never get to the rostrum? Always somebody bought it at the door, said George, and he could sell half a dozen if he had them.

October 1981

St. Luke's Summer

The St. Luke's Summer which we are in at the time of writing is a continuation of the wonderful harvest weather and makes us more than ever thankful for the blessings of 1969.

At Askerswell Harvest it was good to see a glass jug of water sharing the place of honour at the chancel step with the harvest sheaf – a reminder that we can live for weeks without food, but only days without water. Sprays of blackberries gathered by the children represented the fruits of the hedgerow.

At Loders Church on the second Sunday in October large morning and evening congregations gave the harvest a rousing send-off. Sheaves of corn from the other churches, and the late Mr. Harry Legg's corn dollies, made the church look like an old-time harvest-field.

The evening congregation trooped out of church into the darkness and a light fall of welcome rain. A rustic gentleman said: 'I always come to Loders Harvest. The singing is bloody good'.

November 1969

Taking the plunge

The Harvest Supper in Askerswell Village Hall was a very jolly affair, and its eighty participants, young and old, certainly tested the seating capacity of the Hall. The commissariat of the Hall tested the eating capacity of the guests with all sorts of delectable viands, and defeated it. (Their drinking capacity came through with flying colours, but then, nobody in Askerswell makes cider now).

After the feast the company surrendered to the blandishments of Miss Perkins, who shepherded them through the prancings and pirouettings of country dances, including a very sober piece called The Askerswell Reel. Miss Perkins coaxed the Rector and a visiting Papal Knight [Leonard Clark] on to the floor, but two former submarine commanders looked on, afraid to take the plunge.

November 1971

Loders Harvest Supper

'The Hut' as Loders Village Hall is still affectionately known, looked ideally rustic for their Harvest Supper, to which about a hundred guests sat down. At present the new rafters still await the attachment thereto of a heat-conserving ceiling. For this occasion they had been so festooned with greenery that a Tarzan act by Robin Upton as part of the post-prandial entertainment seemed not altogether beyond the bounds of possibility. But Mrs. Netta Taylor is not one to go swinging about in trees. With feet firmly on the floor she delighted the company with her anecdotes in the Dorset dialect. Colin Varndell, the champion of the barn owl, followed suit with an engrossing story of a fight between Romans and Britons at Maiden Castle – but why he had to travel all that way for a setting when the hill fort of Eggardon was at hand is best known to himself.

The entertainment ended with community singing with Chris Read at the piano – if the winning of the raffle of a toy dog by Tom Fox, the dentist, be discounted. Ample helpings of lamb and pork etc., cheese and rolls, gâteaux and coffee, made a very satisfying dinner. Those who had forgotten to bring something to drink could win bottles of pomagne if they were lucky. The happy faces of those who stepped out of the hut into the moonlight must have been rewarding to the Entertainment Committee for all their hard work.

November 1980

Masculine monotony

The noble order of grandparents is enriched by the addition of Mr. and Mrs. Ron Thomas of Loders and Mr. and Mrs. Savage of Askerswell. The former's son Andrew and wife have produced a son and the latter's daughter Susan and husband Paul another son. Susan and Paul live in Purbeck Close, Uploders. The Close goes in for boys in a big way. There are now ten and no girls. The neighbours say they are all nice little boys. What their mothers think we have not heard. To break the masculine monotony, our Mr. and Mrs. John Samways of West Milton have had a daughter.

November 1975

Hallowe'en

Our Brownies kept Hallowe'en in the traditional manner with gusto and invention. Their meeting-room seemed to be swarming with witches, skeletons, devils with entangling tails, and the lighted-up faces of pumpkins from the church harvest festival. There were apple-bobbing and buns on strings, and very good eats, cooked by the Brownies themselves to win a badge.

December 1974

Guy Fawkes

Bonfire Night will be corporately celebrated near Askerswell village hall on the fifth. This is a great time for fathers who let off the fireworks in the interest of their offsprings' safety, and for mothers who feed the brutes with soup and hot dogs.

November 1974

November the Fifth

The evening of November the Fifth was at first lacking signs that this was bonfire night. As we passed through Loders and Uploders a fire here and there was blazing merrily with children prancing round it. But the sky over Askerswell was strangely dark, making us wonder what might have happened to the communal bonfire. It was there all right, near the village hall, and so were a crowd of villagers. A drenching of rain earlier in the day had made the bonfire reluctant to light up. This was good for the hot soup stall, which did such a roaring trade as to be defeated finally by the demand. With that and hot dogs the multitude were quite content to watch the firework display, which this year showed the advantage of collecting money round the village and buying, with it, a good selection of fireworks.

The crowning event of the evening was the draw for the gallon bottle of whisky which had made a profit of £100 for the church fund raising committee. Mr. Elliot Andrews, chief executive officer of the West Dorset Council, pulled out the winning ticket, and the bonfire, already gorged with paraffin, saw there was nothing left for it but to burst into flame when Mrs. Bellis made off with the whisky. It delighted everybody that her public spirit (for she is full of good works) should be capped by the other kind.

December 1975

Evaporating the Guy Fawkes rain

Guy Fawkes night was unpleasantly wet. From the general absence of bangs and meteors in the sodden sky, it seemed that only Askerswell were celebrating. They overcame the difficulties and a good time was had by all. George Bryan operated a terrific bonfire which evaporated the rain before it could fall on the spectators. Stanley Barrow and Donald Marsh kept the higher heavens fizzing and popping with £25 worth of fireworks whisked item by item from the shelter of a van. The ladies served hot-dogs and soup from a charcoal brazier bought for the Queen's Jubilee, and just the job for such a night. Attendance was gratifying.

December 1979

Remembrance Sunday

The sum sent to Earl Haig's Fund from our Remembrance
Sunday services drew a grunt of congratulation from that great
servant of the British Legion, Mr. Shoobridge of West Milton.
A feature of the Loders service is always Handel's *Dead
March* in *Saul*, superbly played by the organist Mr. Bill
Tiltman. Few who heard him on this occasion were aware that
the pedal work so characteristic of this piece was being done
by swollen feet which had had a manhole-cover dropped on
them a few days before.

* * * * *

The church collections for Earl Haig's Fund at our
Remembrance Sunday services were a record £86.50. Half
muffled peals were rung before and after the service. Captain
Harry Crabb, seen on the road before and after Remembrance-
tide with a suspicious-looking sack over his shoulder, had not
been rabitting. He had been muffling or demuffling the bells.
What it owes to him for servicing the bells the parish will
never know, much less pay.

December 1974–December 1978

Ploughman's supper

A ploughman's supper, we thought, was ideally fat bacon and
beans. But Loders Women's Institute has other thoughts. At
the village hall on Thursday December 4th, it is offering a
ploughman's supper of cheese, cider, pickled onions and
Dorset applecake, with the option of tea or coffee for the
squeamish. What's in a name? This will doubtless taste as
good and swell W.I. funds, as intended.

December 1975

Parish Social

Restrictions on the use of energy had no ill effects on the
parish social in Loders Village Hall. There was a crowded
attendance, and a thick blanket of fog outside had not kept

relatives and friends from round about at home. Indeed, the slight nip in the air of the hall put a sort of winter sports energy into the games and dancing, which was stoked up with an abundant supply of sandwiches, sausages, cakes, cheese puffs, mincepies, and Cox's orange pippins, from the kitchen.

It was a truly family occasion, ranging from small children through teenagers and middleagers to white-haired senior citizens. The M.C., Mr. Derek Skeats, cut a fine fatherly figure, catering for everybody with persuasiveness, courtesy and humour. Mr. Hurst, of Punknowle, was in attendance with his accordion band. The coach of the young Loders singer, Miss Thelma Record, was regrettably absent and ill, but with Mr. Tiltman at the piano, and Alan Read and Kevin Tiffin giving a lead, they acquitted themselves splendidly, it being whispered among the audience than Alan was to be *The Artful Dodger* and Keven *Oliver* in Bridport Operatic Society's next presentation. Mr. Meaden, of Bradpole Church choir, obliged with a full-throated drinking song that could have stood many encores. Then the handbell department of the Bridport Operatic Society made the welkin ring with old favourites like *The bells of St. Mary*, *Linden Lea* and Brahm's *Cradle song*. A couple of carols were a final reminder of only twenty-seven shopping days to Christmas. Altogether a highly enjoyable evening, proving that home-made entertainment can be the best.

Rustic Glen

A cold wet morning might have disinclined the unknowing to attend Mr. and Mrs. Lowle's *Rustic Glen* in Uploders for the annual sale of cards and calendars by the Dorset Naturalists Association. But those knowing Mrs. Lowle's flair for hospitality, and the Glen's ability to become a Snuggery, crowded to it, with the result that a couple of nice gossipy hours relieved them of £125, which nobody regretted.

December 1976

Business as usual

Worms boring deep into the earth and a rash of hawthorn berries on the hedgerows were signs of a hard winter that had not arrived by Christmas. Warm air, lush green grass, ceanothus in flower, a lone lupin, primroses and the cooing of a dove made the time of year seem more like spring. At midnight on Christmas Eve the air was balmy, and a moon was running with the clouds. Not surprising that so lovely a night should bring a record crowd to the service in Loders Church. Latecomers had standing room only.

By dawn the weather had changed out of knowing to torrential rain with a high wind. It made child's play of the defences the builders had put over their repair-work on the tower roof. Water rained on the ringers on the ground floor as freely as if it had not had to get through the bells and two floors first. But they swept the water through the door, manned their ropes, and a 'business as usual' peal brought parents and children to the family service, in which the Sunday School sang carols by the Christmas tree, and received sweets from it and prizes for good attendance.

January 1975

School play

Loders School, like the church, plays a vital part in Christmas and we hope the headmaster, his wife and family, and his school staff, are not worn to a frazzle by their exertions. These they embark on with an enthusiasm which is in itself one of the real spiritual fruits of Christmas.

The concert with which they open the mission sale is always different, and the current one always seems to excel the preceding one. This time it had a flavour of Greek drama. A chorus of children, accompanied by recorders and fiddles, etc., sang about Christmas, while shepherds and magi threaded through them to pay homage to Mother and Child. Child actors are unpredictable, and fortunately for the producer there is nothing the audience likes better than, say, for one of the Three Kings to be giving another a clout. Here the Mother was musical, jogging the Child to a beat so animated that He would have died of hiccups had He not been a doll.

January 1975

The Ayatollah Khomeini at Well Plot

The Boxing Day frolic on the Well Plot playing field had a melodramatic background that the ladies and gentlemen playing hockey and rugby combined were unaware of. It appears that the Ayatollah Khomeini had got wind that one of the players would be – and was – our Commander Jimmy James, who had lately been posted from Whitehall to an assignment on one of our most sophisticated warships. The Ayatollah never underestimates a potential enemy. On his hot line to Kuddles, the star of the Boxing Day frolic, he requested a report on the Commander's moral fibre, as revealed by the frolic. Kuddles siezed this chance of diddling the Ayatollah.

But he had to be careful. He rightly suspected that the stranger in the red balloon-suit pacing the touchline was an Ayatollah agent checking on him, and that the lone car parked on the other side of the river housed another Ayatollah agent checking on the checker. So these were his tactics:– instead of himself he had a college lecturer, Chris Hill, refereeing the match in an undertaker's top hat to show how seriously the English take their sport. On a corner of the pitch he had a bamboo cage called the Sin Bin, for the incarceration of foul and cowardly players, with the vicar in charge.

The Commander was the only player – surprisingly – that the referee relegated to the Bin, and the Commander exposed the depths of his own degradation by foraging in his kitbag as soon as he got into the Bin and swigging the liquor abhorred of the Ayatollah. Kuddles cunningly left the agent to inform the Ayatollah, and headed for *The Crown* and the hot punch freely bestowed on all comers by the amiable Maurice Lawson, whose life's work now is to stage this annual frolic. But the said Maurice was stripped of the Parochial Information Office and promoted – on the strength of the punch – to the Public Relations Office. He had been absolutely unaware of his part in foxing the Ayatollah!

The pantomime that the Loders Entertainment Committee were to have staged in January is now to be in March – perhaps to relieve the rigours of Lent?

January 1980

CHAPTER 3

Pre-occupations

There is a thin dividing-line between a mission and an obsession. Rev. Oliver Willmott believed in a number of things with a fervent passion. His quiet obsessions were the foundation of his ministry. They included: the preaching of the gospel, simply; the visiting of all souls and sundry; the maintenance of the fabric of the three churches; the encouragement of village traditions, new and old; the welding of all people together, where possible; the nurturing of the wider family of the church, including expatriates and parishioners who moved in and out; the furthering of the local school, and the enjoyment of village outings, especially those of the bell-ringers.

He came up against the churchyard, with its hours of back-breaking labour, and its lack of public support; local politics, with its absence of communal participation; the Squire, with his designs on the churchyard wall; and a few other causes for contention. A note of tetchiness appears in the latter phase of *The Parish Notes*. When some parishioners consider spending £100 for a council election for one councillor, he unashamedly refers to them as being 'thick-headed'.

On occasions there is the sad picture of a fine mind caught up in small matters – exhausting for the Vicar's spirit, and that of all others involved. In retrospect, some of the battles may now appear heroic, and not Luddite. He fought long and hard for the retention of local priests instead of team ministries. He campaigned for the preservation of one of the Church of England's richest assets – the magnificent, historic country parsonages. In November 1980, at the height of the final débâcle, he proclaimed, 'Ecclesiastical machinery being ancient is usually cumbersome.' Obsessive reporting was equally cumbersome, and unappetising.

Fortunately, the disharmony that percolated the last editions, particularly concerning archdeacons, was tempered by an unstoppable good humour. In village affairs Dogberry ruled: the affectionate depiction of bungling officialdom. Some of the old hobby-horses were laid to rest: the arrant male chauvinism of Chapter Four of *'Yours Reverently'* was transmuted into praise for the female clerk to the Parish Council (p. 104). The report of the marriage of Prince Charles and Lady Diana was full of vitality, and far away from the pains of parting from his parish into retirement (at 72). There was time for a quip:

And now to close, an anecdote from the Rector of Bart's the Great. Interviewing a prospective bridegroom, he asked whether the bride would want to promise in the service to obey him. The bridegroom replied, 'She told me to be sure to tell you she did, and I always does what she tells me.'

Common sense prevails

Loders Parish Council Election gave parishioners a choice in the matter of maintaining the churchyard, whether to graze it, or to go halves with the Church Council by contributing £50 annually from the rate, thus putting the churchyard on an equal footing with the cemetery. The verdict was for a rate. So the indications are that commonsense has at last prevailed, and that we need think no more about churchyard or cemetery until it is time to be going there.

* * * * *

About 70% of the electors voted, which is very high for a local government election and equal to a general election. It had an energising effect on the sick of the parish. Mr. Charlie Gale and Mr. George Randall rose up from their couches to vote and

The Vicar goes to court.

Mrs. Frank Gill foresook her wheeled chair. The oldest inhabitant, Mrs. Beatrice Clark, now in her ninetieth year, came
from Uploders with the roses of June already in her cheeks and
with the express intent of voting for Mr. Wilfred Crabb,
'because he is a very nice man,' and for the Vicar, 'because he
ain't all that bad'.

June 1968

The Uploders Room and The Hut

The Charity Commission have taken ten years to merge the
Uploders Room and the Hut in one trust!

* * * * *

The fire buckets which were once a feature of Loders Hut
seem to have vanished. While the heating still depends on old

oil stoves the W.I. think the Hut should have fire-fighting equipment and have put in a petition to the Hut Committee for some. But that Committee is to be commiserated with, for its plan of improvement to the Hut is held up by the legal tangles which have prevented the sale of the Uploders Room. Somebody says that for the Hut to go up in smoke would be the best way out of the deadlock. The same body was neither Mr. Bradshaw nor our policeman, whose homes hug the Hut on either side. It would be too warm for their comfort.

* * * * *

We hear that the trustees of the Uploders Room and Mr. John Ellis, the owner of adjoining property, have come to an agreement which will allow the long delayed sale of the room to materialise.

* * * * *

Loders Parish Council breathed a sigh of relief when they heard from their clerk, Mr. Harold Brown, that the twelve years of negotiation with the Charity Commission were about to end with the offer for sale of the Uploders Room. An unforeseen and lucky consequence of the delay is that the site has rocketed in value, and grants to parish halls have proliferated. When Mr Derek Skeats and his committee set about renovating the present Village Hall they should not be hampered by lack of funds.

November 1968–February 1972

Locking the church door

A special meeting of Askerswell Church Council decided to accept Mr. Fry's estimate of nearly £700 for relaying the north side of the church roof.

The lock on the church door was again discussed, as it is year in and year out. When Mr. Garrard offered to try to make it work, there was a stunned silence, as if the council were being robbed of an everlasting bone of contention. We have since heard that Mr. Garrard already has the lock working perfectly. If anybody becomes suspicious of a comparative newcomer who is an expert with locks, let it be said that Mr. Garrard's antecedents are impeccable.

April 1972

Loders Village Hall

The annual meeting of Loders Village Hall was also very much taken up with finance. It appears that the net proceeds of the sale of the Uploders Room are £3,435. The meeting was delighted with the plans drawn up (gratis) by the secretary, Mr. Harold Brown. These envisage the encasing of the present wooden building with reconstructed stone, a refreshment bar (backed by a kitchen) opening on to the main room, a fixed stage with dressing room, a games room, a committee room, a store room, a covered entrance porch with a pull-in, and electrical heating. When this has been done, Loders Village Hall should be the most commodious in the neighbourhood. Thirty years hence it should also have a substantial annual income from the interest on the charity, for maintenance. For these inestimable benefits the parish has to thank that poor little eyesore of an Uploders Room, the mad rise in property prices, and the dilatoriness of the Charity Commission, which kept this particular property off the market until the right moment.

August 1972

Long-winded meetings

The Askerswell Village Hall Committee ask us to publish their scale of charges, which include caretaker but not electricity. All ordinary Askerswell functions 10/-. Outside ones, four-hour sessions 20/-; bingo and whist 25/-; dances and wedding receptions 35/-; political meetings 30/-. Anybody suffering from long-winded meetings in the winter would be wise to hold them here. When the shilling in the slot expires the hall is plunged in darkness and the warm glow of the electric fire fades. This happened the other night when the Church Council were trying to answer the eighty-odd questions on the Bishop's Visitation forms. And it happened several times before the forms were filled. It seemed like mind over matter. When a specially obtuse question numbed the mind the lights went out and only the urgent need to find a shilling restored consciousness.

February 1970

Drainage for Loders and Askerswell

Mr. Lucas and Group-Captain Newall our representatives on the Rural District Council, have both given assurances to public meetings that the sewer will be begun in 1970, if not in the autumn of this year. Connecting up should impose no great financial burden on any householder.

April 1969

For the statistically-minded

Loders rate was unavoidably raised to sevenpence: it is hoped for this year only. The following crumbs of comfort are offered to Loders ratepayers: comparisons with other parishes may be misleading because it is not the rate alone that determines what you pay, but also the rateable value of your premises, and the rateable value of Loders houses is surprisingly low (we hope this may not get to the rating officer). For instance, a penny rate extracts £200 from neighbouring Bradpole, but it takes an eightpenny rate to extract a like sum from Loders. As the population of Bradpole is four times that of Loders, and a Bradpole penny rate produces eight times that of Loders (where a penny rate produces £25), it follows that the rateable value of Bradpole is about twice that of Loders. The current circular of the National Association of Parish Councils says there are 7,500 parish councils and their average expenditure was 'only £370 each' in 1966–7, with a sevenpenny rate Loders Parish Council expenditure is only £175. This said, it is hard to see how rates can be kept down while wages and other costs keep on rising.

April 1969

Unwelcome fame

At the Loders Parish Assembly the civic head of the parish [Mr. Wilfred Crabb] had a few uncomplimentary remarks to make about these *Notes*. Neither he nor anybody present dreamt they would reverberate round the country. They hit the headlines in the world's highest circulation daily, the *Mirror*, and the *People*, and the *Sketch*. As if that were not enough, the B.B.C. collared the Vicar for a television interview, and a *Radio Four* interview, both with John Tidmarsh, in their studio at Southampton. The television interview was preceded by cartoons of a pig on a sofa and a man with a wooden leg shuffling through snow, referring to paragraphs in the *Notes* which had amused not quite all our readers.

Western Television showed a film of a glamorous Sarah Barnes putting the real pig through his paces at Bilshay Farm. The whole episode has produced much comment and letters which, if printed, might make the ink blush. One came in a bunch of comics from an inmate of an institution in Glamorgan. We will not hazard a further wounding of delicate feelings by specifying the kind of institution, but leave it to be inferred from the letter, which began: 'Thank God for men like you, Sir. I must admit you have made me think a lot over your article in the *Daily Mirror*, April 14th, re. rumpus re. comic cuts, etc. Personally I do not belong to any place of worship, for special reasons of my own, known to the Almighty and myself, but I love two things, my Bible and those comic cuts . . .'

Urgent appeals not to change the character of the *Notes* came from a Mr. L.C. Hill, of Poole, who says he used to play Loders organ years ago, and from Mrs. MacDonald, of High Wycombe, who says, she is an old Loders girl, and, 'Let the people laugh'. A news agency and a radio and television agency both offered fat subscriptions to be placed on our mailing list with extraction rights! Needless to say, they were declined, for we hope, all this notwithstanding, to retain our virtue as a humble sheet, recording our very local doings for our own edification and that of our friends.

May 1969

To the parishioners of Loders

The Vicar, the Rev. O.L. Willmott, wishes to make this personal statement:- 'You may have read in the local and national press reports of some remarks made about these *Notes* by Mr. Wilfred Crabb when he presided over our parish meeting in March. The other remarks he then made about me you will not have read. The press did not publish them because the reporter present thought they might be defamatory. Mr. Crabb made allegations which in effect charged me with having obtained £5 by false pretences from his wife, and also having falsified the church accounts for the year ending December 31st, 1967. I immediately drew attention to the gravity of the charge, and asked him to withdraw it, which he refused to do. A few days later I received a solicitor's letter confirming that what Mr. Crabb had said at the meeting was correct, and asking me to apologise to his wife. This I cannot do, for the charge is completely untrue. I wish he had made it to the police.

Instead he chose to make it at a parish meeting – the wrong sort of parish meeting at that – and without the courtesy of prior notice to me. It is now seventeen years since I succeeded Colonel Scott as church treasurer. For many years I have also done the collecting for the church fête. In view of Mr. Crabb's accusation, I would prefer not to continue in these capacities. The accusation was not garden-gate gossip, which could have been ignored, but what appeared to be a prepared speech delivered by the civic head of the parish to the annual parish meeting. Accordingly I have resigned these offices, and doubt-less the June meeting of the Church Council will appoint a successor.'

June 1969

Friends in need

At its meeting in June, Loders Church Council passed unani-mously a resolution that it disbelieved the charge of dishonesty made publicly against the Vicar, had complete confidence in his integrity and wished this to be recorded in the *Notes*. The Hon. Alexander Hood proposed his re-election as treasurer, but he declined, thanking the Council for their faith in him, and assuring them he had not betrayed it. Miss Muriel Randall, who already negotiates the tax repayments on the covenants, was unanimously elected treasurer in his place.

July 1969

Closing the Chapter

The Chapter of Clergy of Bridport Deanery died at the birth of the new Lyme Bay Synod, which comprises most of the old Lyme Regis and Abbotsbury Deaneries and the whole of the Bridport Deanery except Toller. The last of the Bridport Chapter was presided over in Bridport Rectory by the expiring Rural Dean, the Rev. W. Rowley, whose office like that of the Rural Dean of Abbotsbury, is merged in a new one filled by the present Rural Dean of Lyme Regis, the Rev. G.V. Syer. For the Bridport Deanery clergy it was an occasion for sad reminiscence. They all signed the minutes book after the chairman.

It is to be hoped that the minute book will not perish with the Chapter, if only because some of it was written by one of those individualists for whom the C. of E. is famous, the Rev. C.B. Moss, a good classical scholar and former county cricketer for Worcester. Mr. Moss was allergic to the then Rural Dean, Canon Clare. The latter's would-be masterful conduct of meetings was somewhat deflated by the former's deadly sniping. As Chapter Clerk Mr. Moss exercised his talent for irony and sarcasm in the minutes at Canon Clare's expense. Once the worthy Canon could stand it no longer when Mr. Moss was reading the minutes. 'Blast you, Moss, you're always getting at me,' he shouted and rushed out of the room. Mr. Moss appeared not to notice, finished the minutes, handed them to be signed to the empty chair, and said, 'Dear me, I had the impression, the Dean Rural was here when we started'.

Rationing continued into those post-war days, and the clergy would bring a contribution of food to the tea with which the Chapter ended. Mr. Moss used to make and bring a confection called 'parkin', whose main constituent was black treacle. At its first appearance the clergy wolfed it down. But only once. Ever afterwards when the tea party dispersed the pile of parkin remained untouched, which did not deter Mr. Moss from continuing to manufacture it. The clergy had discovered its medicinal properties!

Another ornament of the now defunct Chapter was the Rev. Claude Streatfeild, Rector of Symondsbury. But neither space nor time is to spare for the saga of the famous voyage to the Chapter meeting at Rampisham, when Mr. Streatfeild, who was guide to three other divines in an open sports car, missed his way in a country lane, and took the car through several fields of mowing grass (it was June) through a hedge and down a steep bank on to the main road. Small wonder that he fell asleep at the ensuing Chapter and annoyed Canon Clare by his intemperate snoring.

February 1970

A clash of tastes

A gasp of consternation was the reaction of Loders Church Council to their architect's proposal to remove the stained glass window from over the altar, and replace it with clear glass. The window is not a work of art by any means, but when one enters the church from the west it catches the eye and focusses it on the altar, and is altogether pleasing until one is close enough to see the detail.

The generality of Loders people love it, and a surprising number of visitors write in the book that it is one of the many pleasant features of the church. The architect was proposing to replace three lesser windows, as well, and to eliminate all colour except for the medieval and Flemish fragments in the Ladye Chapel, and the Norman window in the Chancel. His predilection for clear glass might suit a post-reformation church but is here historically incorrect, for Loders Church belongs very much to the pre-reformation when church walls as well as windows were a blaze of colour.

As custodians of the money put up by the parish for essential work, knowing also that the present windows still have years of life in them, the Council agreed unanimously to clamp down on the architect and direct his attention to the exterior work that needs doing.

March 1972

Closing country churches

Looking back on Easter, we relish the memory of happy services in churches beautifully decorated for the 'Queen of Seasons'. Those who advocate the shutting of small country churches would do well to ponder the attendance at ours.

Askerswell, with a population of 130, had Easter congregations totalling about 80; Dottery, with a population of 60, also had congregations of about 80; and Loders, with a population of 540, had 114 communicants, and such a crowd at matins that the congregation filled the chancel as well as the body of the church. The singing was gay and vigorous.

May 1972

Pastoral reorganisation

The takings of the three-day festival of flowers at Askerswell exceeded expectations at £255, and were a decided rebuff to the inclement weather. Commenting on the latter a friend writes: 'I think God must love Askerswell deeply, because He certainly doesn't make things easy for us. Just think of last year – the one really cold miserable drizzly day of the whole summer, and yet our fête was a real success. And last weekend at the children's dancing on the lawn, in spite of there being metaphorical icicles on my tea, I've never felt so warm and happy inside. Perhaps it was the general spirit pervading the whole village in spite of the weather. Never have I known a village so completely involved in a job of work for its church.'

The children of Loders School and their parents pushed prams three miles to the church and three back. The church has never been more crowded than it was for the festal evensong, when the West Walks Choir led the singing and gave an anthem, and the Dean of Salisbury preached. The Dean was surprised and delighted, and this will do our three parishes no harm when the pastoral reorganisation committee gets to work.

July 1972

Group Ministry

On September 11th the Lyme Bay Deanery Synod will vote on the proposals of the Pastoral Reorganisation Commission inasfar as they affect us locally. P.C.C's concerned have already debated the issues and made their attitudes known. Powerstock, West Milton and Poorton are not antagonistic to union with Loders and Askerswell, and the cession of Dottery to Bridport, but Loders, Askerswell and Dottery are. Bradpole and Allington are reluctantly agreeable to being merged in a team ministry in Bridport; Bothenhampton and Walditch are strongly opposed.

Bridport St. Mary's is in a state of schizophrenia on the issue. The voting 'that we accept a *team* ministry in principle' was 9 in favour and 12 either against or abstaining. The voting that 'if it be really necessary we favour a *group* ministry' was 8 in favour, and 13 either against or abstaining.

September 1972

Circulating

The January *Parish Notes* can never be out on time because of the Christmas holidays. So, belated new year greetings herewith to all our readers. How many these are, and how widely scattered over the world, we cannot know, but the number may be around a thousand, for our circulation has crept up to three hundred.

January 1974

More churchyard appeals

'The flowers appear on the earth, the time of the singing of the birds is come, and the voice of the cuckoo is heard in our land.' With apologies to the *Song of Songs*, the time of the mowing of lawns, and of churchyards, has come also. The arrangements for keeping in order our three churchyards need to be re-stated.

Askerswell churchyard is cut by volunteers under the guidance of Captain Lumby, and the Church Council has equipped them with a new mower. The trimming of all the mounds and curbs and tombstones is too much to expect them to do, and is the responsibility of the surviving relatives of the deceased. Relatives should take this duty seriously. It is not asking much. A few unkempt graves spoil the appearance of an otherwise well groomed churchyard.

Loders churchyard is mown by Mr. Dunford and Mr. Kick, at a total annual cost of around £100. The borders, paths and yew hedges are cared for by volunteers. But here again, mounds and curbs are the responsibility of relatives of the deceased. It is a relief at Dottery to have Mr. Turner willing to continue the cutting in spite of his removal to Allington. The pay is small, and he cannot be expected to trim the graves as well. Many hands make light work, so would relatives kindly 'get cracking'.

May 1974

Of closing churches and take-overs

A meeting of Askerswell Church Council heard with mild surprise and much gratitude that Captain Aylmer had sought out woodworm in various parts of the church and attacked it with Rentokil. The operation had begun in the Captain's own home. When the fighting spirit of the Navy is up, there is no containing it. As to the controversial coconut matting on the floor of the nave, having solemnly decided that it must come up, the Council solemnly decided that it must go down.

The Council were wary of a proposal by the insurance company that the church should be more adequately insured – at double the present premium. With an eye on Powerstock's efforts to close West Milton Church, and with the awful possibility of a Powerstock takeover of Askerswell in mind, the Council feared that the doubled insurance premium might eventually be to some foreigner's advantage, and will take further advice.

November 1972

Loders School

The managers of Loders School met recently under their chairman, Mr. Charles Miles. The headmaster, Mr. Ronald Price, reported that there were 56 children in the school, that the playground had been resurfaced, and a tape-recorder acquired. He was grateful to Mr. Cooper for auditing the school fund. To remedy the lack of space in the school he proposed asking the County to build a small extension, or supply a hut, taking up to ten children and holding stores. The managers supported this. In a discussion of the newspaper reports of new primary schools in Dorset, the managers inclined to the view that it might be cheaper, and as efficient, to enlarge the present Loder's School rather than build a new site.

November 1972

The photographer

Dottery is unusually flush with news this month, of a wedding and a double christening. The wedding was that of Miss Julia Ann Smith, of New Close Farm, and Mr. Danny Green, of Pymore Terrace. She was the last of the several children that Mr. & Mrs. Stanley Smith have seen to the altar at Loders, and everybody was pleased that after his long spell of illness Mr. Smith was able to be there and give his daughter away. With a pair of pretty bridesmaids to match the bride, and a lovely afternoon, the wedding was highly photogenic.

The photographer was much in evidence, and obviously had no qualms about getting married inadvertently as he muscled in on the heart of the ceremony. He knows his job, and the pictures were works of art. The christening concerned Mr. and Mrs. Maurice Turner, and his father, who is sexton of Dottery. It was like old times to see all the clan walking in a body down to church from where they had left their cars. They half filled the church, and the baptismal candidates were quiet enough for a short sermon to be preached. They were named Hayley Michelle and David Anthony.

September 1974

Loders public buildings

Loders is a fortunate parish public buildingwise. At the height of the property boom the village hall received well over £3000 from the sale of the Uploders Room. Much of this windfall has already been used to improve the hall. A portion was returned to the Charity Commission to recoup this particular charity, and when this is accomplished (not for some years) the hall will have the interest on £3,000 odd in perpetuity. When Mr. & Mrs. Morris came to live in New Road, this was a blessing for the Uploders Chapel, which is a gem of Regency village architecture. They brought it to life and saved it from redundancy. By enlisting outside help, they have repaired it externally so that it looks smart in its new creamwash, and they hope to be lucky again in doing up the interior.

It is fairly common knowledge that Loders Church has also had good fortune. The late Mrs. Olive Legg, of Well Plot, who worshipped in the church all her long life from the age of three, left the residue of her estate, £3,000, for its repair, with special concern for the great stained glass window over the altar, which is in poor condition. The Church Council will doubtless invest this money to produce a useful annual income. Her generous help should inspire the parish to still greater efforts in the fête, for the repair fund of a place like Loders Church can never be oversubscribed.

September 1974

Modern theologians

Promotion for Dr. Martin Thornton. His friends here and over a very wide area indeed will welcome the recent announcement that he is to be a canon residentiary and chancellor of Truro Cathedral. He, his wife Monica, and daughter Magdala, will be leaving *Trinity Cottage*, Loders, to take up the appointment next June.

To the question, What sort of a job is this? we venture the answer that it is largely an educational one: Dr. Thornton will have the training of ordinands, beside his duties as a canon of the cathedral. He may be hard put to find time to continue writing his theological books, which have a faithful and enthusiastic readership here and in America. His latest book comes out on Nov. 4th. Its title is *My God: A reappraisal of normal religious experience*. We shall like to discover whether the author finds the present norm of religious experience so feeble a thing that his 'My God' is an expletive. This would fit his wry sense of humour. Mowbrays the publishers have commissioned a book of essays in honour of Dr. Ramsey, Archbishop of Canterbury, on his retirement this month. Dr. Thornton contributes one of the essays. It is called *The cultural factor in spirituality*. He and the other contributors will present a leather-bound copy of the book to His Grace at Lambeth Palace on Nov. 13th, the Archbishop's seventieth birthday.

November 1974

Dottery windows

The windows of Dottery Church keep on attracting the attention of mischievous boys, and now three windows are either broken or badly cracked. This is no joke at any time, much less the present, when repairs cost so much. There is evidence enough to make a court case, but the churchwardens offer 'one more chance', and trust there may be no repetition.

March 1975

Of church unity and midges

The coffee evening on the lawn of Loders vicarage turned out to be a pleasant exercise in church unity in spite of the midges, and produced a useful £110.50 for the redecorating of the interior of the Uploders Methodist Chapel. It was a way chosen by Askerswell and Loders churches to celebrate the ninth centenary of the diocese of Salisbury, and had the backing of the chapel members and some of their friends in Bridport. Loders Brownies lent a hand by making packets of fudge to sell and by circulating notices of the event.

To their delight, the Rev. Norman Skinner, who ministers to the Uploders Chapel, fished an accordion out of his car and paraded the lawn playing ditties they could sing. The Vicar and Mrs. Willmott have since received letters of thanks from Mr. Skinner, and from Mr. Morris, the steward of the Uploders Chapel. Mr. Skinner says: 'I write to thank you and your wife and the friends in the parishes concerned for their kindness in organising and supporting the coffee evening in aid of our little Uploders Methodist Church. The result was quite staggering and we are grateful not only for this practical support but also for the very fine ecumenical spirit which prompted it. This has given local meaning to the Spearhead campaign and I would like to express our gratitude for this outward going Christian love and fellowship. Please thank all concerned. This kindness has meant a great deal to us'.

July 1975

Re-organisation

Re-organisation, like re-form, is reckoned to be improvement, but improvement is not inevitably their concomitant. Look at Loders Parish Council. Four of the old council did not seek re-election. Only six people were nominated for the seven seats on the new council, and these included for the first time two ladies. Under the old system the six councillors could have filled the vacancy by co-opting a seventh. Under the new system co-option is disallowed, and the vacancy has to be filled by an election, which in Loders would cost the ratepayers around £70. So if the vacancy is filled strictly by the new method, we could have an Alice-in-Wonderland situation – six of the councillors there only in virtue of having been proposed and seconded by a parochial elector, and one elected by the parish at a cost of £70.

May 1976

Seeing the light

The older residents of Askerswell will like to know that we have heard from Miss Wilkinson (now living at Hove), one of the four retired teachers who used to live in Mrs. Findlay's house in The Square, known to the peasantry as 'The Ladies'. She writes: 'Exactly twenty years this very month have passed since we left Askerswell. Much has happened in that time. Both Miss Croxson and Miss Webb have passed on. Miss Norah Croxson is now living in Heathfield Priory. In those twenty years the *Parish Notes* have never missed coming to me each month, and I do enjoy reading the activities of the village, although, naturally, the names of some residents are new to me ... In the new year I shall often be turning my thoughts to Dorset. My best wishes to you all.'

We wonder if Miss Wilkinson can recall that general election when The Ladies had a picture of their candidate inside their front window, and somebody fitted a picture of a rival candidate exactly over it on the outside of the window. Thus did the posters remain for some days until somebody congratulated one of The Ladies on 'having seen the light at last'.

February 1977

North Sea Oil

In 1974 the Secretary of State approved the proposed closure of Powerstock school, and the building of a new school for a hundred pupils at Loders. Nothing more was heard of this during the economic blizzard. But now that North Sea Oil is calming the troubled waters, the proposal has surfaced again. The Assistant Education Officer in charge of planning and development has informed the Loders managers that the Education Committee has received from the Premises and Support Services Sub-Committee 'a recommendation that consideration should be given to the inclusion of a replacement school for Loders in the 1979–80 building programme'. But the Assistant Education Officer is not giving a guarantee that any concrete achievement will emerge from this welter of inter-committee activity.

He ends his letter thus: 'If the proposal is approved, it will still be some time before the project is firmly accepted by the Department of Education and Science, but I felt that you would wish to know that the school's replacement is again actively considered.' The Assistants' mention of the school's replacement being 'actively considered' confirms our long-standing suspicion that some matters are 'inactively considered' at County Hall. Finding a site for the new school will be quite a problem. The site at Uploders is now mostly covered by Purbeck Close, and the owners of the best site in Loders have said, 'Only over our dead bodies.'

February 1978

The Village School

Economy cuts, so it seems, are not going to delay the building of a new school in Loders. Negotiations are proceeding for one on the site above High Acres, and the cost is visualised as being around a quarter of a million. The County are dead set on doing nothing to remedy the deplorable state of decoration of the old school, and the ladies among the school managers are equally dead set on doing the redecorating themselves. They will not believe in a new school before they see it. They will begin work these holidays. The headmaster has made a grant from the school fund to get them started. They hope that a jumble sale will supply the rest. The male managers – both of them – are keeping to what the media call a low profile. To be houseproud is a female affliction.

January 1980

The School and the responses

Loders Easter vestry and annual church meeting was not well attended. The congregation seems well content to let the vicar rule without parliament. One young lady called him the Ayatollah Willmott: had it been the name of the great John Paul the Second she had taken in vain, she might have gone across his knee. The proposed new school, being a church one, figured appropriately on the agenda. The owner of the site above High Acres, insisted upon by the County, lamented that the County would shortly get its way, having rejected an alternative site he had offered which would have spared the inhabitants of the quiet enclave of High Acres the traffic of the new school.

The annual church meeting is one time of the year when the laity are free to express an opinion about the church services. But how great a fire can one spark kindle. A layman asked whether the responses at matins could not be speeded up. The fuse reached the choir in no time and they, naturally, blew up the vicar for not defending them. He thought when their spokespersons upbraided him that he had lost choir and organist for ever. But there they were on the following Sunday as if nothing had happened. The spirit of turning the other cheek had prevailed over the tetchy artistic temperament.

May 1980

An ecumenical event

The church unity service comfortably filled the Uploders Chapel on a weeknight. It was conducted by the Reverend Norman Skinner, of the Bridport United Reformed Church, who said the chapel was one hundred and fifty years old this year. The vicar gave the address. Almost certainly he was the first vicar of Loders or of anywhere to have done this. Seven different Christian denominations were represented at the service.

February 1977

The shrubbery

The great heap of shrubbery on the public green at Well Plot looked like a provision for the Queen's Jubilee bonfire, but it was not. It was only a headache and a backache for Mr. and Mrs. Nicholas Woollard, the new occupants of the late Mrs. Good's bungalow. They had to clear all this out of the garden to find the garden. They could not burn it on the garden, for that would be too near the bungalow, and they were not allowed to burn it on the green, so Mr. Woollard is taking it away, one faggot at a time, tied to the roof of his car. We thought it best not to ask its destination.

We hope this will not cure him and his wife Moira of their love for the Dorset countryside. Mr. Woollard is no stranger to many of us. He is a social worker based on the Bridport Health Centre. His wife was teaching until ill-health forced her to give up.

* * * * *

The heap of shrubbery on Well Plot Green, Loders, which at first sight seemed something to do with the impending jubilee bonfire, has drawn a lengthy letter from Mr. Frank Good, son of the late tenant of the bungalow out of whose curtilage the heap was extracted. He maintains that it came, not from the garden proper, but from the hedge dividing the bungalow from number fourteen which both neighbours had allowed to grow by agreement to secure their respective privacies. That 'the heap had to be cleared out of the garden to find the garden' by the new tenant was untrue, because 'last year, 1976, my wife and I spent most of our time there clearing and cropping the garden . . . Other residents of Well Plot know very well these are the true facts of the matter and we're upset by your report.'

And so it will be seen that our two sources of information disagree, although they are both first hand. We make our exit in the spirit of Shakespeare's *Midsummer Night's Dream* – 'If we offend, it is with our good will'. The heap has now gone, and not all in parcels tied to the roof of the new tenant's car. Finding the hire of a lorry too costly, he burned the rest of the heap in the garden of the bungalow, helped by a sympathetic neighbour.

March–April 1977

Jumble sales

Our thanks to the Askerswell people who responded so well to our appeal last month for things to sell at the jumble sale in Bridport. It raised £30 for the church roof. The ladies who manned the stalls might benefit by a course in siege tactics from Major Evans before they next face the Bridport jumblers, whose initial onrush all but obliterated them. They are now wise to a few tricks of the trade, notably that of trying on a garment from the stall and vanishing, leaving the too-busy vendor with the discarded one. Jumble sales bring out the worst as well as the best in human nature.

October 1972

Quality jumble

Having drawn the outside world into Askerswell to explore and admire the gardens of the village, and relieved it of £130 in the process, the church fund-raising committee ventured into the outside world of Bridport on a sunny September Saturday and relieved it of another £260 by selling it jumble, produce, white elephants and cups of coffee. The proletariat of Bridport appear not to dislike being fleeced. On the contrary, the crowd outside the United Church Hall seemed so restive that the Askerswell commander-in-chief panicked and gave the order to open before time (for fear of being lynched, she said).

The white elephant pitch did a furious trade. The purveyors of jumble, anticipating the pressure to which they would be subjected, had sorted their inferior stuff into grades of tenpence and upwards, leaving the prices of the more desirable things to be haggled over. One of the Askerswell gentlemen doing the serving said the bargains were such that only the fear of coming to church in a suit that might turn out to have been his next door neighbour's saved him from investing.

But the gem of the sale was not recognised until sold and gone. It was an authentic suit by Montague Burton when he was The Fifty Shilling Tailor, in good condition. The salesman who let it go for a song is still wracked by the thought of what the Victoria and Albert Museum might have given for it.

October 1976

Of jumble and church organisation

Our Christian Aid collections produced £130.77 for that very worthy object. The Help the Aged appeal for clothing gave the Vicarage the colley-wobbles this time. How on earth were we going to produce anything after the spate of local jumble sales? But 'the faithful' never fail. Parcels appeared in the garage, at the door, up the stairs, in the study and so unobtrusively that we rarely saw the donors to thank them. We had seventeen sacks for the HTA ladies' truck and most of it good enough to sell in the HTA shops, which helps the cause more.

But why do these appeals come in such a dollop? As the HTA ladies were in the study gathering up their sacks, the Christian Aid agent was at the door delivering the posters and collecting-tin for that, and we had only just got the collection for C of E children's homes off our chest. A change is as good as a rest, so it was refreshing to be called to the door that same evening by a nice girl with a tin for the Red Cross and later by another with a tin for Cancer Research, to be invited to give instead of to collect.

But the refreshment was short-lived. Ere long the church treasurer was in the study with a circular letter to all churches saying that parochial quotas were being raised by 50% to bring clergy stipends up to £3,500 p.a. As the Askerswell quota is £385, and the Loders £1,353, that means an extra £869 p.a. to be found on one item alone of the two churches' budget. It boils down to the parson having to beg for his keep, and to beg from a good-hearted minority of the community when the whole community has a legal right to his services. Hospital, service and prison chaplains of recognised denominations are paid by the State. The churches might have been better exercised in negotiating this privilege for all their ministers than wasting their time changing their form of government and worship.

June 1979

Verbal duels

We are all feeling deeply for the widow and five sons of the fifty-one year old Vicar of Broadwindsor, who died after clearing snow. Rumour first had it that the victim of this fatal heart attack was Canon Rowley, of Powerstock, and that the cause was not clearing snow, but his spirited verbal duel with the Archdeacon of Sherborne at the recent meeting when the latter heard local objections to the plan for putting the parishes of Powerstock, Loders and Askerswell, deprived of their resident parsons, under a Bridport team ministry. The meeting was unedifying in all respects. Only the Church Commissioners seem to know what the plan is. When the aggrieved parishes are let into the secret they will be able to appeal.

March 1978

Manning the parishes

To understand the Vicar's piece in the paragraph to follow this one, readers will need a rough-and-ready picture of the present system of manning the parishes of England with clergy: (a) Some areas are served by a team of clergy under a captain called a team rector. The team are called team vicars. But here 'rector' and 'vicar' are only courtesy titles. Legally they are priests-in-charge, licensed for a specific period, with no freehold. They may officiate in any church in the team area, at the captain's discretion. The church councils of the team area are reduced to 'district councils'. Their important functions are transferred to a new church council for the team area. (b) Some areas are under what is called a group ministry, but that need not be explained here. (c) The rest of England is under the old parochial system, where a rector or vicar serves his flock, with a freehold and a self-governing church council.

Because of the desperate shortage of clergy several flocks are put under one pastor, but the pastoral relationship as opposed to the team is preserved, though in a diluted form. The team system is supposed to be spiritually superior to the pastoral, which is supposedly riddled with parochialism. The team system is said to be more economical of clergy. But this remains to be seen. When the new priest-in-charge gets to Bradpole the Bridport team ministry will be five clergy serving six churches in a small compact area. The Loders–Askerswell–Powerstock pastoral ministry would be one clergyman serving five churches in a large area where the population is spread out.

* * * * *

The proposal that the Vicar should add Powerstock to his responsibilities is beginning to look like a dead duck. The very week that the committee informed the Vicar that vicars and rectors were not appointed these days, the *Western Gazette* told how a former cowman, only ordained in 1975, had been appointed rector of the four country parishes based on Winterbourne Whitechurch, near Blandford. It also carried a picture of those assisting at his institution and induction to the freehold, and they were the 'top brass' of the diocese – the Bishop of Salisbury; the Bishop of Sherborne, the Archdeacon of Dorset, and the Rural Dean of Milton and Blandford. To have begun life as a herdsman, or better still a shepherd, is an excellent qualification for a country parson, but it will be hard on parsons who have come by the usual route if the freehold is to be limited to those who have had the former advantage.

So, the Vicar of Loders and Rector of Askerswell will soldier on for as long as circumstances permit. Of these, the most important will be whether he is still getting a good congregation. The churchyard is proof enough that nobody in this world is indispensable.

September 1978

The Chancellor's stick

The Lord Chancellor of England attended matins at Powerstock a few Sundays ago. Around that time two 'distinguished-looking gentlemen' were seen inspecting the old and the new Loders Vicarage, one of whom was walking with a stick. The Lord Chancellor was using a stick at Powerstock, which is due to be joined with Loders and Askerswell in a country Plurality, and he is patron of Loders for this turn.

August 1981

Short and sweet

All that the last paragraph has to say this month is short and sweet. The machinery has been set in motion for Askerswell, Loders and Powerstock to become three self-governing parishes united in a benefice under a vicar with a freehold living in the vicarage being built at Loders, all confirmed by

Her Majesty in Council. The Archdeacon said this could not
be done with the present vicar still in possession of his
benefice, but it is being done.

November 1981

Of church-going, and the collection plate

These winter days are a measure of the importance we attach
to the worship of God. To stay in bed when the outside world
is dark and freezing is tempting indeed, yet a pleasing number
of last year's confirmees have got to the early Communion.
When church could be got to, others have turned out well to
matins, and made up missed contributions to the plate without
parsonic admonition.

February 1979

Statistics

Congratulations to Christopher and Janice Clay on the birth of a
son, Robert Andrew, at Portwey hospital on 11th May. Their
home is at Askerswell, and this event was a timely reminder to
the parish that people can be born as well as die. Mrs. Clay was
told that five babies were born at Portwey on the day hers was,
and the hospital suspects a population explosion to be under way.
The hospital bookings for three consecutive months are a most
unusual 90–80–90. It could merely be that certain times of the
year are getting popular for hatchings. But the point to take note
of is that the statisticians predict a progressive reduction in
births. A few years back they predicted a dramatic increase,
which did not come to pass. It may well be that the extra teacher
training colleges built for the predicted increase, and now
disposed of, will be needed for the predicted decrease.

June 1980

Records of death

At Dottery church the evensong on the second Sunday in
January was a family occasion for the Marsh clan. It was
followed by the burial in the family grave of the ashes of one
of their long lived matriarchs, Anne Marsh Marsh, a widow of

98, who had died at Axminster. Her husband, Frederick Charles Marsh, of Charmouth, died at the age of 49 in February 1931. John Marsh, churchwarden of Dottery, says that Frederick Charles had the misfortune to shoot and kill himself as he was getting through a hedge rabbiting. His widow endured life without a husband for nearly fifty years.

On the principle that a good story deserves embellishment and a bad one needs it, legend asserted that he was also the first to be buried in the churchyard given to Dottery by his family. Those who cherish this legend had better not look at the Dottery burial register, which records that John Lenthall, of Belshay farm was the first to be buried at Dottery, on 10th June 1924. Frederick Charles Marsh was the eighth.

February 1981

Parish Assemblies

The Askerswell Parish Assembly gathered in strength to hear an expert from County Hall, Colonel Woodward, explain the difference between government by parish council and by parish assembly. At their annual meeting, when the question was raised, there seemed to be a bias towards continuing with a parish assembly. The bias remained after Colonel Woodward's exposition, in spite of his surprising revelation that the chairman of a parish assembly has much more power than the chairman of a parish council, rather like a president of the United States compared with a British prime minister. This derives perhaps from the time when a small parish consisted usually of a squire and his varlets, and it was assumed that the squire would be elected chairman.

But Askerswell is now peopled with retired officers of all three armed services, and others who have made their mark in industry and business. There are more chiefs than Indians. It is as well that the parish assembly chose as their chairman a truly feminine and intelligent and humble lady before the awful powers of the chairman were generally known. She has summoned the assembly to meet again to settle what the parish shall do to celebrate the royal wedding in July [Prince Charles and Lady Diana Spencer] – a nice, homely, non-controversial matter.

June 1981

The fête and the fabric

It does not mean that because August the Second, the date of Loders Fête, is now within sight, and the vicar has said nothing about it, that he has not been thinking about it. The recent changes at the vicarage have made no difference to the church; its fabric wears out a little year by year even if the wear is not immediately apparent, and our policy of making annual provision against it is a sound one. So, in the week before the fête, the Vicar will be round in his ancient rôle of beggar of things to sell on the stalls. To those who are justly tired of his face he offers the consolation that it cannot be long before they see a younger one.

July 1980

Of Parish Councils and female clerks

Eight parishioners and five parish councillors attended the annual assembly of the parish of Loders in the village hall. Mr. George Hyde, the chairman, welcomed those who had turned out in such unseasonal spring weather. As a countryman himself he knew that had it been good gardening weather the attendance could have been still thinner. Mrs. Jessica Dunn, the rights of way liaison officer, reported that a new bridge over the river at Well Plot was being dealt with by the county council. At Locks Lane the persistent ploughing up of a right of way had been stopped 'by negotiation and a threat of prosecution.' If parishioners would walk their rights of way, owners would not put pig pens on them, as one did, 'because nobody uses it.'

As wardens of woods and rivers Mrs. Dunn and Mr. Hyde reported that many dead elms still needed removal. Preservation orders had been made on two woods at Matravers, one at Black Hut, two at The Leazes and one at Hillway. Loders Court Woods, Waddon Copses and Bunkers Hill already had tree preservation orders on them. To the relief of the clerk-for-nearly-55-years, Mr. Harold Brown, the meeting ended with the news that Mrs. M. Dent, of Yondover, had agreed to succeed him. She has had experience in local government.

June 1981

The Parish Notes

Readers of these *Notes* have usually been eager to get hold of them as soon as they are published. Because they are intensely local, perhaps, hands seem to be waiting inside letter-boxes to grab them. If they are late, some readers call at the vicarage and ask innocently if there is a mistake in their almanack. The publisher is deeply grateful to the distributors, who carry on in the spirit of the first distributors, the late Mrs. Olive Legg and Mrs. May Osborne.

At Askerswell Mrs. Christine Savage has been functioning for nearly 28 years; at Dottery Miss Rene White has been serving a readership scattered over several parishes, and doing it for over eleven years – on a bicycle. The distributor of the greatest number is Mrs. Willmott, in Loders, who also does most of them that go by post. Mrs. Nash and Mrs. Plows look after High Acres. Lower Loders is lucky to be under the wing of Mrs. Record, who takes them round hot from the press with the daily papers. The glory of Uploders is that distribution there has been an ecumenical effort. For nearly seven years it has been presided over by Mrs. Jessica Dunn, who is a Roman Catholic, helped by Mr. Joe Morris, who is a Methodist, and relieved at holiday times by Mr. Maurice Lawson and Mr. Phil Young, who are High and Low Anglicans respectively. Many hands make light work, but not invariably quick work – apparently – and the Vicar was much asked if he could not expedite the Uploders distribution.

Fearful of upsetting its ecumenical character, he raised the matter as tactfully as he could with Mrs. Dunn, offering her more help, but some of the correspondence will show that he only exploded the ecumenical effort. He is sorry for this, but assures Jessica that he still has a very soft spot for her.

March 1980

Universal Declaration of Independence

Both the fair and the exhibition have suffered grievous loss by the unexpected death of Richard Plows, of High Acres, who was the organiser of both, a prodigious worker, and an engaging personality. He was seventy. When he was eight he got pneumonia so badly that the Holy Church gave him the last rites. That resolved him never to be ill again, neither was he until the other day, when pains in the chest prompted him to drive himself to the doctor. He died in the surgery.

The attendance at the funeral in Loders church, which preceded cremation at Weymouth, was a measure of the sympathy felt for his family, and especially for his widow Ray, who is as public-spirited as he was. In the funeral oration the vicar referred to the success of the parishes of Loders, Askerswell and Powerstock in fighting off their proposed absorption into the enlarged parish of Bridport. He had regarded Richard as an ally in trying to keep the village a lively entity in its own right.

July 1980

West Milton Church

Observations on the fête: Local patriotism persists in these parts, and hats off to it. But Loders need not be irked because Burton fête has taken over the lead by about £80, topping £1,000. It has the holiday camps. The issue is not in doubt as to which is the better fête financially, when one with 500 paid admissions takes £921.80; and the other with 1500 paid admissions takes £1000. Loders owes its success to the unfailingly good giving before fête day, the measure of which is £236 in cash, and offerings in kind which sold for about £400 on the day. All sections of the community 'do their stuff', not least the old-age pensioners, new parishioners and former parishioners, and friends from far and near.

Cash donations this year were swelled by a quite touching and substantial offering from 'the friends of West Milton Church' in recognition of the Vicar's help in their efforts, (unsuccessful), to save their church, which was declared redundant after an operation that looks more like murder.

September 1974

End of a churchyard

Loders Church was tightly filled for the funeral of Mrs. Ada Samways, of Lynch Farm, West Milton. The sun broke out of its black winter prison and beamed on the flower bedecked coffin in the chancel for a memorable service. In his address the Vicar said Mrs. Samways' life had been uneventful and dull by present reckoning. Nearly all of it had been lived in West Milton. A reporter of a daily paper would be hard put to write something about her that his editor would print. Yet there was that in her conduct as a wife and a mother and a neighbour and a pillar of the church that brought together this great gathering to pay their last respects.

Years ago the Reverend Brian Issac had been on holiday in West Milton. Mrs. Samways was one of the first villagers he met. Her sweetness and the feel of the village decided him to retire to West Milton if he could. Well, he did, and he would be taking the burial service in the churchyard of the church she worshipped in until it met its untimely end.

April 1979

The Parish Notes and the terrorists

These *Parish Notes* are not intended to be a diary of events in our domain, but a record of things worthy of note. Just lately the parish has been noting something in the great outside world that is getting horribly familiar – terrorists hi-jacking a plane and holding passengers hostage for the release of fellow terrorists in jail. Pilots are threatening drastic action if they are not protected against this, and the United Nations are worrying their heads off how to stop it.

Our country air is clear of the smog that seems to envelope the world's conference chambers, and we see a simple solution. When terrorists have been caught, tried, and found guilty, they should be executed, then nobody could be held hostage for their release. When an offence is committed against an individual, he can turn the other cheek, according with the Sermon on the Mount. But the civil power cannot turn the other cheek to murderers and the like, and is not expected to. St. Paul, following his Master's precept about rendering to Caesar the things that are Caesar's and to God the things that are God's, says (*Epistle to Romans, New English Bible*), 'The civil authorities are God's agents working for your good. If you are doing wrong then you will have cause to fear them; it is not for nothing that they hold the power of the sword, for they are God's agents of punishment for retribution on the offender.' St. Peter concurs. He says (in his First Epistle), 'Submit yourselves to every human institution for the sake of the Lord, whether to the sovereign as supreme, or to the governor as his deputy for the punishment of criminals and the commendation of those who do right.'

The other day Pope Paul the Sixth had a glorious opportunity to give the world the dominical and apostolic teachings on this subject. Instead, he made the futile offer of himself in the place of the hostages. How very odd it is that the civil authorities and the Vicar of Christ should be ready to expend the lives of the armed forces and of the police in the thwarting of terrorists, and yet regard the life of a captured and condemned terrorist as sacrosanct!

November 1977

Stormy weather

The storm of December 27th which took tiles off the vicarage and plaster off the south wall, and let water into the dining-room, led to an inspection by the archidiaconal surveyor, who reported to the diocesan parsonages board that the south wall of the fifteenth century part of the vicarage is leaning outward under the weight of the superstructure added a century ago, and needs rebuilding. This would be a major work. It would make the dining-room and probably kitchen and study uninhabitable for a while, and the bathroom and bedrooms above them.

The vicar has agreed to the suggestion that he might move to Bell, and continue the cure of souls from there. Seeing that Powerstock is to be united with Loders, that the retired priest now caring for Powerstock wishes to be relieved of it, and that a more convenient house has to be provided for the incumbent of the new plurality, it seems probable that the vicar would not return to the vicarage. He could continue his vicarial duties from Bell until his successor was ready to take over.

February 1980

The new Vicarage

A sketch design for the new Loders Vicarage is being studied by the Parish Council. Their first impression could be well conveyed by the word 'posh'. It is a well-conceived bungalow, twice the size of an ordinary bungalow (indeed, floor space 175 square metres to meet official requirements), and probably costly to build even on a site which costs nothing. The local planning authority is known to disfavour bungalows in the Loders conservation area, but may be persuaded that the environment of the new vicarage requires that it be literally low profile.

Meanwhile the Vicar is feeling slightly episcopal for the first time in his life. A church which contains a diocesan bishop's seat is a cathedral whether the building be a nissen hut or a minster. Any house in which a vicar of a parish lives with official approval is a vicarage. The vicar now lives in Bell, so Bell is for the present Loders vicarage. The former vicarage has done what he did when he reached 70, come of age, and for the first time in its near 500 years is now 'the old vicarage'.

May 1980

Forward planning

Loders vicarage. A meeting of the Sherborne Archdeaconry Parsonages Board on June 20th informed the vicar that they had told their architect to submit to the planning authority a design of a 2-storey 4-bedroom house for the vicarage garden which they hoped would succeed. A month has elapsed and the plan seems not to have penetrated these parts yet.

August 1980

The end of the saga

Loders Vicarage. The Vicar writes: This final paragraph of *The Notes* seems to be the one nobody skips. It is becoming like something out of Trollope.

* * * * *

March the Tenth was a portentous day for believers in astrology. For the first time since the year 1803 and the last until 2357, the sun's nine planets, including the earth, were all within an area of 96 degrees on the same side of the sun. Disasters from India to

California were predicted – earthquakes, riots, outbreaks of disease, etc. and perhaps tidal waves. Thousands of people were reported to have flocked to mosques, temples and churches in Kashmir for prayers to ward off the predicted catastrophe.

But nothing happened. This, of course, can be interpreted in two ways: either the prediction of the astrologers was wrong, or they were right and the prayers in mosques, temples and churches were answered by God in the affirmative. Astrologers who are not prayerful may be comforted to know that on March 10th the long régime of the Rev. O.L. Willmott as Vicar of Loders and Rector of Askerswell came effectively to an end. On that very day he happened to write the letter of resignation which ended his régime and extinguished him as a vicar and rector. It also extinguished the longest tenure of an incumbency in the counties of Wiltshire and Dorset that comprise the Diocese of Salisbury.

One of Shakespeare's dicta came readily to the Vicar's mind: 'When beggars die there are no comets seen; the heavens themselves blaze forth the death of princes'. But this seemed not to apply to him. As Vicar he had been a beggar, certainly, but not a prince of beggars. The latter, surely, are those professional tear-jerkers who raise a lot for deserving charities and pocket fat commissions. Perhaps the words put by Thomas Hardy into the mouth of the exiled Napoleon make a better epitaph: 'Great men are meteors that consume themselves to light the earth: I am in the burnt-out stage.'

July 1981–April 1982

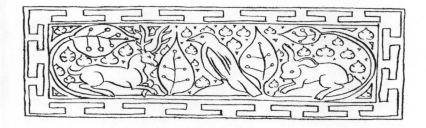

CHAPTER 4

Staying put, passing through, passing on

One commentator upon the draft version of *Yours Reverently* proclaimed irreverently – 'Who would want to read a sequence of obituaries, for a whole chapter?' He had a point, though the genre has its fanatical aficionados, as the broadsheet newspapers know well.

Inevitably, the form of the obituary was used for a substantial portion of *The Parish Notes*. I have not stopped to count how many the Vicar wrote – it must be in the region of 1,000. He had the art of writing immediate, intimate, warm obituaries, often humorous, always perceptive, and knowing how to deal with the sensitivities of the departed, and their relatives. He wrote very straight obituaries, even for his critics. And where possible they were balanced by happy births, merry weddings and accounts of eccentric people.

There are some portraits of formidable village aristocratic ladies of the Lady Bracknell school. Their male counterparts are reminiscent of Justice Shallow in their faded hankering for the good old days when they were 'wags'. Aristocracy, judges, doctors and lawyers met farmers and humble folk in the pub, at the Fête, at Well Plot Green, or on the lawns of genteel garden Open Days.

The mix produced what Falstaff noted of Justice Shallow and

his servingmen in rural Gloucestershire: 'It is a wonderful thing to see the semblance coherence of his men's spirits and his: they, by observing of him, do bear themselves like foolish justices; he, by conversing with them is turned into a justice-like servingman.'

The Vicar, sadly, began to accept the parish as 'somewhere where people came to die'. He took the funerals. He wrote the obituaries. Obituaries need not be morbid. They are a celebration of character, and love generated, and of a community noticing. Where possible he wrote with joy. Obituaries can also be funny – wait for the account of the hearse on ice (p. 143). They were only part of his Dorset philosophy absorbed from Thomas Hardy of 'noticing such things'. In this instance it is not so much Nature as human nature, which fascinated him.

The spirit of the true countryman

That 'The perils and dangers of this night' prayed against at evensong are not obsolete was shown by the recent high winds. A giant ash tree near the Old Rectory at Askerswell was blown over. Mercifully it fell in the one place where it could not hurt the house and main outbuildings, and it flushed Captain Aylmer with firewood. He, in the spirit of the true countryman, lamented that so many of the animal kingdom had lost a home. The tree was hollow. What would the tawny owl and his feathered neighbours do now?

December 1972

The passing of Captain Aylmer

The Old Rectory of Askerswell without Captain Aylmer is now as lonely and mournful as Jeremiah's lodge in a garden of cucumbers. His three pet Guernsey cows still feeding beside it, cannot blind us to the fact that his death, at 82, has ended an era. The congregation that filled the church for the funeral service seemed aware of this, and the pealing of the muffled bells proclaimed it to the countryside he loved so well. In the funeral oration the Rector remarked that his appreciation of the countryside and his zest for country pursuits seemed greatly to exceed that of those who had lived all their lives in the parish, probably because with them it was 'Easy come, easy go', but with him his twenty-eight years of enjoyment of Askerswell was bought at a price.

People enjoy what they really earn, and nobody was more deserving of the delights of home life in the country than he. For forty-one years he had served in the Royal Navy, with the disruption of home life and moving about that that entails. In the two world wars he was in destroyers, submarines and anti-aircraft cruisers, in the thick of the fight to save this country's lifelines, and himself bearing a charmed life. Even in his spell of shore duty as captain of the Naval College at Dartmouth he was bombed out, and had to evacuate that establishment temporarily.

The death of his wife had done to him what the might of the German Navy could not, knocked him out for many weeks, but with the help of other naval veterans in the neighbourhood he had pulled through, and resumed his useful rôle.

The Rector did not say it, but to him one of life's minor mysteries is that so often warriors born to command, like Edward Aylmer, have a partiality for commanding wives. On the wall of Askerswell old rectory hung the bell of his submarine the *L23*, at the ringing of which his crew jumped-to. Here it was his late wife Phoebe who rang it imperiously when he was wanted from the garden, and he who jumped-to.

December 1974

Squirearchical symptoms

A human birth in Askerswell is a rare event, so the knowledge that there was to be one kept the village in a state of pleasurable but discreet excitement for some weeks. The happy event occurred in Bridport hospital on August 15th, when Christopher William was born to Francis and Jennifer Hemmings, who live in the bungalow formerly occupied by Mrs. Swaffield, near The Square. The excitement has subsided into a calm feeling of communal achievement: the village is not moribund.

To the deep-thinking among the parishioners, the real signif-icance of this indigenous increase of population is that it should have occurred so far down in the village as The Square. For years the spirit of fertility had looked to be permanently settled up at Legg's Mead. But now the spirit of that great Askerswell character, the late Mrs. Phoebe Aylmer, of the *Old Rectory*, seems to be at work. She had squirearchical symptoms, and once told the present Rector that on her way back from shooting at Nallers she had had the good luck to meet the miscreant from Legg's Mead 'who had just added a sixth to his five lovely children, and had told him it was time he was "put down"'. Her moral right to say this was impregnable: she had produced only one. But she was forgetting that the rector was the father of seven.

September 1977

Dizzy heights

One of the summer visitors to call recently at Loders vicarage was our village bobby of long ago, the former P.C. Edrich. He is now so high in the Force that the vicar felt in need of oxygen to converse with him in his rarified atmosphere. But his son Eddie is the marvel. Eddie used to be the naughtiest and nicest boy in Loders Sunday School. (He stayed at the vicarage while his mother was in hospital and got a spanking for eating part of the old tithe map after squeezing a crumpet full of hot butter over the table-cloth). Well, he ran a London West End cinema so successfully that the Rank organisation sponsored him to London University, where he took a first class bachelor of science in economics. He is now working for his master of science, and runs a successful business college!

August 1979

Kiss for the Vicar

A Christmas Carol Service at the Uploders Chapel, led by some of the choir of the Methodist Chapel in Bridport, produced a collection of upwards of £3 for Christian Aid. It happened to be the ninetieth birthday of Mrs. Beatty Clark, the oldest inhabitant of Loders. She was sung *Happy Birthday* to, when she came into the chapel for service. Earlier in the day her ancient cottage in Uploders had been a beehive with people calling to congratulate her. She took them all in her stride, showing them her cards and presents, but getting on with the housework as well.

When the Vicar made his call to offer the homage of the parish he noted her eye travelling to the bunch of holly above his head, and heard her saying that it was only there temporarily until the mistletoe should arrive, which was late in coming. He was not one to let the nature of the appendage mar the luck of The Cloth, and seizing the opportunity with both arms, became the envy of the males of the parish.

In the early evening of the birthday the Church Choir began their Uploders carolling at Granny Clark's. After their recital she called them in – not easy of accomplishment in so small a house. They found her sitting in state in her armchair by the fire, enjoying the attention hugely. At her command a retinue of neighbours issued from behind the chair and dispensed wine and birthday cake.

January 1969

The best place!

When Granny Clark, the oldest inhabitant of Loders, did not appear for a few days, and milk bottles and newspapers accumulated at her front door, neighbours feared the worst and mounted a ladder to her bedroom window. To their relief they saw the grand old lady sitting in bed, muffled to the eyebrows and well supplied with food. She had been there several days and said it was 'the best place this weather'. There was snow at that time.

February 1971

92-years-young

June was mostly a dismal month. Cold wet days, with blackened hay lying about, were hard to stomach after the glories of May and April. How inspiriting then to hear the 92-year-old Granny Clark, the oldest inhabitant of Loders, say, 'To the devil with the weather', and watch her set about the lush crop of weeds at her cottage door with a bill-hook.

When she came more into public view to deal with the ivy on her boundary wall it needed no eye for detail to see that she was in a trouser suit, the seat prodigiously padded against a fall. The spectacle confirmed the grand old lady's contention that she is 'Ninety-two-years-young'.

July 1971

A glad triumphant setting out for home

Loders lost its oldest inhabitant by the death at Sidney Gale Home of 'Granny' Beatty Clark. Whether she was ninety-four or ninety-five was something she had argued with the benign Master of the Home. He seems to have had the last word, for it was ninety-four on the disposal certificate. She had told the Master the hymns she wanted at her funeral (in Loders Church) and these were duly sung: *A few more years shall roll, and There is a blessed home.* An Epiphany carol, *As with gladness men of old*, was added for good measure. The church was still in all its Christmas finery, with lighted tree and crib.

This made the funeral a glad triumphant setting out for home, an appropriate send-off for so long and good and colourful a life. She was buried at the cemetery in the grave of her husband, who died in 1958.

Soon after this there were signs that her crumbling old cottage was being turned out. A bonfire smoked in the overgrown garden which she was still trying to cultivate when she was well past ninety. Presumably the cottage will be pulled down. This seems slightly sacriligious, for those stones must have absorbed the prayers that the old lady learned at her mother's knee, and continued to say, aloud, each night when she went to bed.

February 1974

Great-grandson of Parson Thomas

The great-grandson of Parson Thomas, Vicar of Loders 1887–1914, has come with his wife and two-year old daughter, Vanessa to live at *West Winds* in Uploders. He is Mr. Nicholas Prideaux, who had been a farm manager in Cheshire, and has now taken a similar post with Messrs. O. and J. House, at Powerstock. His grandmother, Mrs. Prideaux, is well into her eighties, and lives at Weymouth. As the young Miss Thomas, she played the organ at the thanksgiving service for that part of the restoration of Loders Church completed in 1900.

Parson Thomas cleared the church of its box pews and three-decker pulpit and west-end gallery, made good the floor of the nave and Ladye Chapel which was honeycombed with vaults, and removed the lathe and plaster from the walls, exposing the doorway to the pulpit and roodloft and the architectural delights concealed in the north wall of the chancel. He did not deal with the roofs, which still held a little wear in 1900. The nave roof was restored in 1952 and the Ladye Chapel roof in 1967. The chancel roof has still to be done.

A comparison of costs is a salutary lesson on the decline of the value of money. In 1900 Parson Thomas's entire restoration cost £1,200. In 1967 the Ladye Chapel roof alone cost over £2,400.

Desmond Bye

It took the very successful village fayre at Well Plot to discover to the Vicar his most remarkable parishioner. He was watching the annual tug-o'-war between Loders and Uploders for the soup plate when a bystander drew his attention to the Beggars Opera mob that seem always to swarm on the Uploders end. One of the mob was Desmond Bye, who had told the Vicar on coming to live in Uploders only that he was a 'retired bank manager with a tin leg.' Such is the characteristic reticence of the armed forces of the Crown.

Desmond Bye was a Spitfire pilot who fought in the epic defence of Malta in 1942. The Liberator in which he and fellow pilots were returning to England crashed into the sea near Gibraltar and several were drowned. He was rescued from under water minus a useful leg and eventually invalided out of the R.A.F.

His tin leg is no passenger. He not only wins tug-o'-wars with it, and gardens, but plays golf. We can hear our own valiant golf addict, George Houghton, saying, 'It's the golf that does it.' He also saw hot service in the R.A.F. The weather for the fayre was perfect, and the wonderful roses in the Scotts' garden at the top of Well Plot welcomed a goodly attendance. The Wessex Morris men were on form, and their practised precision made the flutterings of the young ballet dancers the more appealing. In the hall a display of old village photographs was alone worth an afternoon of spectating.

The little parson in cassock, surplice and outsize stole was none other than the Reverend David Thomas, to whom Loders owes the intelligent and thorough restoration of its church at the start of the century. His stalwart great-grandson Nick Prideaux, who was at the fair, must have marvelled at the rock whence he, Nick, was hewn.

August 1981

Preaching at over-80

Mr. Fred Vacher, a former luminary of the Methodist Church, gave the address at Loders morning service on the Sunday preceding the Bishop and set the high standard that the Bishop was to maintain. The vigour of Mr. Vacher's mind, and the strength of his voice, quite belied his eighty-two years. Age has mellowed him: he was still more loveable, and a shade less critical of our sins. He insisted on speaking from the chancel step, where his happy married life began.

September 1969

Fred Vacher

Toronto, Canada, saw the obsequies of another Fred, also a true son of Dorset and a frequent benefactor of Loders Church, Mr. Fred Vacher, husband of the former Marjorie Budden, of Loders. It will be remembered that they were both in Loders last summer, when at the age of 82, and after a very serious operation, Mr. Vacher gave the address at matins on the chancel step where he had been married thirty one years before. At his request and expense, the Vicar flew out to take the funeral, which was the simple English service in the elaborate American frame. Mr. Tony Budden (nephew) flew from New York to be a bearer. Another nephew, Mr. Bill Budden, being then in Spain, was unable to be present. As friends in a constant stream came to offer their condolences at the open casket, and sign the book, the Vicar was impressed at Mr.

Vacher's standing in Toronto, and his rare combination of business astuteness with compassion.

Tenants of his house told how he refused to take rents at the prevailing level because he thought it was too high. His lawyer told how he would only take two thirds of the current mortgage rate because in his opinion it was ridiculous. A girl from the blind school told how every Christmas he sent them all five dollars each to help with their Christmas shopping. Clearly the huge array of floral tributes was not perfunctory. His dead hands clasped a bunch of violets from Loders. Later, a few simple flowers from his funeral appeared on Loders chancel step, and despite their long journey, seemed to refuse to die.

May 1971

Peripatetic Bill Budden

We would like to wish our readers a Happy New Year. They continue to grow in numbers. Sometimes we try to visualise them en masse. They could fill a cathedral. Paper may be a fragile thing, but it does us good service. Some copies of the *Notes* get read by one family, re-folded, posted, read by another family and then posted to another. They meet their end, some of them, in distant parts of the world. It would never surprise us to hear from that amiable peripatetic Bill Budden that he had had fish and chips served up to him in an old copy in Baghdad.

January 1976

Peppered with Buddens

Mr. and Mrs. Bill Budden, who are no strangers to Loders, and their daughter Caroline fortified by a degree in Law newly acquired from Bristol University, have at last come to live in their imposing new house. It dominates the High Street from the school westwards, and commands the pass to Yondover eastwards.

The earthworks are merely the convulsions of a beautiful front garden being born, and not a defence against Mrs. Anthony Sanctuary and her Civic Society. Bill is so nice a character that he will soon have lived down his rough handling

of Mother Nature. Nobody in Loders has a better title to living
here high and lifted up than this. His is the oldest Loders
family. The three and a half centuries of parish registers are
peppered with Buddens, and nobody else going up to the house
of God to worship has to worm his way through the altar tombs
of his ancestors as Bill has.

July 1976

One of Nature's aristocrats

Mr. David Thomas was buried beside the lamp in Loders
churchyard, the spot he himself had chosen. The hymns sung
at the funeral were his choosing. It was doubtless to his
liking again that the lesson was read by the Lay Rector, the
Hon. Alexander Hood, and that his friend Mr. Bill Tiltman
could be at the organ.

Mr. Thomas was a parish clerk in the old tradition. Had
our three-decker pulpit survived the 1900 restoration he
might have been leading the responses from its bottom deck.
At the west end, and among the congregation he was incon-
spicuous, but the moral support of his 'answers' was
fearfully lacking when his last illness kept him away from
church. His long and faithful service of the church was
inspired by a devotion akin to what he had felt as a ploughman for his horses. He was one of nature's aristocrats, a
living ornament of the church. We and countless visitors
cannot think of the church without thinking of him, too. So
he passes into the church invisible with whom our earthly
worship is joined.

September 1968

Parish Clerk

Mrs. Thomas, widow of the late parish clerk of Loders, has
been appointed verger in his place. As a parish clerk must be
a man, this office, so fittingly performed by Mr. Thomas, is
in abeyance for the time being. It is not to be confused with
the office of clerk to the parish council, a new creation. The
parish clerk's is an ancient office. In the Middle Ages he was
in minor orders. Canon 91 says, 'The parish clerk shall be

twenty years of age at the least, and known to the parson to be of honest conversation, and sufficient for his reading, writing, and also for his competent skill in singing, if it may be. And the said clerk shall have his ancient wages without fraud or diminution, either at the hands of the churchwarden, or by his own collection, according to the most ancient custom of every parish'.

An Act of King William the Third says that 'a parish clerk, for assisting at a marriage without banns or licence, shall forfeit five pounds for every such offence' and five pounds was a small fortune to a poor man in those days.

November 1968

Neighbours in life and death

Loders was shaken by the quite unexpected death of Mr. Harry Sanders. He was 74. He had been about to light his fire, when he fell ill and called a neighbour. Before the doctor came he was gone. For him an ideal departure – active to the end, and no pain – but for his invalid wife, whom he looked after with great devotion, a shattering experience. She was moved into Bridport Hospital, where, conscious of the sympathy of a multitude of friends, she has borne herself bravely.

Mr. Sanders had been an officer of Loders Church for forty years – twenty-four as sidesman and sixteen as people's churchwarden. His ample figure and regular attendance made him very much a pillar of the church. He and his wife would have celebrated their golden wedding on April 12th. For both of them Loders Church was about their only interest outside their home and they knew from the inside its domestic history in the past fifty years. He sometimes recalled 'the elevenpenny ha'penny evensongs' of the early 1930's, when 11^1/2d was the usual collection and the church had no competition from cars, television or Sunday cinemas! He was buried alongside his former next-door neighbour, the late Mr. David Thomas. Not often are next-door neighbours in life next-door in death as well.

March 1969

Mrs. Caroline Thomas

Loders Church was well filled with friends of the late Mrs.
Caroline Thomas lamenting her death which came unexpectedly when she was seemingly well and active. She was 77, and
showed the love for the church of her late husband, Mr. David
Thomas, who was parish clerk and verger for many years. To
within a week of her death she rang the minute bell for the
early communion, took the collection, tolled the funeral bell,
and rarely missed matins. In his funeral oration the Vicar
recalled the accident that incapacitated her husband years ago,
and how nobly she had played the part of bread-winner to her
family. She had an innate refinement of character, and knew
how to make the most of her personal appearance.

At a village fête some years ago the stage celebrity Vic
Oliver had judged her the most glamorous grand-mother out of
a pretty bunch of competitors. She was proof that genuine religion need not be long-faced. In the heyday of village whist
drives she was the keenest of players, much given to trumping
her partner's ace, yet seeming always to emerge with a prize.

April 1974

Summer Time

Jack McDowall, Churchwarden of Loders, advanced his ten
clocks by one hour on the eve of Sunday, 22nd March, because
his diary said Summer Time began that day. He found he had
risen for church an hour too soon, the day having been postponed a week to suit the European Community. He is still sore
over the loss of an hour's sleep.

But his discomfiture was as nothing to the Vicar's years ago,
when David Thomas brought in summer time prematurely,
chiming the bells for early service when the Vicar was half
dressed and unshaven, milking the vicarage cow.

April 1981

The late Mrs. Sarah Brown

By her death Uploders has lost a gracious old lady of ninety
on whom the ever-rolling stream of time seemed to have no

effect. Immobility, which kept her indoors, was her only apparent physical defect. Se had a clear, objective mind, well-versed in the events of the day, and an amazing fluidity of expression which never faltered, however tired she might be.

She was a native of North Allington, and when a girl entered service in Loders Court under the Nepeans. There she met her husband-to-be, Mr. Sidney Brown, who was coachman. Thereafter she was a working partner in his small-holding and carrier's business. Old people's institutions are good and necessary places, but 'home is best', and Mrs. Brown was always praising the devotion of her son and daughter which enabled the closing years of her long life to be spent at home.

November 1971

Clerk to the Parish Council

By a nice coincidence it was Nov. 11th, 1926, when Mr. Brown became clerk to Loders Parish Council, and November 11th, 1976, when at the social Mr. Ronald Price, present chairman of the council, called on Mr. Wilfred Crabb, a councillor for forty-six years, to present Mr. Brown with a cheque for £100 and an inscribed pewter tankard. The cheque was a large hand-painted one, which he says he will frame. The cash, he says, is earmarked for a long awaited holiday with his lady wife.

Like most of us, Mr. Brown was vastly amused at the flash-light photograph which appeared in the *Bridport News*. Something on the reverse side of the thin paper had given him a toothbrush moustache. It consoled him that if he looked like Hitler, Mr. Crabb looked like Hess. But two less warlike characters are hard to imagine.

December 1976

Retirement

Bad news travels fast, so Loders is likely to know already that its parish council clerk for fifty years, Mr. Harold Brown, has asked to retire with effect from 31st March, 1977. He was appointed on Nov. 11th, 1926, at the tender age of twenty-one. Ill-health is the reason for the resignation. He says playfully his doctor tells him he is suffering from Four A's – Arthritis,

Angina, Anaemia and Anno Domini. The thought of Loders
parish council minus Harold seems preposterous. He *is* the
parish council. Where will it be without his truly professional
management of its affairs, he a mountain of a man at a mouse
of a salary? We hope in next month's *Notes* to be free enough
from funeral reports to return to the subject of Harold.

February 1976

The Exeter by-pass

Mr. Harry Crabb, Captain of Loders Ringers, and the only
surviving champion of the Ringers' annual 'Out In,' has had
his faith in the therapeutic value of that institution severely
jolted. This year our Ringers joined a trip to Newquay, organised by the Netherbury Ringers, who left out of their reckoning
the horrors of the Exeter bypass on a summer Saturday. In
consequence, Harry was marooned for five hours with a bottle
of lemonade, and the coach never got to Newquay.

September 1969

Teething troubles

The ringers of St. Bartholomew the Great, London, much
enjoyed having Mr. Harry Crabb, the Loders captain, as their
guest, first in the tower for ringing practice, and then in their
snuggery at *The Hand and Shears*. We hear, incidentally, that
Harry had teething troubles with his new colour television.
The programmes kept changing of their own accord, which
displeased him. It transpired that the set is hypersensitive, and
flies walking over it were the culprits. So *Rose Cottage* now
has a super fly-paper!

July 1975

Rose Cottage

Rose Cottage, the tiny thatched home of Mr. and Mrs. Harry
Crabb that looks like something out of Grimm's *Fairy Tales*,
was the pulsating heart of Loders as well as Uploders on
September 17th, their Golden Wedding Day, for Harry may be
captain of the Loders Ringers, but Lizzie his wife is the wise

woman of Uploders whose kind heart and capacious medicine cupboard are the first resort of anybody in trouble, physical or spiritual.

The first of the many callers on the great day were Post Office engineers who connected the cottage to the telephone, this being the gift of the children and grandchildren whose intuition was a sound one that nothing could please more than to improve her means of communication. As the family gathered to celebrate in the evening, the bell-chamber of Loders tower filled with ringers who sounded the bells in praise of Harry's fifty-odd years of devotion to campanology. It was the ringers' turn to be royally entertained at *Rose Cottage* the following night.

And then Mrs. Harry opened her heart a little. She said she had made no preparations for the anniversary in case it didn't occur. She was the eleventh of eleven children, and she had not forgotten how her sister had died only three days before *her* golden wedding. Neither had she forgotten old Granny Hyde at the village shop, who got so excited about hers, that she was in bed with a heart attack when the rest were eating her lovely ham and pickles in the Uploders Room. These fine sentiments are not shared by Harry. When his other Odd Fellows emerging from their monthly meeting in the Chapel two days before the golden wedding took him round the corner to *The Crown* to celebrate, he hadn't to be dragged. 'A bird in the hand . . .' is his motto.

As hostess talked and ringers listened, a bell tinkled, and there was dead silence. 'It's the telephone,' said Harry, as he climbed over the ringers to answer it. In that snuggery of home-made wine and burnished horse brasses a telephone seemed incongruous. 'It's Wilfred for you, Missus. Wants to know how bist.' Putting down the phone, Harry clambered back to his place. As Lizzie picked up the phone, he cautioned her, 'Mind thee speaks into the right 'ole'.

October 1975

Captain of the outfit

A former landlord of the *Loders Arms*, Mr. Frank Osborne, has given us a sheet of the *Bridport News* and *Dorsetshire,*

Devonshire and Somersetshire Advertiser, dated Friday, September 5th, 1884. It was given to him by the last landlord of the neighbouring but now defunct *Farmers Arms*, Mr. Bill Maddison. It contains a letter by John S. Stewart, the then Vicar of Loders, appealing for funds to repair Loders bells. The letter is interesting, but so uneconomical of words that it would take more than a whole issue of these *Notes* to reproduce.

Precisely what the money was needed for is hard to elucidate, but some quaint things are said about the bells, namely:- the treble has a beautiful shape and tone and was cast on the spot at Court Close; the ugly bell is the second and its tone is not as good as the rest; the third bell is an old friend with a new face for it had cracked and been recast; the fourth bell was recast from an old bell, in Court Close, but is too sharp in tone; the fifth bell is four feet across and more than 200 years old, the clapper being as old as the bell and having dented the side of the bell with its blows. It would seem that the bells needed rehanging. The belfry was full of jackdaws' and pigeons' nests, proof that our Harry Crabb was not captain of that outfit.

March 1979

Of Harry and hot air

A little girl from Shrewsbury, being shown Loders Church, said she liked 'the chimney'. Her puzzled father elucidated that she meant the tower, which does indeed emit hot air sometimes, especially when Captain Harry is telling the young ringers – and often the old ones – 'Yule nivver make a hringer'.

May 1979

Premature death

The seventy-six year old captain of Loders Ringers, Harry Crabb, surprised and dismayed their annual meeting by showing a premature sign of dying. He said the time had come for him to stand down as captain. In itself this was nothing, because it was always his opening gambit.

But this time not all the beguilements of the lady ringers could change his mind. He nominated Frank Good as his successor, and David House as vice-captain, and these were duly elected, Frank agreeing to continue as secretary and treasurer (it is always the busy people who are landed with extra work: he has his hands full of St. John's Ambulance and is a lively member of the Loders Entertainment Committee). Where the ladies failed, the Vicar succeeded. Harry grudgingly agreed that the machinery of his beloved bells was safe in no hands but his, and accepted the office of tower-warden.

July 1979

Harry's true age

We apologise to Harry Crabb for giving his age as seventy-six. It is seventy-seven. He 'proved' it to be seventy-seven, not seventy-six, by pulling up the tenor bell in front of the vicar, single-handed. The tenor weighs nearly a ton.

August 1979

Order of merit

The life size Teddy Bear on the children's stall was bought by a Canadian for £4 to take home to Canada. It had been made by Mrs. Rob Wrixon, whom we wish a speedy recovery from her present illness. Our Order of Merit goes to Mr. Steve Newberry for supplying the tea-tabernacle with a tarpaulin in emergency. He had emptied the tarpaulin of newly shorn fleeces which he could not think where to put.

September 1971

Ready for the operating theatre

Mrs. Rose Newberry is back home at Yondover Farm from a major operation at Weymouth General Hospital, still smiling after her unnerving experience. When she first went in for the operation she was sent home without it because the surgeons were busy with the casualties from the submarine explosion at Portland. On the second occasion she was trussed and ready for the operating theatre when the sterilising equipment broke down, and the operation had to be postponed for a few days more. Were Mrs. Newberry the sort to ask, 'Why should this happen to me?' the answer would be, 'Because you can take it.'

November 1971

The clan

Sunday, February the seventeenth was a great day for the farming clan of Newberry's in Loders. It was the fiftieth anniversary of the wedding of its head, Mr. Harry Newbury senior, and his wife, Rose. It was also their last family gathering in the farmhouse at Yondover, for they are shortly retiring – in the village fortunately – and the farm is up for sale. Members of the family from afar converged on the old farmhouse on the night of the seventeenth for a feast of good things, and a 'tell' about old times.

No farmer worthy of the name is addicted to the bath. On this occasion the smile on Mr. Newberry's newly reaped face, and the shine on his whole person, suggested that he did not regret it. The joy of the company of his large family obliviated his rheumatics. For Mrs. Newberry the highlight of the evening was to step into the yard and listen to the bells ringing in honour of the event. She confessed afterwards to being deeply touched by the fact that four of her grand-daughters were ringing that night – Sheila and Dulcie, Cynthia and Linda, with Captain Harry Crabb and the Vicar manning the two heaviest bells.

Thanks to Harry Crabb the campanological programme survived the breaking of the rope of the fourth bell, which did not disconcert Cynthia, who was ringing it. With an agility believing his seventy-odd years Harry was up the stairs to the belfry, down with the errant rope, splicing (or 'marrying' as he called it) the broken ends, up the belfry again, and down to ring. What Loders Tower would do without him, heaven only knows.

March 1974

Newberries and Crabbs

By custom the sheaves of corn that adorn Loders harvest festival are given to Mrs. Jude Greening, the widowed daughter of that magnificent Dorset character the late Shepherd George Crabb. How exactly she disposes of the corn came to our ears by accident. She keeps it till Christmas, which she spends with her daughters. The Newberrys, of *Cloverleaf Farm*, see to her hens as well as her few sheep while she is away. On Christmas Day, on her strict instructions, they put the sheaves in the hen-house for the hens to scratch about in. 'They be God's creatures just as we be, so why shouldn't they have a little Christmas treat?' demands Jude in that tone of voice that nips any contradiction in the bud.

November 1980

Champion at bowls

Mr. Jack Verrinder, of *The Crown*, Uploders, was in the convalescent side of Portland Hospital at the time of writing, hoping to be transferred to Bridport Hospital. The spirit in which he resigned himself to the amputation of his right leg, just below the thigh, is beyond praise. He keeps his visitors cheerful, and is already figuring out whether it is possible to have an artificial leg and still be a champion at bowls.

February 1969

Local hero

A local hero very much in the minds of Loders people at present is the landlord of *The Crown*, Mr. Jack Verrinder. When he had a leg amputated a year ago, and by sheer will-power got himself back to serve at the bar, everybody hoped his troubles were over. But his other leg has now been amputated. Contemplating the stumps as he lay in Dorchester hospital with amazing sang-froid, Jack recalled his naval days at the Battle of Jutland and remarked on the strange way of things that a little sugar could do what hours of exposure to the sea could not when his ship went down.

One thing the grim operation could not deprive him of was his balanced outlook on life, and his innate cheerfulness. His looks still belie his seventy years. As he reads this we hope he will be conscious of the sympathy and admiration of us all. An observant reader might well query how a man of seventy could have fought at Jutland. Like some other headstrong boys, he put his age up.

November 1969

Legal tombola

With respect, may we offer our warmest congratulations to a
faithful member of Loders church, Mr. David Hirst, Q.C., on
his appointment as a judge of the High Court. In that capacity
we are not likely to see him running the bottle tombola again
at Loders Fête.

February 1982

Hot-foot to communion

That there is also virtue in sheer stamina was well illustrated
by the doyen of the Loders congregation, Mrs. Dora Boyd,
now in her ninety-second year and still a regular communicant. She had returned from London to Dorchester by train
and stepped out of it where the platform was not, falling
heavily on to the line.

Everybody feared the worst, but she got up and, armed by
two gentlemen, walked to her son-in-law's waiting car. She
declined all the offers of sedatives and stimulants and appears
only to have been slightly bruised. The first account we heard
of this alarming episode illustrates the maxim that a poor story
needs embellishment and a rich one deserves it. We were told
that she was brought to the station door on a stretcher and
insisted on getting off it to go home rather than to hospital.

January 1976

The Boyd Trophy

Mrs. Dora Boyd, of Uploders House, is famous for having
celebrated her ninety-second birthday by flying to Washington
in *Concorde*. Now, in her ninety-fourth year, she is famous for
having broken her hip and got it mended. She was 'the life and
soul' of Weymouth hospital. On Grand National Day she ran
a sweepstake, with a pound note as The Boyd Trophy. She got
the house surgeon to draw the horses 'to prevent any suspicion
of fiddling'.

May 1978

The Queen Mother remembers

Tribute was paid in her eightieth birthday celebrations to the Queen Mother's amazing gift for remembering old friends in all walks of life. An instance of this appeared through the oldest member of the congregation of Loders church, who kept her 96th birthday on July 14th – Mrs. Dora Boyd, an example of fortitude if ever there was one. Her husband was killed in the Great War, her only son was killed in the Second World War, and both her daughters died prematurely of cancer. The Queen Mother remembered the son as having been Guard Commander for a spell at Windsor Castle, and his death in Belgium in 1940. She wrote to Mrs. Boyd asking the honour of the latter's attendance at her special Garden Party at *Buckingham Palace*, and this was followed by a formal invitation from the Queen. Friends of Mrs. Boyd drove her to and from the Palace in a day, and Miss Mona Edwards gave a small dinner party in her honour at *Raikes*.

August 1980

Nurse Fooks, David Thomas and Harry Newberry

Our valley had the good fortune to escape the serious effects of the tropical storm which hit the West Country one night in July. There was a lot of water about, but the only noteworthy incident we have heard of is that Nurse Dorothy Fooks was barred at the railway bridge from getting to Mr. David Thomas to give him his injection until Mr. Harry Newberry came to her aid with a tractor. Right gallantly he drove her all the rest of her journey, waited outside while she officiated, and took her back through the flood.

* * * * *

Miss Dorothy Fooks has taken two years leave at Askerswell to do another stint of work for her old love, the Grenfell Mission, but this time in the province of Quebec. She will leave a gap in the regular Askerswell congregation, among the ringers, and at the Bridport General Hospital where she ushered new babies into the world. We wish her a fruitful and happy tour of duty and a safe return.

August 1968–May 1973

Sir Edward Le Breton's Bell

The memory of the late Sir Edward and Lady Le Breton is still green and revered in Loders. The P.C.C. were taken aback to learn, 'off the record', that their intention to place a memorial plaque in the church was not received with a like enthusiasm by the advisory body in Salisbury. Some of the advisory body knew the Le Bretons and what they meant to Loders, and have been concerned to point out that their objections are entirely aesthetic. They maintain that Loders is a church of exceptional beauty, that it contains as many monuments as it can absorb, and any more would upset the delicate balance that has been achieved. The P.C.C. chewed the matter over, and came reluctantly to the conclusion that the advisory body was right.

One councillor thought up a bright idea that has since been acted upon and won universal approval. On the chancel step is a bell with a brass plate explaining why the bell was put there by Sir Edward. This bell seems to interest visitors beyond measure, and its brass plate is more read than any other inscription in the church. The councillor's proposal was to replace the plate with a bigger one, re-worded as a memorial. So the plate now reads: 'This bell is a memorial of the late Colonel Sir Edward and Lady Le Breton, who lived at Loders Court 1921–1961 and worshipped in this church. For three hundred years the bell hung in the tower. It was placed here in 1927 to save it from being melted down. Sir Edward gave another bell'.

Why anybody should have wanted to melt down such a venerable bell is too much of a story for the plate. By 1927 the bells had got into a bad state. They had to be re-tuned and re-hung on a new frame. Try as he would, the engineer from England's oldest firm of bellfounders, Mears and Stainbank, could not bring the third into tune with the others and proposed melting it down and recasting it. To avoid the destruction of a Charles the First bell, Sir Edward paid for a new replacement. Incidentally the church minute book gives the names of the ringers in 1927. They were: Messrs. H. Sanders, E. Greening, C. Greening, W. Symes, W. Crabb, R. Williams and R. Butcher. No ladies then, be it noted. Now the bells are very dependent on lady ringers and over the country as a whole they seem keener than the men.

October 1970

Crowning the May Queen

The May Fair at Loders school is a delightful memory in every respect. Coming at Whitsuntide it basked in the perfect weather that went before the wintry 'spring' holiday, and drew a record three hundred spectators to the school playing field. It made a record £280 for the school fund. Lady Laskey apologised for not being the Archbishop's Grace of Canterbury, but made a prettier job of crowning the May Queen (Wendy Miles) than a mere man could have. O that all speeches from The Throne were as pleasant and innocuous as Wendy's!

July 1977

Head Gardener honoured

The imaginations of all who know Mr. David Crabb should be stirred by a ceremony of which he was the focus at Loders Court after morning church on Sunday, August 24th. Before a gathering of the outdoor and indoor staff, the Honourable Alexander Hood presented him with an inscribed silver salver to mark his completion of fifty years of faithful service to Loders Court. Mr. Hood was supported by Mrs. Hood, the Viscount Hood, Mr. and Mrs. Malcolm McDowall, Commander and Mrs. John Streatfeild and Mr. and Mrs. Rob Wrixon. Mr. Crabb had an escort of wife, children, grandchildren and sister-in-law.

Words might well have failed him on an occasion so fraught with emotion, but he took it calmly and was applauded. He being of an unretiring disposition, Loders will continue to benefit by the picturesque touch he imparts to it. In the shirt-sleeves of a worker, and with his dog Major, he is as natural to the village street as the houses themselves. When little difficulties occur, as they sometimes will, he can appear like magic to lend a neighbourly hand, or to offer advice distilled from years of intense observation of village affairs. Anyone assuming that he seeks the limelight would be entirely wrong. His friends in – and out of – the village could testify that it is a cardinal principle of his generous nature to try to do good by stealth.

* * * * *

The death of Mr. David Crabb at the age of 70, so soon after his retirement as Head Gardener of Loders Court, was not unexpected locally, but came as a surprise to some of his large circle of acquaintances. As his type of Dorset worthy dies out it is never likely to be replaced. Born in Loders, he seemed never to wish to venture beyond it. His neighbours, any visitor, and the changing seasons, were the limit of his interest, apart from children, and he was very fond of them indeed. The sons of the Vicarage remember him with affection for the country lore he taught them, and wonder how the dog who was his inseparable companion will live without him. The service at Weymouth crematorium drew a large congregation of friends as well as family mourners, in spite of the hazards of the holiday traffic. On Easter morning the Vicar paid tribute to his memory before the crowded congregation in Loders Church.

September 1969–May 1973

Each man to his allotment

A little town girl who explored Loders Church and then looked over the churchyard wall at the Court Garden beneath, exclaimed to her companion, 'Oh, what a beautiful allotment.' The Honourable Alexander Hood on his allotment is quite a thought.

October 1978

An act of homage?

Anxious enquirers after Mr. Leslie Smith, the Askerswell lay-reader, who had a fall during the Loders midnight service, will like to know that he was little the worse for it in spite of his hip operation a few weeks ago, and was on duty in Askerswell church on Christmas morning. In the dim light of the Loders 'midnight', he was on his way to the altar to assist the Vicar in the administration of communion when he tripped over a step, and fell at the feet of the Viscount Hood. Frank Good, a St. John Ambulance officer in the congregation, was quick to see that this was an accident, and not an act of homage, and came at the double to the rescue. Fortunately his skills were not much needed.

January 1980

The Sixth Viscount Hood

In the late evening of 13th October the Vicar was told over the telephone by Alexander Hood, now the 7th Viscount, the sad news that his elder brother the 6th Viscount (Lord Hood to all of us) had died in his London home, having wished his ashes to be buried in Loders, which he regarded as his church. The Vicar went down to the tower, pulled up the tenor bell (the 'death bell'), rang it for quite a while, lowered it, then sat in the church for a breather before going home, as the bell weighs nearly a ton. The church was still in its harvest festival glory, and the light of the hunter's moon at full shining in made it something out of this world.

Lord Hood had filled his seat in the chancel whenever he was in Loders, and for eighteen years had been partner with us in the family joy of Christmas, the solemnity of Good Friday and the triumph of Easter. At the church fête he came out of his shell (being shy by nature) and shewed visitors the paintings in Loders Court in which his illustrious naval ancestors figured. Sometimes on a summer's day he would get a packet of sandwiches from the kitchen and walk our lanes and copses. Any stray local fortunate enough to meet him was not likely to forget the neighbourly chat that ensued.

When the Vicar got home from church the 'phone rang again. This time the voice was that of Harry Crabb, the tower warden, who said that Frank Good, the ringers' captain, had heard the tolling of the tenor bell, and had rung Harry to ask why. Harry was certain he heard the bell before Frank. And so the sad news was racing round Loders on the night of the 13th.

Next morning the national newspapers carried Lord Hood's obituary notices, and we could read his distinguished career in 'the corridors of power'. His funeral in Loders church was deeply impressive. The casket with his ashes was on the chancel step banked by white chrysanthemums. His nephew, the Honourable Henry Hood, read the lesson from Ecclesiastes which says there is a time to be born and a time to die; the naval hymn *Eternal Father* was sung; then his brother Alexander, the new Lord Hood, carried the casket out into the churchyard to a little grave near the chancel door. A muffled

peal rang out from the tower. But a memorial service in St.
Margaret's Westminster will have the last word.

November 1981

Mr. Charlie Gale

Mr. Charlie Gale was the only survivor of the parish's once
considerable number of blacksmiths, and the line has died with
him. His forge in Uploders, where he shod horses, and whither
farmers in distress with their implements resorted, was a whiff
of the old world whose passing we lament. He was a public-
spirited man, giving freely of his time to Parish Council, Rural
Council, the Special Constabulary, the Ex-Servicemen's Club,
the Agricultural Discussion Club and the Oddfellows.

He was a man of forthright views. However widely one
disagreed with him, one respected his sincerity and integrity.
He was kind and generous, and in business was the rare type
who as often as not had to be told that he was not charging
enough for his work. Many a job did he do for Loders Church,
and a request for a bill was always countered with, 'I don't
come as much as I should, so take it as my collection'.

* * * * *

Mr. Albie Wells

Mr. Albie Wells was also a public-spirited man, and a member
of many organisations, of which his home, Loders Post Office,
became the spiritual hub. The wide area over which he was
known, and liked, became apparent at his funeral. Scores of
cars lined the approaches to the church, which was not big
enough for the congregation. The funeral procession from the
Post Office to the church was impressive, the hearse having a
large escort of police, of which he had been a member.

Loders will not be the same without him. He was young in
spirit, a schoolboy who had never really grown up, full of fun
and enthusiasms. In his company it was impossible to be moody
for long. An optimist he was, and generous perhaps to a fault.
His like are in too short supply for him not to be missed.

September 1968

Miss Albertina Pearson

Services at Dottery seem woefully different without the familiar figure of the late Miss Albertina Pearson. Come rain or shine, heat or cold, she never missed. The name she had given her cottage – *Content* – was the keynote of her life. Her sturdy self-reliance in these days when so many look to the Welfare State to crutch them along, was a shining lesson to us all. It was fitting that the last service she attended should be Harvest.

November 1968

Aussies abroad

One of the nicest bits of Christmas came a few days after, when Mrs. Reg Ascott called at the *Vicarage* with a letter from her son Stuart, in Australia. The letter had been meant to arrive for Christmas. It contained Stuart's best New Year wishes for the church and a five dollar-note for the funds. Incidentally, he is not convinced that Australia is all that better for a young man than England, and reckons to be home again by the end of 1969.

January 1969

Ecumenical landlord

Mr. Fred Smith, of the *Loders Arms*, is in the good books of the C. of E. Children's Society. He divides the proceeds of his *Christmas Snowman* between that Society and the Catholic counterpart. Each receives £1.15s. this year.

February 1969

For sale

An estate agents' notice of sale outside Miss Edwards' lovely cottage at Askerswell fills the village with sadness. When she goes Askerswell will no longer be a miniature Cranford. She is the embodiment of all that Cranford esteemed. Like generations of her female – and male – forebears, she was clever with her hands and had the leisure to employ them in every parochial cause, raising an amount of money known only to the Recording Angel's book.

To successive generations of Brownies and Cubs she was Brown Owl and Arkala. The Guides were her charge as well. At one time her children were drawn from five different schools, and her cottage must be deceptively elastic to have contained them. A village body without Miss Edwards on it would have been unviable, so she was on everything – community club, school managers, church council, folk dancing and all the committees. The handsome carpet in the chancel of the church will long be a memorial of her.

Miss Edwards came to *Folly Cottage* to join her late sister and Mr. Norman Adams, in 1941. She moved to her present cottage in 1947. Advancing years have made the contemplated move inevitable and she hopes to be settled in a bungalow in Parkstone before the summer is out. But it would take more than a furniture van to abstract her from the affections of Askerswell.

June 1969

Canon Percy Smith

The Mothers' Union will hold their corporate communion in Dottery Church on Thursday, June 22nd, at 10 a.m. Their May meeting in Loders village hall was notable for an address by Canon Percy Smith, of Pilsdon, and for a toothsome birthday cake made and given by the Enroling Member, Mrs. George Bryan.

It happened that the hall got booked by the M.U. and the County Fire Officer for the same afternoon. When the M.U. tried to get in, they found the key was with the Fire Officers' party, who were nowhere in evidence. Mr. Robin Wells sawed a way in for the M.U. The Fire Party was surprised to find the M.U. in possession, but listened courteously to the proceedings, and were rewarded with tea and birthday cake.

June 1972

Mr. Herbert Bartlett

Mr. Herbert Bartlett, of Matravers, celebrated his eightieth birthday on May 8th and after only one day in bed, with his sense of humour active to the end, slipped quietly away out of this world on May 13th. It was a triumph of mind over matter. He had been gravely ill for four years, but the encouragement of a devoted wife, and the large clan of his relatives, helped him to keep up the reality, as well as the appearance, of 'business as usual'.

Born into a large family at *The Crown*, Uploders, he passed through the village school and an apprenticeship to a village carpenter. After war service in the Royal Navy he turned his talent to animals, of which he was a shrewd judge, and thenceforth became a familiar figure at sales, shows and farms over a wide area. He appreciated the whole Dorset countryside, but his travels seemed only to convince him that no other parish could quite come up to Loders. He served for years as a parish councillor and a trustee of parish property. The inside of Loders Church used only to see him on festivals and Remembrance Sunday. He was wedded to the quaint country notion that only the good are entitled to attend church, and did not see it as a sort of doctor's surgery. However, the church, like others, has reason to be thankful for his kindness and constant support, and will miss him.

June 1973

Captain Lumby

Bad news seems always to travel faster than good news. The story was circulating in Loders that one of the key figures in Askerswell, namely Captain Michael Lumby, churchwarden and village hall chairman, had been badly thrown in the hunting field and had broken his neck. This turned out to be true, except that events were given in the wrong order. In hospital the X-rays disclosed that his neck had been broken before the fall. It seems that he had broken it without knowing at rugger in his college days at Dartmouth, and it had mended itself.

This fearsome accident only kept the Captain away from church for one Sunday. He was on duty at the Family Service, wearing a surgical collar, and showing no sign of the pain that strained ligaments must have been giving him. Everybody was glad to know that his horse hadn't to be put down. Remembering how Lawrence of Arabia came through all his wars in the desert only to die on a motor-bike in the Dorset lane, we were thankful indeed that Captain Lumby did not do the same sort of thing – for he, as a submarine commander, had survived many a desperate situation in the war at sea.

February 1974

Three local stock

Three Loders families suffered bereavement in September, and they are the focus of much sympathy. The funeral of Miss Florence Brown was at Loders on Sept. 7th, and she was buried in the grave of her grandfather Malachi. She was in her ninetieth year, and was an authentic specimen of old Loders. Her father used to run the carpenter's and wheelwright's business near the Uploders Chapel. He acquired such skill in bandaging cut fingers and the like that mothers sent their children to him when they needed this office, and the girls were wont to come home heads adorned with curly shavings of wood.

Mr. Eric Bunnell, whose funeral was on September 9th was only 53. It could well be that his death was a merciful release from a rare illness which is often protracted and always painful. The former Rural District Council, which was represented at the funeral, valued him highly as one of their best workers. When the illness really had him in its grip, he would cycle home from work exhausted, and yet feel sufficiently strengthened by the night's rest to resume next day. (If we all took our work as seriously there might be no inflation.) For some years he was a ringer, and was always good company, coming out with remarks that could seem absurd, and yet be profoundly wise. He has left a gap in his neighbourhood.

Mr. Frank Russell Wood, of Matravers, was cremated privately at Weymouth on Sept. 24th, having been so reticent about his illness that its seriousness was not generally known. A comparative newcomer to the parish, he was never drawn from his remote station at Matravers into the vortex of village affairs, but those who lived near found him, and for that matter his wife, the best of neighbours. He was devoted to his sheep, and it was when he was seeing to them that his tall, massive figure graced our fields and lanes. Nobody will miss

him more than his dog, who seems disconsolate, but Loders
Church will. He disclaimed being a churchman, but was a
generous and secret contributor.

October 1974

The Parochial Information Officer

The ecclesiastical authorities have in their wisdom decreed that
parishes must have a new official, called The Parochial
Information Officer. Loders is notoriously unresponsive to the
crack of the official whip, but is inclined to do something
when the cracking degenerates into nagging. Looking about for
a worthy recipient of this honour, the Vicarial eye alighted on
Mr. Maurice Lawson, of Knowle Farm, who is a man of intelligence, prudence, and of pleasing presence.

In a spirit of obedience becoming to a soldier of the Church
Militant, Maurice accepted the news of his appointment with
only the ghost of a wince. In due course, the authorities may
indicate who the recipient of the parochial information is to be.
For the present Maurice is feeding it to the Vicar, and tasty
stuff it is.

February 1975

Bishop Tiarks

Bishop Tiarks, formerly chaplain to Archbishop Ramsey, and
at present suffragan Bishop of Maidstone, is to be installed as
Rural Dean of the Lyme Bay Deanery at Powerstock Church
on Friday 1st October, for a period of three years. He will be
living at *Primrose Cottage*, Netherbury, which was the home
Colonel Donald Scott a churchwarden of Loders, went to on
leaving the *Old Mill*.

Bishop Tiarks was well known and liked by many of us when
he was Vicar of Lyme Regis. Incidentally, with him there will
be nine retired bishops and two hundred and seventy retired
clergy living in this diocese. Bishop Tiarks will have the care
of fifty-five retired priests in this archdeaconry.

June 1976

The venerable Samuel and Sidney Fry

'That car' was how the village-proud inhabitants of Askerswell referred to an incipient car cemetery on a patch of grass in full view of The Square, and just beneath the cottage homes of the venerable Samuel and Sidney Fry. Nobody liked to tell Sam or Sid what an eyesore it was, for fear of hurting nature's own gentlemen, and Sam and Sid could not bring themselves to tackle the owner, because he was young and hard up. When somebody was on the point of painting it at dead of night, to improve its appearance for the fête, a recovery truck came and towed it away, not without breaking a rope, because the car had taken root, and not without a near accident at the dump, because the car seemed allergic to it. The car gone, and The Square clear of it, Samuel and Sidney dropped their low profile, and in their Sunday best mingled with the crowd, to everybody's delight.

August 1977

The Johnstons of Dottery

Mr. Henry Johnston, of Ash Farm, Dottery, and his sons have again distinguished themselves in the Melplash show hedging and ploughing matches. They do this so often and so consistently that it is ceasing to be news. A family that acquits itself so well against all-comers year after year is something to be proud of.

Our Dottery churchwarden Mr. Cecil Marsh also has a proud record. He is an honorary vice-president for life of the Melplash Show, and for around sixty years has been marker for the ploughing match. The doctors who were topping him up with blood at Dorchester released him in time to attend the Show banquet given by President Palmer at the Old Brewery, Bridport.

Mr. Marsh was ever a thoughtful man. He asked the Vicar 'how come' that he ascended seven flights of stairs in the Brewery to the banqueting room 'easy as winking', whereas he puffed like a grampus to get up the one flight to his bedroom at Higher Pymore Farm? Something to do with that blood, perhaps. Followers of *Huntsman Ales* could point out that Dorchester is Eldridge Pope country.

October 1977

Hearse on Ice

Much sympathy was felt by the Loders congregation for Mr. Kingsley Wenlock, in the sudden loss of his wife Margaret. Theirs was one of those marriages made in heaven. She in her quiet gentle way was a great Christian. The Vicar for one felt it was he who had had his battery recharged after a pastoral visit to her.

It was snowing hard for her funeral at Yeovil crematorium. The cortège took two hours to get there, and two to get back. The Vicar was glad he was not driving: he found a niche in the hearse, alongside the coffin. He reflected how the journey would have tickled Margaret's sense of humour.

At East Chinnock the driver injudiciously broke from the queue of cars crawling up the hill, and took a short cut to the crematorium up a steep lane on the left. Seeing two cars skidding about ahead of him, he backed down to the main road, where the hearse gyrated about like a shying horse before it found its feet. The queue ascending and the queue descending came to a reverent halt while the hearse was being assimilated, taking a cautionary lesson perhaps from the coffin.

On the way back the hearse was in another queue crawling through West Coker. It found itself halted near the turning to East Coker. As the wait was getting long, the driver switched off the engine. When the queue moved again, it would not start. But the Lord God had caused a van to be stopped outside the village stores hard by. The Funeral Director, immaculate in tails and pinstripe trousers, disappeared into the shop. He emerged with the driver of the van, who raised its bonnet. The driver of the hearse raised the bonnet of the hearse, and producing a coil of wire, connected therewith the battery of the hearse and that of the van.

The hearse's engine started, the Funeral Director thanked the van-driver, and the hearse moved off at a spanking pace to catch up with the rear of the queue in front. The queue behind had been too fascinated by this unusual scene to pass and fill the gap. They might have thought they were in on some exploit of the Count Dracula.

February 1979

Jack and Molly Stevens

Saturday, 20th September was a notable and happy day for Jack and Molly Stevens, who in a few years have embedded themselves in the 'establishment' of Askerswell, to the latter's undoubted advantage. It was their golden wedding anniversary, and their large family assembled seemingly from the ends of the earth to celebrate. At the reception in the village hall the toast was proposed by their son John, who, with his wife Betty, and their five daughters, is a flying missionary in Zululand.

Next morning the family swelled the congregation at church, where John told how he switched from being a commercial pilot to serving the Lord by flying sick Zulus to hospital, greatly helped by Betty's command of the language. Later he showed slides at the spacious home of Geoffrey and Doris Bellis. The family left for Zululand with Askerswell's imagination stirred by their example of complete dedication to the Lord's work. But they cannot live on admiration. Here is a worthy object of financial support.

* * * * *

The Reverend John Stevens and his wife Betty and five daughters have sent a long, newsy, epistle-general to their friends in Askerswell, thanking them for the gift of £150 which reached them in their Zululand mission station just before Christmas. The letter itself is being circulated in Askerswell. It gives an instance of the sad side of his ministry. He flew a white baby who was desperately ill to Durban. The night was dark and stormy. The doctor aboard trying to keep the baby alive got him to radio the hospital, to have an ambulance with special equipment standing by at the airstrip, but the baby died as they were coming in to land.

October 1980–February 1981

Kenneth Allsop

The Country Fayre on the Playing Field at Well Plot found favour with a clerk of the weather who has bestowed very few this year, and completely achieved its object of providing home-made amusement unconnected with the raising of money. Judging by the programmes sold, some 400 people attended, and receipts will well cover expenditure. It was all a feather in the cap of the entertainment committee, who had taken up the torch dropped by the late Richard Plows and put in a lot of hard and skilful work. The annual tug-o'-war was won by Uploders – the 'Uploopers Lot' as the late Kenneth Allsop liked to call them.

The ponderosity exuding from sheer weight of numbers made their victory probable: the niceness of the Loders lady who was referee made it certain. She was the new Mrs. Malcolm McDowall, performing her first public function in Loders. She is a true lady, whose sympathy is naturally with the underdog. Whether Harry Richards is a true fireman is still open to question. His 1926 Dennis fire-engine, with its plethora of brass fittings polished up to the nines, was observed to have on the running board a tiny Pyrene fire extinguisher for use on itself.

The honesty of the traders at the fayre was apparent: the lady who sold for 10p the fine camera that a customer had accidentally left on the bric-à-brac stall retrieved it for him. The vicar acknowledges – in case it was meant for him – a seeming mark of respect emanating from the comic band when he drew near. A bawdy song suddenly turned into the hymn *The Lord of the dance*, done in a way that churches might well emulate.

August 1980

Lady Crutchley

The sympathy of the older members of Loders congregation concentrated on Admiral Sir Victor Crutchley, V.C., at the death of his wife at Mappercombe. They were a devoted pair. A sense of duty as Loders' biggest landowners used sometimes to be their excuse for playing truant from Powerstock church to attend Loders matins.

Lady Crutchley could be endearingly irrelevant (typist please note, not 'irreverent'). She was head of Powerstock Mothers' Union. At one of their meetings she welcomed the Vicar of Loders as guest speaker with: 'I have had only two ambitions in life – to nominate the Vicar of my own parish, and to pull pints of beer from those long and pretty handles in a village pub.'

October 1980

Jack Dare

The late Jack Dare, who lived near *Loders Mill* at *Holehouse Farm*, was buried in Loders churchyard after a sung service in the church on the Tuesday of Holy Week, a large congregation attending. He was 72, and a native of Wootton Fitzpaine. He had lived in Loders for 33 years. A kick from one of his cows was for him the beginning of bad health, which ended in an agonising illness that he endured with unflagging fortitude.

He was proud of being old-fashioned – of being the youngest of a family of twelve, of having maintained the tradition of family farming, of having a steadfast wife whose devotion came to full flower in the arduous nursing of him. And his favourite hymns were the old-fashioned *Jerusalem my happy home* and *For ever with the Lord*, which an apparently old-fashioned congregation sang with all their hearts.

May 1981

Ernest Boon and Maureen Lander

A rare event in Loders church on 18th June was the funeral of a highly regarded and ninety-year-old veteran of the Great War who had come through its fiercest battles unscathed, preceding by only three hours the funeral of a much-loved local girl of eighteen, who had been killed, with one of her two companions, in a motor accident on the peaceful Weymouth–Bridport coast road at three in the morning. The veteran was Ernest Boon, and the girl Maureen Lander. Each funeral was largely attended, choral, and well garnished with floral tributes.

Those who attended Maureen's funeral as well as Ernest's were painfully aware of the perverseness of life, that a peaceful end in Port Bredy should be the old warrior's lot, and a horrifying end on a quiet Dorset road early on a June morning should be the lot of a young waitress who had endeared herself to many.

The Vicar made this apparent perverseness of life the theme of his address at Maureen's funeral, to which many teenagers were listening. He tried to show that the horrors of war and of most deaths on the road could be traced ultimately to man's misuse of freewill, and not God, who had given it. Without freewill we would be only automata, or animals acting on instinct. Freedom was rightly one of our most cherished possessions, but if it were not used in accordance with God's will, it could be our destruction.

The Vicar expressed the deep sympathy everybody felt for the foster-parents, Mr. & Mrs. Stubbs, to whom Maureen had always been as their own child.

July 1981

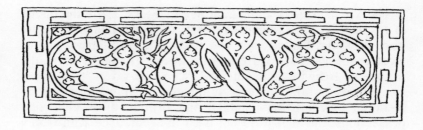

CHAPTER 5

Vic and his quiverful

The Vicar's 'family' extended well beyond the immediate. He was the eldest of a family of four girls and three boys. The family of seven children that he helped rear was only so extensive because he had a yen for a boy, and Mother Nature served up five girls first in quick succession (and then another boy to keep the elder company). With his eye on nature, he referred to births as 'hatchings'. His parish people were his 'flock', which is why he felt great affinity with shepherd and bellringing captain Harry Crabb.

His readership of people who were emigrants from Loders, or friends, relatives or holidaymakers, was extensive. His apparent smallworld vision, with the Squire in his chancel, was underwritten by his commitment to the Church Missionary Society (and his voracious reading of the daily papers, and constant attention to news broadcasts). His readership now would astound him, whilst giving him a small smile of pleasure. The telephone was never his medium. The Internet came later.

The phrase 'Vic and his Quiverful' was concocted suitably at *The Marquis of Lorne* pub, Nettlecombe. This was how he was traditionally greeted (even when the Quiverful weren't present) by Charles Amor, Charlie Greening, Bill Score and his brother 'Beauty', who seems to have had no other name. Beauty did have the capacity to chat up 'grockles', a West Country term of contempt for lucrative holiday-makers from the Midlands – so as to ensure his next pint of Palmer's Ale. This has nothing to do with Uncle Tom Cobleigh. Their true portraits remain at the pub. The opening-time clubs at *The Marquis* and later *The Crown* were an important extension of his family.

There were his deep friends in the bell-towers, who spoke a mysterious language of number computation and arm movement that even now only the initiated understand. They also spoke plain English, and knew where the nearest pub was. They came on tour, or they invited him up to St. Barts the Great in London. They even became female, which might surprise a few readers of *Yours Reverently*. It was a development that certainly surprised his innate prejudices. There were his friendly professional 'rivals' on *The Western Gazette*, *The Bridport News* and the *Dorset Evening Echo*. He enjoyed beating them to a scoop, and pointing out to them a failure in statistical detail.

He loved the Fête, in spite of, or perhaps because of the collecting, which caused him immense pleasure, and only a little pain. The pain was anticipation: the pleasure came during the afternoon, when his quiver was definitely full, and afterwards, when he got down to statistics.

A paradox of life in a country vicarage was that the goings-on there were known intimately by all and sundry. The place was open-house and vied with the local pubs ('the best public house in the village'). Nevertheless, as with royalty and the famous, the full nature of the life of a vicarage will never be known – except to its full-time members. I have never intended to comment biographically on home.

Nevertheless, as *The Parish Notes* progressed, there were more mentions of the Vicar's wife and family, and cats and dogs. Not many people reveal their all about their dear friends. But my father was able to refer to Bishop Pike of Sherborne as 'our dear friend'. Perhaps it was because he had been a 'rugger'-player, and was Irish (p. 164). Other Bishops and Archdeacons receive less favourable mention, particularly after April 1977, when the Prebendary of Loders in Salisbury Cathedral was presented to a vicar from Poole, and the Vicar of Loders was invited to attend. In the same *Parish Notes* (p. 170) 'Bishop Tiarks came to preach in Askerswell ... This was the first service in Askerswell to be graced by a bishop in sixteen years.'

Barchester Towers contains it all. For the most part, bitterness about the 'family' of the ecclesiastical hierarchy was transmuted into good works back at the parish.

He had a soft spot for mischievous boys:'Mr. Malcolm Trickett of Gribb Farm, Uploders, was married to Miss Linda Margaret Jones, in St. Mary's, Dorchester, on April 8th. Malcolm has undergone a sea-change on moving into matrimony. Malcolm used to be the soul of mischief in Scripture lessons at Askerswell School.' May 1972.

Like Francis Kilvert before him, he also had an eye for radiant belles, of whatever age. At the Queen's Silver Jubilee celebrations ... 'Sitting on bales of straw, the company did justice to chicken and sausages being fried by a bunch of rosy wenches without ... July 1977'. His eye was more innocent than that of the curate of Clyro. He delighted in his extended family including 'the vast family of less fortunate children cared for by the Church of England Children's Society'. December 1972.

Leonard Clark, Her Majesty's Inspector of Schools, poet and friend from the Forest of Dean, provided words, company and stimulation, as did Fred Vacher, Methodist, from Whitchurch Canonicorum, and Toronto – as much as anything, because he knew the Bible like the back of his hand.

Modestly tucked away, but nonetheless prominent, were the central tenets of Anglican, Protestant, ecumenical, Christian faith. 'Unity, without uniformity,' was perhaps his deepest love.

He loved Bell Cottage and the Bell Hills. Bell Cottage, situated on the outskirts of the village, had already been the birth-place and living-place of countless Loders folk. It had also been a pub, and the lodging-house for Irish navvies working on the Maiden Newton railway-line. On the Vicar's retirement it became the replacement Vicarage for entertaining his quiverful. It is conveniently next door to *The Marquis of Lorne*, by a mile, up-hill.

Then, of course, *The Parish Notes* were the most telling expression of the extended family in action: they were his baby. The Fête was his favoured method of re-stoking the 'family' exchequer, and leaving three churches in fine fettle for posterity. He was a family man, with the strengths and the weaknesses of someone wanting to be at the hub. Visiting every parishioner, at their home or in hospital, was his means of meshing his flock. ('The New Year Party at Askerswell had about it the bewitching

feeling of one big family at play. The Psalmist's "young men and
maidens, old men and children" were all of an age.'

February 1978)

Shoulder to the wheel

Looking back on Loders Fête, we can see why it was such an
outstanding success this year. All the ingredients that make a
good fête were present at one and the same time. We had not
only stalls laden with good things, but a crowd of people to
buy them. And by great good fortune some of the Vicarage
family, accompanied by useful husbands, were able to get
home and put a shoulder to the wheel. Mr. Richard Lloyd and
Miss Juliet Willmott burnt the midnight oil devising attractive
posters and put them at strategic points in the holiday camps.

In consequence the gate was up by a third, proving Mrs. Hood's point as to the importance of advertising.

Dr. Ken Gray needed no lesson on advertising. What at first seemed a voice from heaven, speaking when the band stopped, proved to be his, coming from the top of the church tower, and not a few people paid a shilling to join him up there. For the record, it was not his voice that made the pony cart bolt and break a shaft, but the merry noise of the pram derby.

September 1968

The adopted daughter of the Mothers' Union

The Rector of Burton Bradstock (the Rev. Cyril Ridler) succeeded against a hot fire in keeping our Mothers' Union awake when they met in the Vicarage to hear a talk from him on China. Which is saying something.

The meeting had other delights as well. Mrs. Lenthall, her leg still in plaster, but feeling sprack in herself, was there for the first time in four months; Mrs. Sanders had managed to negotiate the steps even with a surgical frame; and Mrs. Mabel Crabb was there again as though she had not been out of the parish for years.

The branch sent a record token for £6 to their 'adopted daughter', Miss Juliet Willmott (who is at Bart's) for her 21st birthday. We heard from her direct how deeply touched she was by this. It needs to be explained that Juliet was the first child to be born in Loders Vicarage in many years. Because she was only a girl, and the fifth at that – she got no bells, as did the brother who followed her. So the M.U. made amends. Juliet bore the ringers no grudge. Indeed, she is now one of their number, and rings also at St. Bartholomew the Great.

* * * * *

We leave our readers to imagine what was said across the Vicarage breakfast-table one morning, at the beginning of the Christmas rush, when Mrs. Willmott opened a letter inviting her to a meeting for clergy wives in this part of Dorset, to hear the new Principal of Salisbury Theological College lead a discussion on, 'Should clergy wives be trained, and if so, for what?' Since the publication of the Paul Report there has been a lot of discussion on the best use of clergy manpower. Have Principals of theological colleges nothing better to do?

December 1968

When our own time comes

Congratulations to Mr. Herbert Bertram Wheeler and his wife, Amy Elizabeth, on reaching the fortieth anniversary of their wedding. They were married at Charminster on December 20th, 1928. Their family was born and brought up in Loders. Its internal ties were always strong. Children and grandchildren all gathered in the old nest for the celebration.

Mr. Wheeler is one of the rare and decreasing body of men still willing to dig graves. He is sexton extraordinary to several parishes besides Loders. But the great test of his skill is Loders churchyard, where much burying has made the ground friable. We have never known one of his graves to cave in.

As we watch him digging away with calm assurance, in his tasseled woollen bonnet, and pulling at his fragrant pipe (only decent baccy on a job requiring such reverence) we find ourselves hoping he may still be operative when our own time comes. If he isn't, he has an apprentice son, who may become a chip off the old block.

January 1969

Change at the helm

Visiting preachers are by no means a feature of our services. The Rev. Eric Wastell will be welcome to Loders pulpit at matins on July 6th. He will preach for the U.S.P.G. He is Rector of St. Mary in the West Indian island of Antigua.

July 1969

Series two

The Bishop of Sherborne has written to thank all concerned in the inspiring service in Loders Church at which he preached in August. Church and chancel were quite full and included the former Governor of Gibraltar, Sir Dudley Ward (and Lady Ward) an old friend of the Bishop. The sermon was to everybody's deep satisfaction. The service, says the Bishop's letter, was a real uplift to him. He probably found a straight matins relaxing. Adjustment to the local variations on the Series Two theme must call for fearful concentration on the part of a visiting officiant.

September 1969

The Vicar's waistcoat pocket

The first whist drive ever to be held in connection with Dottery Church was an unqualified success, and a credit to the organisers. The Vicar was called on to draw the winning number for a box of groceries. Shouting out the number, and getting no response, he eventually found it in his own waistcoat pocket. The donor of the box may like to know that he gave it to the Loders Mission Sale, where it made a further £3 for another good cause.

February 1970

From afar

Two letters have come from ladies who once lived in Loders Vicarage. Mrs. Prisca Barrow Dowling (née Hutton) writes from Port Alfred, South Africa: 'I was so interested to see in our daily paper, The Eastern Provence Herald, a news item from Loders. I was waiting for my car to be serviced and reading the paper when the name "Loders" caught my eye ... I was so interested because my father was Vicar of Loders from 1914–1935 ... My husband and I came here in 1956. Your wife kindly allowed me to show my husband over my old home'.

The other letter is from Mrs. Charles Palmer, whose husband was Vicar 1939–1946. She says, 'I often think of you in that beloved happy place and feel grateful for the time we spent there'. She enclosed a colour photograph of the church at harvest festival two years ago. Her home is now in Swavesy, near Cambridge.

February 1970

Grand Turk

The senior members of our Mothers' Union, hard workers all of them, who usually fall into a little nap during the address at the monthly meeting, did not 'drop off' last time, and are glad that they kept awake. The speaker was a man, and a young man at that, Mr. Michael Willmott.

For the best part of an hour he held them enthralled by his experiences on the island of Grand Turk, in the West Indies, where he and the son of the chaplain of Mill Hill School did a stint of Voluntary Service Overseas before they went their respective ways to Cambridge and Oxford.

Mr. Gerrard contrived to show colour slides illustrating the talk, with an expertise not noticeably cramped by the thirty bodies squeezed into the vicarage dining-room. Members who sell their garden produce were especially interested in a place where cabbages fetch six shillings each.

May 1970

Music vs. the Election

The choice of June 18th for a General Election is thought by some of our friends to have cancelled automatically the visit of the choir of Selwyn College, Cambridge, to Loders Church, fixed long beforehand on the same date. But the young gentlemen who compose the choir think that if something must indeed give way on this date, then it should be the General Election. They will come according to plan. There is no need for either to be cancelled. A feast of choral music from the year 1,500 to the present day, served up by young enthusiasts in the dispassionate calm of Loders Church at eventide, should take away the taste of the election and nourish us with less ephemeral food. Last summer they sang in the Lorna Doone country, including Oare Church. They are keen to see how the Hardy country compares.

June 1970

To the Editor

A lady writes: 'Dear Sir, I do hope you will pardon me bothering you. My reason for writing is this: A year or so ago we spent our holidays in Dorset and one Saturday you had your garden fête. We came, and enjoyed such a pleasant afternoon, I am wondering if you are having one this summer? If so, I should be grateful if you would let me know the date, please, as we are hoping to spend our holidays again this year in lovely Dorset'. The letter is signed 'Mrs. Kathleen Gardiner'.

She is probably unaware of the real compliment she pays the setting of Loders Court and so of the fête, for she writes not from among the dark Satanic mills – but from 3, The Village, WINDSOR GREAT PARK! What has Loders that the Queen lacks?

A few years ago your editor came near to being snowed up in Windsor Great Park and never regretted it. The tracery of the frost on the great trees of the forest, especially the old oaks, was breathtaking in its beauty.

January 1971

Mrs. Willmott's Words

The Mission Sale this year was held under the threat of an electric power cut which did not materialise. Faith triumphed again, though somewhat vitiated by a furtive provision of hurricane lamps, 'just in case'. The little sale which follows the concert produced £51, the highest ever, and Mrs. Willmott thanked all concerned. She was so overwhelmed that she confessed to a loss of words, which interested her husband.

January 1971

Pauline Follett

The death of Mrs. Findlay, better known to Uploders and Loders as Pauline Follett, was received here first with incredulity and then with grief that could be painful. Her husband was a pilot when she married him in Loders Church, and is now a schoolmaster. They had three boys, and then, to their delight, a girl, who is now seven months old. Their home is at Comrie in Perthshire. There, without knowing that she was ill, Pauline died of a coronary in the early hours of February 13th. She was 32. Her parents live at Corscombe, but her aunt, Mrs. George Hyde, is with us, and other aunts, Mrs. Elston Paul and Mrs. Hostler are frequently here.

We know how devoted they were, and feel for them in the heavy blow they have suffered. Our own memories of Pauline are fragrant and wistful. She was the live wire among the children of her day and an enthusiast for the Sunday School, calling for the small children who lived near her, and bringing them Sunday by Sunday to class. Years later, when she was married and in Scotland, she did a long ride on a scooter to a Sunday morning service the Vicar was taking as a locum in St. Mary's Dunblane.

Why the good should die young is a problem that vexes the faith of many and is topical as Lent leads up to the remembrance of the 33-year-old who was crucified on the first Good Friday. The problem is not solved, but may have the sting taken out of it by reflecting that if freedom from affliction were the reward of goodness, then goodness would become the world's best insurance policy – and cease to be goodness! Goodness has other rewards.

March 1971

Hymn for Loders

The poet, author, educationist and broadcaster, Mr. Leonard Clark, has written a hymn for Loders Church, which he hopes Mr. Richard Lloyd, organist and master of the choristers of Hereford Cathedral, will find time to compose a tune for. Its sentiments are strong and simply expressed and autumnal in mood, arising from a deep appreciation of the Loders scene. How nice if we could sing it next harvest! (p. 222)

May 1971

Three belles

Weddings are a great feature of Easter in areas more populous than ours. At Loders one had the stage all to itself and was memorable for those concerned. The bride was Isobelle Jane, daughter of Mr. & Mrs. John Ward, of Uploders, and the bridegroom Keith William George, son of Mr. & Mrs. Charles Cadman, of Allington. The church was gay with flowers, the bells set the air vibrating outside, and hymns and Mr. Tiltman's organ voluntaries animated it within. Only sunshine was needed for the finishing touch, and the sun obliged.

A member of the congregation has since confessed that she spent the service debating which was lovelier, the bride or her mother, and couldn't make up her mind! Beauty is more than skin deep. The debate would have been even more difficult could the bride's grandmother, Mrs. Sarah Read, have been present.

May 1971

Captain Gulliver

A coat of arms carved in wood and embellished with colours would look well on one of the interior walls of Askerswell village hall, thinks Mr. Brook, of *Dayspring*, and he has offered to make one. The hall committee liked the idea very much, and have asked Mr. Brook to explore the possibility of making an Askerswell coat-of-arms. He had suggested a conflation of the County and Bridport arms. Mrs. Brook's aptitude for design may come in here.

Several possible motifs spring to mind – a well and an oscar of some sort for the old manor of Oscarswell; or Eggardon and its ramparts. The 18th century smuggler, Captain Gulliver, who owned North Eggardon, is rich in motifs. His gang of fifty wore white wigs. A lighted beacon on Eggardon warned them of danger. Within living memory horses ploughing have fallen into the pits which hid his kegs and contraband.

July 1971

The Vicarage Fire

Mothering Sunday coincided with a rumbustious north-easterly wind which came down the chimney of the big Tudor fireplace at the vicarage, and kept blowing some of the log fire on to the carpet. The house was filled with smoke more potent than in Isaiah's vision, and the fire had to be put out – the first time the present incumbent had had to do such a thing. But the wind was powerless to deflect a large congregation from the morning service at Askerswell.

April 1972

25th Anniversary

April 22nd, 1947 was the day on which the Vicar and Mrs.
Willmott began work in Loders. To mark the 25th anniversary of
this, the Church Council presented Mrs. Willmott with a delectable box of chocolates, the Vicar with a survey of the historical
monuments of West Dorset (skilfully inscribed by Mrs. Thornton)
and both with an oak garden-seat. Mr. McDowall made the
presentation after the Easter Vestry. The surprise caught the Vicar
at a loss for sensible words, and showed Mr. McDowall to be as
good at speechmaking as he is at cross-examining. But Mrs. Wells
has presided over village communications at the Post Office for
more than 25 years and Mr. Brown has dedicated more than 40
years of his life to the clerkship of the Parish Council. What have
the Vicar and his lady done compared with these?

The Bishop of Salisbury [George Reindorp] sent the Vicar and
Mrs. Willmott a kind personal letter about their twenty-five years
in Loders, and regretted that his engagement list prevented his
coming to preach on the occasion. The poet laureate of Loders,
Mr. Leonard Clark, kindly sent a poem. (He has lately been
awarded the thousand dollar prize of the International Poetry
Society for the best published poem of 1971, which he shares
with another poet, and could have been forgiven for forgetting
Loders). The poem to mark the Vicar's 25th anniversary is
headed *Easter at Loders 1972* and continues:

> The woods come green again, the meadows walking:
> Lambs charge at nothing on the hills,
> And what a din the crazy rooks are making,
> With April but a name for daffodils.
>
> The lanes look primrose and first blackthorn's showing;
> Five spots of ladybird are going for a walk,
> And here the ploughing's done,
> And there the barley's growing.
>
> A drowsy mouse is nibbling at a stalk.
> A shower of rain, three magpies for a wedding,
> As now on Waddon's slope the shadows creep,
> And half across the sky a glorious rainbow spreading,
>
> And only moles on Eggardon asleep.

May–June 1972

The Mission Sale

There is no working party making things to sell for weeks before-hand. Like Nelson, Mrs. Willmott expects all the kind friends of the Sunday School to do their duty, and they never fail.

December 1972

Family ringing

A rare combination of circumstances enabled the Vicar, his wife, and four of their children to ring the six bells of Loders in honour of the Queen's twenty-fifth wedding anniversary and Miss Juliet Willmott's twenty-fifth birthday. Cpl. Nicholas Willmott was in Loders en route from St. Kilda to Germany, Mr. Michael Willmott had the day off from Watford Grammar School because of the Royal Wedding [Princess Anne and Mark Phillips], Miss Juliet Willmott had time off because she had been on night duty at Bart's, and Mrs. Gray (née Rosamund Willmott) was able to come from her house in Bristol. Moreover, two friends of Mrs. Marjorie Vacher from Toronto happened to be in Loders on a day trip and were thrilled to watch the exercise in the tower.

December 1972

Mr. Fleming

We would like to offer our sympathy to the printer of our *Notes*, Mrs. Fleming whose invalid husband died recently after years of suffering which draw amazing devotion and care from her and her family.

* * * * *

'May I say 'thank you' for these very kind remarks. My family and I have felt the warmth of the prayers of our many friends. A. Fleming.'

December 1972

A Brownie's prayer

Brown Owl asked our Brownies each to compose and write out a harvest prayer. One began, 'Thank you Lord, for the harvest. Thank you, Lord for the Vicar'. As the harvest was exceptionally good, the Vicar will have something to live up to.

November 1973

Greatcoat and biretta

Dottery people showed how highly they regarded the late Mrs. Lucy Turner, and her husband the sexton of Dottery, when they turned out and filled the church on a day of hurricane-type weather for Mrs. Turner's funeral. The undertakers' men had a wetting, to avoid which the Vicar donned greatcoat and biretta. It is the first time he has had to do this at a funeral, if he remembers rightly.

Mrs. Turner had lived most of her long married life in Dottery. She was as cheerful in her distressing illness as she always was when neighbours met her going to post or to town. A cheerful face, come wind come weather, is a service to the community.

February 1974

A change is good – and a rest

A change of preacher will be afforded the long-suffering congregations of Askerswell and Loders on Sunday, February 17th. The address will be given (Askerswell at ten, Loders at 11) by Mr. Roy Rusbridge, the dynamic young area Secretary of the Church Missionary Society.

February 1974

Confirmation

A Confirmation service comes our way only about once in four years because bishops are extremely busy men, and we have not enough young people to merit more frequent visits. We have been notified that the former assistant Bishop of Bath and Wells will hold a Confirmation in Loders Church on Palm Sunday, April 7th, at 6.30 p. m.

Those of our readers who do not know what Confirmation is, may welcome a word of explanation. When a baby is christened it is made a junior member of the Church. It does not know what is being done, but then, we are always doing good things for babies before they themselves know how to choose. And when they are mature enough to choose the choice cannot be unbiassed, because we do not grow in a vacuum, we absorb subconsciously some of the manners and outlook of the family we grow up in. That is why, at the christening, the godparents promise that the environment the child grows up in shall be Christian.

At Confirmation it is the child, now come to years of discretion, who confirms what his godparents did for him, and is admitted to full membership of the church by the laying on of hands of the Bishop, who is in the present-day Church what the Apostles were to the early Church. Confirmation qualifies the candidate for receiving Holy Communion, which is a Christian's highest privilege.

In many churches today, Holy Communion is THE service, attended by all and sundry. There is much to be said for this. There is also much to be said for the practice of the saintly Tractarians (based on ancient precedent), which we follow, of making matins or evensong a kind of evangelistic service for all and sundry, and reserving the inmost mystery of Holy Communion for the committed.

February 1974

Central tenets

Standing up to be counted as a follower of Jesus Christ is one of the ingredients of Confirmation. We wonder whether all people attending service on Easter Day will see themselves as partaking in an act of witness to the fact of Jesus' Resurrection?

They should do, because they are. The accounts of the Resurrection in the New Testament do not stand alone. They are supported by a living company of believers in every age, which existed before the accounts did. Those who will be attending Easter services received the message from the preceding generation, and the preceding generation received it from its predecessor.

So the unbroken chain of living witness reaches back to Bishop Irenaeus who was a pupil of Bishop Polycarp who was a pupil of St. John and others who had seen and talked with Jesus Christ when he was risen from the dead. Changing the metaphor, it is the business of our generation to pass the torch firmly and convincingly to the next.

April 1974

Shakespeare's Bells

The Ringers of St. Bartholomew the Great, London's oldest church, will be ringing in towers in this neighbourhood in the first weekend of July, and because Miss Juliet Willmott is one of their band, will make the Vicarage their base. They hope to attend Loders matins on July 7th. The bells of St. Bartholomew the Great are all pre-Reformation, and the oldest in England. Shakespeare must often have heard them when he was acting at the Globe playhouse.

July 1974

Mr. Pettigrew

Mr. Leonard Clark was kept very busy signing copies of his new children's book in Hine's Bridport. It is called *Mr. Pettigrew's Harvest Festival* and is 'going like a bomb', in the parlance of the proprietor of Hine's.

It is about a family of mice which poetic licence has allowed Mr. Clark to transfer from Dottery Church, where they dwell beneath the altar, to Loders Church, where none is ever seen unless as an offering deposited there by Tiddles, the junior cat at the Vicarage, who is quite devout. Mr. Clark has dedicated the book to the Vicar, the latter's first ever, with an assurance that he is not Mr. Pettigrew. Parishioners evidently skip the title page, for they keep telling the Vicar that he is Mr. Pettigrew 'to a tee', and that the illustration, which could be of a balding grocer, is exactly like him.

July 1974

Rio Pongas

The Bishop of Sherborne [Victor Pike] preaching to the people of Askerswell, Loders and Dottery on Sunday morning April 6th at Loders, is something we are looking forward to, and is a timely reminder that pleasant things have in the past emanated from Ireland even if they don't now. Victor Pike is Anglo-Irish, a former rugger international, and a former Chaplain-General to the Forces. (Rugger seems to help promotion in the Army Chaplain's department: a room junior of the vicar's at college is now Chaplain General, and he was good at rugger).

Bishop Pike's mother must be the most remarkable woman in the world. She begot three bishops, and perhaps as an after-thought, a colonial governor. The bishops are their lordships of Meath, Sherborne and Gambia – and – Rio Pongas. At one of the Lambeth conferences a trendy reporter described the third bishop as 'The Bishop of Gambia and Miss Rio Pongas'. Bishop Pike finds this perennially useful in his after-dinner speeches.

March 1975

Sunday School Outing on Bell Hills

When faced with the problem of what kind of an outing to have, Loders Sunday School decided that as multitudes of holiday-makers take the trouble to come long distances to Dorset, they themselves would be foolish to go away, so, with the kind consent of Mr. Steve Newberry, they had a picnic on the Bell Hills, and enjoyed every minute of it.

The Vicar was commissioned to choose a site and get a fire going. On a plateau near the top of the hills he collected dead wood from a line of gnarled hawthorns bent the way of the prevailing winds, and made the fire. At something past three o'clock he saw far below a gaggle of the older children hurry-ing along Yellow Lane towards Bell. Soon afterwards a couple of puffing boys' heads appeared on the rim of the plateau, and the fire was soon swarming with boys and girls.

Mrs. Willmott followed at a steadier pace with the infants and the baggage train, plus an odd mother or two, and the business of getting fried sausages on to buttered rolls began in earnest. To the delight of Rover and Beano, the Vicarage Labradors, who finished the sausages, the general fancy switched to Mars bars, apples and bananas, washed down by much Corona. The children have already earmarked the Bell Hills for next year's outing.

September 1975

The Vicar attains seniority

Our last issue of the *Notes* began with a description of Harvest festival at the Uploders Chapel and at Dottery; this paragraph

aims to conclude the story. There was a full turn-out of parents for the harvest service at Loders School. It was taken entirely, and creditably, by the children who afterwards distributed the display of flowers and food to the senior citizens of the parish. Puzzled as to what to do properly with a bottle of elderflower wine, they sent it to the Vicar to mark his attainment of seniority this year.

At Loders Evensong two little farmers' daughters amused their neighbours. The church was filling fast, and they shoo'd people away from the seats of their father and mother, which they had marked with two hymn books, because work on the farm was delaying them. At Matins a mother had given her small son five pennies for the collection. When the plate had passed, she noted that he was still clutching two pennies. 'Here, what's the meaning of these?' she demanded. 'This is the change,' came the reply. Obviously that eagle-eyed sidesman, Mr. Maurice Lawson, had not been operating in this aisle.

November 1975

Sapper 'Chuck' Willmott

A busman's holiday was what the Christmas stay at Loders of the Vicar's soldier son 'Chuck' turned out to be. First, word was passed to him from Captain of the Ringers Harry Crabb that the flagpole on the tower needed taking down and repairing that it might show the flag for Christmas. This was a tall order, but Chuck did it and the Union Jack was proudly riding the breeze on Christmas Eve.

On Christmas Day the electric organ blower broke down just before the family service. A churchwarden bravely operated the handle for ten minutes. Chuck helped by his brother Michael took over from him for the rest of the service. The lack of a lead weight on a string showing the amount of wind in the bellows sometimes caused sounds to emerge that frightened the organist, but we marched out of church to the *Hallelujah Chorus*, Chuck blowing triumphantly. He spent the whole of the next day taking the motor apart and making it work for the following Sunday.

Then the strain of an influx of fifteen visitors on the vicarage water supply caused a malfunctioning of the pump that moves the water from the well to the tank in the roof. 'Where's Chuck?' was again the cry, and not in vain. The influx of visitors had come in cars of dubious performance. These developed ailments which kept Chuck engaged for many another hour. And the moral of it all? Sappers have their uses.

January 1976

Publicans

A good pub, presided over by a congenial landlord with a nice wife, is an asset to a parish. We here are blest with several such. Yet we could ill afford to lose Reg Small, the landlord of *The Crown*, who was buried in Loders churchyard on St. Valentine's Day. He was only sixty-one. He graced this rural scene so well that is easy to be oblivious of our debt to the great metropolis which fashioned him, and of the fact that his reign here was a short one of six years.

'Small' by name, but big in every other way, calling himself 'only a humble innkeeper', but relishing the title of 'Your

Altitude' bestowed on him by one of his more cultured customers, he has left us ruefully aware that there can be more to a pint of Palmer's than the mere downing of it.

The exceptional busyness of the undertakers dictated an awkward time for the funeral – twelve noon on a Saturday. It said much for the affection in which he was held that the church was full. And right to the fore, in a wheel-chair, was his predecessor at *The Crown*, the valiant and legless Jack Verrinder.

March 1976

The Right Rev. Victor Pike

The Rt. Rev. Victor Pike paid his last visit to the clergy of this deanery as Bishop of Sherborne when they met at Litton. He retires in October. The flag flew from the church tower in his honour, and he celebrated Holy Communion in cope and mitre. The Rural Dean well expressed the feelings of the clergy when they drank his health at the Rectory: that they were losing their sheet anchor. But the Church will not be losing his services. He goes to live in Wilton, and to be curate to the Vicar there who has four churches and a considerable population.

April 1976

Publicans at *The Crown*

The Crown Inn at Uploders is now presided over by Mr. and Mrs. Christopher Robin Upton, who have a daughter, Amber, who has quickly found her niche in Loders School. Their interests are not confined to the sale of malt and spirituous liquors, and the serving of snacks. They keep goats and poultry. Mr. Upton is a jobbing builder. Anything he needs to know about pubs his wife should be able to tell him, for she is a daughter of the landlord of the *Fisherman's Arms*, Bridport.

April 1976

The Vicar and the Chairman of the W. I.

Harvest Festival has come and gone once again. At the start of the service the President of the local Women's Institute stepped up to the chancel and asked the Rector to accept and dedicate the colourful array of kneelers displayed on either side of him (these had been made and given by the W. I.). A public confrontation between a parson and a W. I. president is much to be dreaded by him, because the lady, when she is typical, is inhumanly efficient and impeccable. What fears he might have had melted in the genial presence of this one. She addressed him as 'Reverend Sir,' then faltered in a delightful feminine fashion, which put him immediately at ease, so that he did not bumble his words.

November 1976

I. T. V. at Durham Cathedral

From Parson's viewpoint the Christmas services were splendid. At the Loders 'midnight', when the church was thronged, the kindly help of the Askerswell lay reader, Mr. Leslie Smith, in administering the chalice, kept the queue between pew and altar moving nicely. Another kindly soul had put a tilley lamp to light the churchyard path and arranged with certain worshippers to pump it up as they passed.

There was a surprisingly large number of communicants at the eight o'clock on Christmas morning, but not enough to prevent the Vicar getting a glimpse before he went on to Dottery of the magnificent I.T.V. carol service by his son-in-law Richard Lloyd at Durham Cathedral [married to eldest daughter, Morwenna].

January 1977

Fêted at the Barbican

It was the Vicar's privilege to be guest preacher at the famous City church of St. Bartholomew the Great, Smithfield, at the Advent Sunday evensong. In that pulpit where the Heavy Ordnance of the Church are wont to fire their rockets, he felt a mere sparkler. But he also sensed the niceness of the Rector and congregation, which included London members of his family and friends, and he will always remember that evening with pleasure. After the customary coffee with the congregation in the cloister, he and his wife adjourned to a sumptuous supper in the Barbican, given in their honour.

January 1977

Flossie Good of Bell Cottage

Well Plot, Loders has lost Mrs. Flossie Good, who died unexpectedly in Bridport hospital, and was buried in her late husband's grave in Bridport cemetery, after service in Bridport Parish Church. For many years she lived in the defunct and dilapidated *Bell Inn*, as a tenant of *Yondover Farm*. People marvelled that she could live alone and in such conditions on the outskirts of the parish, but she loved it and regretted being moved by the authorities to Well Plot.

Incidentally, passers-by who might well have marvelled at the array of empty bottles outside her front door did not know that they were there for a kind neighbour to fill with water. Her well was full of old bedsteads.

January 1977

New Year's indulgence

The christening of Daniel Raymond Anthony Clark at Askerswell on 2nd January passed un-noted in last months' *Notes*, and so robbed that issue of its main interest for the parents, grandparents, aunts and uncles of the young gentleman concerned. We cannot account for the lapse, although the date – the day after New Year's Day – may have had some bearing on it, and we apologise. Daniel may have had a premonition: we hear that the loving smiles he bestowed on the Rector at the font he made the christening party pay for afterwards.

March 1977

Showing the flag

The beginning of summer time has started a trickle of tourists to Loders Church. One from the Isle of Man has written in the visitors' book, 'May the love of God be with you all,' and another from the same place, 'May the Gospel of the Lord Jesus be proclaimed within these walls.' The Vicar is sorry he was not about to thank them for the blessing, and to assure them that the Gospel is proclaimed.

The Gospel is the glad tidings that the crucified redeemer left his tomb gloriously alive on Easter Day. Were this not

true, there would be no church in Loders, or anywhere else.
So Easter is the day when every Christian 'shows the flag'.

April 1977

Prebend of Loders

Tucked away in the Close of Salisbury Cathedral is a fine old
house which a nameplate proclaims to be *The Loders Canonry*. At
present it is occupied by the Venerable Wingfield-Digby,
Archdeacon of Sarum. The house was originally allotted to the
Abbot of Montebourg, in Normandy, as a lodging when he came
over to perform his duties as Canon of the Prebend of Loders,
whose Priory belonged to his Abbey of Montebourg. At the
Reformation, King Henry the Eighth suspended seven of the
Prebends of Salisbury Cathedral, including the Prebend of Loders.

The present Bishop, Dr. Reindorp, has revived the seven
Prebends, presumably because he has more clergy he wishes
to honour than he has canonries for. It was announced recently
that he had bestowed the Canonry of the revived Prebend of
Loders on the Rev. K. G. W. Prior, Vicar of Longfleet, Poole.
The Dean and Chapter of Salisbury have invited the Vicar of
Loders to be present at Mr. Prior's installation in the
Cathedral on May 30th.

April 1977

Of Holly and the Church tower

As the faithful trooped down the path to Loders Church for the
early Easter Communion they were unaware of the drama that
had occurred shortly before, under the flag fluttering from the
Church tower. The Vicar's younger son, Chuck, who went up
the tower to run up the flag, was followed by his black
Labrador Holly, who jumped the tower parapet and fell eighty
feet to the Court lawn, mercifully not to the tombstone area on
the south side. The impression his body made on the lawn may
still be seen from the tower parapet.

Mr. Cranwell, a vet, happened to be thinking of attending the
Loders Communion when he was telephoned and found himself
tending the wounded Holly instead. X-rays showed that the
injuries, amazingly, were confined to two broken front legs. The

School of Veterinary Science at Bristol University warmed to an enterprising dog like Holly, and operated on him. He is back at the Vicarage, with his front legs in plaster, otherwise fit as a fiddle, constrained for the time being to occasional limps round the lawn. At present he is making a kennel of the study with the Vicar. As Mrs. Willmott's yellow Labradors are entrenched in the dining-room, there are now two rooms in the Vicarage for tramps and tradesmen to be wary of.

* * * * *

So many people have been asking the progress of the Labrador, Holly, who fell eighty feet from the top of Loders tower, that it is as well to say here that he has made an amazing recovery, and been returned to his master at Chatham. He has left his mark on the annals of veterinary surgery as well as on the sward beneath the tower.

* * * * *

Enquiries continue to come in for the health of black Labrador Holly. We have just heard from his master, Chuck Willmott, at Chatham, that he is going from strength to strength. Chuck has presented a much needed St. George's flag to the church as a thank-offering. Worries about the cost of the operation may cheer up. The veterinary department of Bristol University found Holly's adventure so uniquely useful for teaching that they reduced the fee to a half of what was expected.

May–July 1977

Communion

The fear of our church decorators that the primroses and the daffodils might be over before Easter were not well founded. They were in good supply, and were used to fine effect in the company of abundant garden flowers, and those hot house beauties the madonna and arum lilies and carnations. Jubilee had imparted a red, white and blue motif to the borders leading up to Loders church, and they were in their prime on Easter day.

Easter is a time for Communion. If the proportion of our population which made theirs were characteristic of the whole country, then the churches could not contain them. We had 219 communicants in all (Loders 149, Askerswell 50 and Dottery 20).

At Loders matins, church and chancel were tightly packed. The churchwarden was getting eight adults into pews meant for six. Despite being packed like sardines, the choir gave an excellent account of themselves, especially in their anthem, variations on the theme of *Jesus Christ is risen today*. They enjoyed the fortification of Mrs. Deacon, over from Dorchester, and of Commander Jimmy James, who had left the shadowing of the Russian fishing fleet to others. Church collections on Easter Day are, under recent legislation, an important part of parson's stipend. Ours amounted to £139.84. The Vicar is grateful to all contributors, visible and invisible.

May 1977

The luck of the draw

A sophisticated young lady of eight, Miss Sarah Gray, said it was the best fête she had been to, and she goes to many. Writing as from Radlett, Herts, she says: 'I liked Askerswell fête because there were so many things you could buy and they were quite cheap for that sort of thing. The best game I liked was where you had a rod with a magnet on it and had to pick up paper frogs. Everybody got a prize.'

* * * * *

A gentleman who was not at the fête bought fifty pence worth of tickets and won the bottle of whiskey and the two bottles of wine. He can be pretty sure of a pastoral visit in the immediate future.

August 1977

Fête jottings

Loders Fête made a profit of £1,511.72. That is easily the best ever. And it looks to be providential. The fête finances the church repair fund, and the church has recently been found to be under heavy attack by dry rot, which if not contained could do grave damage.

The dry rot began in the north west corner of the church, under the tower arch, in the concrete box that housed the organ blower. It spread west into the ringing chamber, and east along the north wall of the church as far as the blocked Saxon doorway. It has gone right through the thickness of the wall, and is showing in fungoid form on the exterior. The church architect quickly devised remedial measures, and Messrs. Leaf of Powerstock executed them with commendable promptitude. The concrete box was built for eternity and needed a pneumatic drill to demolish it. The affected plaster was stripped from the walls, and the rotten flooring taken up and burnt (mercifully the rot had not quite reached the organ). A blow-lamp was operated over wall and floor to burn up the surface spoor, and then both were injected with a chemical repellent. It is now a matter of waiting and seeing whether this treatment works.

At present the old blower is in the ringing chamber. When last repaired it was reckoned to be near the end of its active life. Its stertorous breathing had come to be audible above the dulcet notes of the organ, and was an annoyance to the organist that only his love of the instrument made tolerable. Modern blowers are smaller and more efficient. The possibility of putting one on the west side of the organ is being explored. This would leave the area of dry rot exposed and accessible. Meanwhile hand-blowing is the order of the day. It is quite an art, as one of our churchwardens could tell, who did it with a vigour that only gave the organ flatulence, and exhausted him.

Now the Navy, the Army and the Parochial Information Officer take turns at the handle and are on the best of terms with it. The secret of success is to watch the ups and downs of a bit of lead on a string which the organist has fixed to the bellows. He, by the way, is highly conversant with the mechanism of the organ, and the spraying he did in and around the blower chamber may well have served the organ itself from infection. For the edification of all our non-parochial readers, his name is Bill Tiltman, and apart from war service he has been Loders organist for around forty years. His skill is happily married to the high quality of the organ.

September 1977

The Typist of *The Parish Notes*

Our old friend Mrs. Fleming has sold her large house in Victoria Grove, Bridport, and moved to a bungalow near her daughter in Yeovil, where she will also be in easier reach of her son. In the old days she used to type these *Notes* and the church guide-books. She hopes that she may be able to combine occasional attendance at Loders church with the care of her late husband's grave.

* * * * *

All the kind people who gave fivers or more to Loders Fête could have been puzzled to see in the fête accounts in the September *Parish Notes* that cash donations totalled only £4.02. The culprit was 'one of those damned dots' abominated by a famous politician. It should have read £402. We think our readers are aware that the price we pay for a typed sheet cannot give us the standard of accuracy of the vastly more expensive printed sheet. The editor would get a proof to correct were it a printed sheet, but with a typed sheet he does not. So he is at the mercy of the typist, and she is often working at high pressure. She is always ready to put herself out to produce the *Notes* just when we need them. She brought us a delectable box of goods for the fête, and the firm let us down very lightly in their charge. So we are not complaining. Neither are our readers. Indeed, before this £402 had become £4.02, they appear never to have noticed any error of spelling, punctuation or grammar. Which may be a sign of the times.

October 1977

Of Mrs. Willmott and rubbish

Last year's drought is probably to blame for the drunken appearance of some of the gravestones in Loders churchyard. They are the responsibility of their owners, and not of the Church Council. Ivy on the walls and on some of the old tombs is being gallantly tackled by Mr. and Mrs. Philip Young, Miss Muriel Randall, and Mr. Maurice Lawson, who felt honoured by a gesture of encouragement from Lady Laskey.

Meanwhile, Mrs. Willmott maintains the borders, as she has done for years, and is a dedicated burner of rubbish.

December 1977

The Vicar and Mrs. Netta Taylor

The *Dorset Evening* in Loders Village Hall added £42 to the Hall funds, and greatly pleased the discriminating souls who attended. One never tires of Mrs. Netta Taylor's *Dorset dialogues* (these are becoming faintly naughty now that she thinks she knows the vicar better), and her Dorset smock, a treasure of the Wells family, made them utterly convincing. Mr. George Hyde's discerning, and often quite beautiful, colour slides of his favourite haunts in Dorset usually had the audience guessing, and revealed unexpected traits of his character. Who, for instance, knew that George was the sort of chap to be out of bed at sunrise taking pictures? Had he gone to bed?

May 1978

An empty wardrobe

Jumble, it seems, will be as greatly in demand in June as it was in May. It is a wonderful commodity, and, unlike money, the root of much good. May Fair at School has a big appetite for jumble, yet Help the Aged, coming only a day or two afterwards, got eight sacks of good quality stuff.

One of our best givers gave generously of cash this time. She said jumble sales had left her nothing to wear. 'Nothing' in the context of clothes has a male and female meaning. The lady of the Vicarage says she also has nothing to wear, but the sight of 'nothing' in her wardrobe is awesome.

June 1978

Snow on Knowle Hill

There was snow remaining on Knowle Hill, Loders, in mid-April, two months after the February blizzard had put it there. Farmer Maurice Crabb swears to this with his hand on his heart, and his wife Pam risked her life behind a young farmer

on a motor-bike to bring a bag of the said snow to the
vicarage. There it was put in a cool corner of the garden, but
soon melted in the wasted heat radiating from the vicarage.

May 1978

What the churchwarden said

Mr. Cecil Marsh, the eighty-five year old Vicar's Warden of
Dottery, has been in Dorchester Hospital for another blood
top-up. The amiable Consultant, doing his morning round,
asked Mr. Marsh why he wanted more blood. 'Well, Doctor,'
said Mr. Marsh, 'I had a Turk of a cold back along, and that
took it out of me.'

'And pray, what is a Turk of a cold?' queried the consultant.
When Mr. Marsh told him, the consultant went into convulsions of unprofessional laughter. 'Put that down, put that
down,' said he to his assistant standing by with notebook. But
we dare not put it down.

June 1978

The *Western Gazette*

Mr. and Mrs. Brian Cook, of Loders, have a son, Duncan
James, born on May 9th. Mr. Cook is the local representative
of our big brother, the *Western Gazette*. So the congratulations
we offer are seasoned with becoming deference.

June 1978

At the Last Trump

The Vicar writes: 'Loders, Dottery and Askerswell are abuzz
with speculation about the proposed union of these parishes with
Powerstock, and I am often asked what is to happen. I do not
know, and because I don't, neither does anybody else. Only time
will tell. Canon Rowley's retirement from Powerstock in
October poses me an awkward problem. The pastoral re-organisation committee say that if I do not take Powerstock from him it
will be merged (against Powerstock's wish it seems) with the
new Bridport team ministry, and Loders, Dottery and
Askerswell will suffer a like fate when I resign them.

I am no chicken, and am failing in some parts of my work, which might respond at once to a 'new broom'. My wife also has to be considered. She cannot for ever tend church borders and run a vicarage the size of a manor-house. I hope prayers will be put up for me to reach a right decision, in the best interest of all the parishes. I have been forty-six years in the service of the Church, if my long monastic training at Kelham be added to my forty years in the ordained ministry, and thirty one years in Loders. Next to Archdeacon Seager, I am holding my parish longer than any other parson in the diocese of Salisbury. He has been Vicar of Gillingham for thirty-two years.

My family and I love Loders like limpets. Neither the attractions nor the scope of other posts offered me have been able to separate us. Probably I am very selfish. The hierarchy for one think that my kind of record is no credit to anybody. But under my régime, Loders Vicarage has produced seven children whose value to the community is not in doubt – four nurses, two teachers, and a soldier. I am relying on them to get me by St. Peter at the Last Trump.

July 1978

Of Don Quixote and funerals

There is a sort of superstition in Loders that whenever the Vicar goes away a parishioner dies. Which could be one of the reasons why he takes a holiday infrequently. Often in the past he has been called back to a funeral. His only night out of the parish this year was 23rd–24th November, when he was in Shropshire watching his son Michael's production of *Don Quixote* at Wem school.

But at eight o'clock on the morning of the 24th Mr. Wilfred Crabb of Yondover died unexpectedly in Bridport hospital after a brief illness. Much sympathy will be felt for his widow, to whose own indisposition he had been such a devoted ministrant. Farming was his forte, and local government his hobby. For nearly fifty years he was on Loders Parish Council, and with the clerk, Mr. Harold Brown, his mentor, ruled it for fifteen years as Chairman.

December 1978

Rover, the Vicarage dog

'*Rover*', the senior of the Vicarage Labradors, died on the afternoon of December 20th. He was so beloved of the tiny tots who
used to attend the Sunday afternoon kindergarten at the Vicarage
that they called it '*Rover*'s Sunday School'.

For a yellow Labrador, and a gun-dog, he was a great age,
nearly fifteen, but perfectly healthy, and active to within an hour
or so of his death. Some of us who are fond of domestic animals
hope that meeting them again may be one of the surprises of the
better world to come.

January 1979

The auctioneer's hammer

A carol party numbering about two dozen serenaded Uploders
and Loders in unpleasant weather, but were well received, and
collected £50 for the Children's Society. The expedition ended
before a big log fire in the Vicarage dining-room, with eats
and drinks to match. How much more of such parochial
conviviality will that ancient fireplace see? The auctioneer's
hammer has knocked so many old parsonages clean out of
village life.

January 1979

Vicarage catacombs

That cats are reliable barometers is now an article of belief at
the Vicarage. Timmey, who was on Christmas holiday there,
went berserk on what turned out to be the night of the great
blizzard. He rushed to and fro along the passages, jumped on
people's beds, and was put out of doors for his pains. In the
deep snow of the next morning, and through the day, he was
not to be found. With pangs of conscience it was noted that the
outhouses were all shut, denying him refuge. Days passed and
he was given up for dead.

Then the Vicarage began to be haunted. Faint mewings were
to be heard, sometimes in the study, sometimes in the music
room. Yet he was nowhere, not even up the chimneys. On the
sixth day, the lady of the house was in the music-room and the

mewing started beneath her feet. She prised up a floor-board. Out crawled Timmey, blinking, looking amazingly well preserved. The theory is that he got into the catacombs beneath the Vicarage floors through a vent to escape the blizzard, and waxed too fat on the mice there to get out again.

February 1979

Knitting

Mr. Michael Stewart and his wife Ruby have come from Maiden Newton to *Upton Peep*. He works at Westland aircraft. She has earned a great reputation for needlework: she has made the exquisite 'Vine' frontal for Askerswell Church. This is the more remarkable because she has long been a martyr to neuritis.

When the Vicar called to welcome her, she was stretched out on a pallet before the fire in the sitting-room, attended by her sister. She was knitting – furiously, it seemed to one who has only done it on a cotton-reel. She was also considering how she could make a British Legion banner on order, and reckoned she might have to do it recumbent.

February 1979

The wheelbarrow

All who know the Tudor fireplace in Loders Vicarage – and they are legion – acknowledge it the best fireplace in the world. It was the deciding factor in the Vicar's acceptance of the benefice thirty-three years ago, and thanks to the manorial lords who have allowed him to feed it on the defunct timber in their rookery, he is its devoted slave. It is beloved, too, of Sunday School, Mothers' Union, Choir, Ringers, Church Council, most of the congregation and his own scattered family, who have revelled in its warmth and aesthetic satisfaction. When he cut wood, his custom was to wheel the tools to the rookery, leave the barrow on the bank, which adjoins the road, carry the tools to the work, and wheel them home afterwards.

One morning a truck drew up, and abstracted the barrow from the bank, when he was out of sight among the trees. It has not been recovered. He misses it. The tools were:- a 14 lb. sledge-hammer, an axe, a crow-bar, nine assorted steel wedges,

and sometimes a chainsaw, a can of fuel, and a can of oil. But the parish misses it more. Their plaint against the Vicar was his inaccessibility – not on the phone, and never in when anybody called at the Vicarage. The barrow pinned him down. The ladies in the Wednesday bus beheld it and nodded knowingly. It performed the office of an angler's float: the worm was out of sight, but not far away.

February 1980

The Parish Notes

This flimsy sheet must be the plainest of parish magazines. But now, at the beginning of another year, it serves, we hope, as a greetings card, and bears the seasonal wishes to all our readers. At *Bell* the rafters of the drawing-room are lined with the Christmas cards that came from far and near. The Vicar for one will study them at leisure and absorb their goodwill. His thirty-three years in the same parish show that he is no rolling stone: he is cocooned in the comforting moss of friendships that have stood the test of time and begotten new ones of like quality. Life is change says the Lord Bishop George Reindorp. (But so is death.)

January 1981

Speed bonny boat

It was not bonny boats, but a benign British Rail that speeded the Vicar to Skye in the busy days leading up to Christmas, and obliged him to miss some village functions that he would not willingly miss. A friend of forty-two years, a Scot of the Scots, Robert Bruce Dundas, died on December 8th. His widow was beset by three Presbyterian divines, each of them confident that the funeral should be in his kirk. The vicar connived at her plan to avoid bloodshed. He conducted the funeral service on a helicopter air strip opened by the Prince of Wales [Prince Charles] as Duke of Rothesay last year. Two of the ministers showed up in the crowd of mourners, and one of them even had the grace to follow the procession led by pipers to a boulder on the hillside where the casket was buried.

One thing convinced the Vicar he had done right – the weather did a kind of Loders Fête act, with the rain stopping and the sun shining just for the funeral. He is sure that his getting from Dorchester to Skye for £2 on the special senior citizens' day trips was not lost on the ministers. But what price the senior citizen of Loders who thought he had been to Afghanistan, radiating a little good will there?

January 1981

The Local Scarlet Pimpernell

The Vicar would also like to thank very much indeed the mysterious person, or persons, who caused two loads of excellent logs to be delivered at Bell, presumably because he had twisted a knee, which retarded his own forestry activities. He is grateful also to the local Scarlet Pimpernell, whose famous 'Get Well' cards assumed the form of logs of his own hewing.

March 1981

Ernest Boon

Ernest Boon was a chartered surveyor by profession operating first with Taylors of Yeovil and then with Lawrences in Bridport. He served in the Great War as a gunner from January 1916 to July 1919, attaining the rank of captain, much mentioned in despatches, and winning the Military Cross, with bar. He was in the front line with 306 Siege Battery in the bloodiest battles of the war – Messines Ridge, Arras, Paschendale, St. Quentin, etc. In the great allied advance of

September 1918 his battery was the first across the hitherto invincible line of German resistance, the Canal du Nord. Through it all he contrived to keep a journal. Like the Gospels it is detached, factual and completely unemotional. It does not say how he got his M.C. and bar, and does not say that he was ever wounded, although it is hard to see how he could be unhurt when his men were so often blown to bits.

On retirement from Lawrences he still attended their office daily as a consultant. When the Bridport churches changed to the new forms of service he became a member of Loders congregation, where he continued to enjoy what he had always been used to. The Vicar first made his acquaintance in 1947, when he was auctioning at the Vicarage the surplus furniture left by the Reverend Charles Palmer. Bidding had begun on the top floor, and was ending on the bottom. Ernest stood on a box between the dining-room and the kitchen. The bidders in dining room and kitchen could not see each other but he could see both. The vicar wanted an electric kettle. He was in the dining room going up by sixpences. But somebody in the kitchen was going up by half crowns. The kitchen one, and when Ernest asked the name of the triumphant bidder it was Mrs. Willmott. He never forgot that.

July 1981

Leonard Clark

The late Leonard Clark, by profession a Schools' Inspector, but making his name as a poet, writer of children's books, educationalist, and broadcaster, had been a frequent guest at Loders Vicarage over the past ten years, and a familiar figure in Loders Church, where he reinforced the choir. He was 76.

London's oldest church, St. Bartholomew the Great, was his usual place of worship, and derived welcome financial support from some of his literary activity. The funeral was there. He loved flowers. As his funeral cortège moved through Smithfield to the crematorium the busy butchers, pausing to pay respect, might have thought they were seeing a bit of a Channel Island carnival of flowers. His ashes are destined half to the ground beneath his seat in 'Bart's the Great', and half to his native Forest of Dean.

The Vicar writes: 'Leonard Clark was a talented man. The English contemporary poets published a book of poems in honour of his 75th birthday. Pope Paul the Sixth made him a Knight of the Order of St. Sylvester for his services to religious education. I shall not forget his partnership with Cardinal Heenan in a fifty minute BBC 1 television confrontation with the atheists Baroness Wootton and Dr. Ayer, former professor of logic at Oxford. The children of Loders day and Sunday schools loved to listen to him. But so did rebellious adolescents – I remember the upper forms of King's School Bruton listening to him on poetry at an evening meeting scheduled to end at 8.30, going on at their insistence and with the headmaster's permission to 10.30. The Italian government commissioned him to render Dante's *Divine Comedy* in simple English for Italian children born here. During his last stay at Loders Vicarage he was working on the *Paradiso*, where I hope our friendship may be resumed.'

October 1981

A tough old bird

In the recent snow the vicar met a fox coming up Yellow Lane as he was walking down it to church. The fox evidently considered the vicar too tough an old bird, mounted the bank with dignity and vanished. On his way back up the lane the vicar met a cock pheasant, which about-turned and ran away. Had Reynard got his timing wrong? What would his tactic have been with a pheasant in the open? In the confinement of the Vicarage a fox had killed a dozen hens and taken one, and eaten the heads off three goose!

February 1982

CHAPTER 6

The answer lies in the soil

❦

It is easy to lose track of just how rural West Dorset is. It is the one county in England with no motorway in it (apart from Cornwall – and that is on the Celtic fringe). It has the A35 shunting all the holiday traffic on to Devon. As a result there is a little pocket of untouched England stretching from the Dorchester to Bridport road, and bounded by Broadwindsor, Crewkerne, Yeovil, and Toller Porcorum. The ancient forest of Powerstock Common, and the bleak heights of Rampisham with the radio masts wailing in the wind, are bounded in by Golden Cap on the coast to the west, Lewesdon and Pilsdon inland, and the hill-fort of Eggardon to the east.

The keynote to the life-style of the inhabitants is probably not one of hardship along the lines of Thomas Hardy's *Tess of the D'Urbevilles*. There was the freak wave off Abbotsbury, (p. 189) and frequent agricultural mishaps. The suicide of Harry Trickett (p. 186) was one bleak farming reference during a time when subsidies and success made farming a safe and productive occupation, unlike at the turn of this century.

But the spirit of the place was more one of rural simplicity, not knowing where luck is. Dorset poet-vicar William Barnes registered the atmosphere 100 years before. The grass is still very green. There was not much time for leisure, but then work was slower and more leisurable. Life was full, but not over-crowded.

From hay to silage

The Licensee of the *Loders Arms* had a good measure of
success against our awful June weather when he tried to get us
celebrating the Longest Day. A lamb was roasted over an open
fire behind the inn by Mr. Albert Wells. A large number of
villagers watched. Then the rain descended, and the delicious
lamb sandwiches had to be eaten under cover. Since that day
the rain has scarcely stopped. Cut grass lies rotting in the
fields and the uncut grass will not be much good. The season
seems to have converted some staunch advocates of hay to
silage.

July 1968

Harry Trickett

Mr. Harry Trickett was a sad case of a farmer who failed
to adjust himself to changed conditions. Ill-health obliged
him to part with his cows, and the control of his land, at
Gribb Farm, and the hard fact that he could not restart
farming unhinged his mind. Sympathetic neighbours attended
his funeral at Loders Church in force. He was buried in the
cemetery.

September 1968

Fire in the shed

The Sabbath calm of Loders was recently disturbed by the
incoming rush of the Bridport fire-engine. To the surprise of
Mr. Raymond Crabb, it stopped first at *Bell Farm*, where he
was feeding the pigs, and informed him that he had a fire
there. As the fire could not be found, the brigade went back
to Raymond's house, in Loders proper, where his wife Hazel
received them gladly. She had called them. The fire, in an
outlying shed, was much more smoke than fire and was soon
quelled.

March 1969

Snowed in in March

The blizzard that swept the south of England did not pass us by, as that kind of thing sometimes does. The swift transition from rain and mud to a white, sugar-loaf world was acceptable to the children, if to nobody else. In the hilly fastness of Nallers it meant no school, although Farmer Tom Foot was able to get the milk over six-foot drifts with his four-wheel-drive tractor. At Dottery, Mr. John Marsh saw to it that his children did get to school, but as they went in the box of a tractor they did not mind.

A rescue squad from the Vicarage climbed the Olympian heights to *Cloverleaf Farm*, and finding the inmates blissfully asleep (it was only 9.15 am) left them to it. At Milton cross-roads they decided that *Lousy Knap* were bound to be all right because they had won the whisky at the social, and turned back into Loders. There they saw that the hygiene wardens, with their usual devotion to duty, had got through, and finding few dustbins, were shouting 'Mack'rel Alive O', which brought heads to the windows. Mr. George Bryan went to open the road to Askerswell. He had a snow-plough on the front of his tractor, and was towing Mr. Robin Well's car at the rear.

At school only a handful of children had appeared and round the stove it was being told how on the previous evening four cars had been stuck on Mill Hill, how Mr. Ron Legg, at the bottom, had helped the three higher up to get away and then found himself helpless.

Askerswell Post Office, however, claims the best adventure. Mrs. Savage was rung by the police at 2.30 am and told that there were two men marooned in the telephone kiosk in The Square, one with a wooden leg which she verified, except for the exact composition of the leg. The two men had turned down from the Dorchester road, had abandoned their Mini at *Hembury* and phoned the police from the kiosk. Finding her electricity was off, Mrs. Savage made do with candles and oil stove and revived the travellers. Although her bungalow is not overblest with room, she bedded them down in a respectable fashion and later sent them off with a good English breakfast.

They found at *Hembury* that their Mini had the good fortune to be blocking the way of an irate milk-lorry, which secured its quick removal. We reckon that this paragraph will amuse our two Canadian readers, Mr. and Mrs. Fred Vacher. We can hear them saying, 'So you think you have had some snow, do you?'

March 1969

A scene from clerical life

In the course of pastoral visiting in Dottery the Vicar stepped into something that would have warmed the heart of George Eliot. Tapping on the back door of *Bilshay Farm* (which is where people on good terms with the Barneses always tap), he was bidden enter, by a voice within. He found the family lingering at table over a late luncheon, and received from them their usual hearty welcome.

When the salutations had expired, some vigorous post-prandial snoring focussed his eye on the sofa, where a full size pig was sleeping the sleep of the just. Robert Barnes countered the Vicar's enquiring look with an assurance that the sofa did indeed seem too small, and might be getting uncomfortable, but would be extended if the pig grew any longer.

Sarah then took up her parable. Billy, she said, was one of the family, and a great pet, and sending her (it is a she) to the butcher could not even be contemplated. It would be cold-blooded murder. Billy was housetrained; wasn't in the least choosey as to what she ate – didn't even object to Robert's trousers; liked a dish of tea with the full farmer's complement of sugar; and sometimes performed frolics capable of scaring away the occasional unpleasant Man from the Ministry.

Billy had begun life as a poor miserable little runt, whose delicate stomach wouldn't hold anything for five minutes and who was going to be knocked on the head. Her present six or seven score of weight is a measure of the love bestowed on her by Sarah.

April 1969

Changing his tune

The cheerful whistling of Mr. Reg Matthews as he goes to and from his work at Boarsbarrow is a tonic to the vicinity of

Vicarage Lane. It is noted that he is not quite insensitive to the weather. When flaming June turned suddenly to Christmas the other day his tune was, *God rest you merry, Gentlemen.*

July 1969

The freak wave

A freak wave which overturned a boat at Abbotsbury took the lives of a young Loders parishioner, Mr. Geoffrey Churchill, and a friend. Deep sympathy is felt for his family and especially for his mother, who is a great sufferer from physical infirmities and was in hospital at the time. Geoffrey had been running the small holding near *Travellers Rest* alone after his parents' removal to West Bexington.

The funeral service was at Martinstown, his former home. The Vicar of Martinstown said the prayers. The Vicar of Loders read the lesson and the commital. The church was full, and a retiring collection (instead of flowers) produced nearly £40. Half of this was given to Loders church repair fund. We would like to thank the family and the givers and say, if we may, how splendid was the fortitude of Mrs. Churchill, who came out of hospital for the service, sat in a wheel-chair at the west end of the nave where she had an unimpeded view of the coffin of her son and returned to hospital when the funeral moved to the churchyard.

July 1969

Standard Time

Standard Time ensures that the mornings are still dark, but hopefuls note that the birds have found something to sing about and are thinking of spring, forgetting that winter can do his worst as late as March or April. Nobody is likely to regret the passing of the present winter. Few houses have been unaffected by ills of some sort. The ubiquitous 'flu caught many of our farmers. Animals have to be attended to, come what may, and some farmers who were bad enough to be in hospital would crawl out of bed to do the milking, and crawl back again, trusting to traditional remedies of their own fancy to put them right rather than doctors.

Farm-work was not helped by the activities of men laying pipes for North Sea Gas. Their trenches scarred the fields, and their great machines, too wide for the lanes, cut into the banks and plastered the roads with mud. A fracture in one of the pipes they had laid took much discovering and delayed their departure. But now they are gone, and those who like to meditate in country lanes, instead of being preoccupied with the hazards underfoot, may think of the hazards to the soul, and the onset of Lent, the time to grapple with them.

February 1970

Agricultural repairs on the clapper

Loders ringers have taken a record collection of £30 from the parish in recognition of their service to the tower. Few parishes can value their bells more highly than Loders. Incidentally, the broken clapper of the tenor bell did not make the long journey to the Loughborough foundry after all. At Sharpe Tone, the agricultural engineers in Bridport, we have in Mr. Philip Symes a friend with Uploders connections. This is the time when the firm are busy with broken balers and tractors, but he saw to it that the clapper was mended in time for Harry Crabb to get it in for the following Sunday's ringing. His good offices will have lightened the bill considerably.

July 1970

Ancillary help

The power-cuts in December were a great nuisance to everybody, but above all to our farmers. Fortunate indeed were those who could fall back on auxiliary generators, which added another word to the Dorset dictionary through the farmer who said, 'We weren't all that put out. We just fell back on our celery engine'.

* * * * *

A good old Dorset farming lady, lamenting with a moist eye the death of a friend, finally consoled herself thus: 'But there, her were quite ready to go. Her had made the Christmas puddins and sent all her Christmas cards. Her couldn't have done more'.

January 1971

'No place like home'

The Ascott and Lenthall families, who had farmed Upton Manor for many years, but now run the West Mead Hotel in Symondsbury, returned to Loders in full strength on January 2nd for the wedding of the younger son, Mr. Stuart Lenthall Ascott, and Miss Jean Susan Sargent, formerly on the staff of West Mead. The big imponderable had been whether a further fall of snow might upset the arrangements, but it did not, and there were no falls of another kind on the icy path leading down to the church, which could only just contain the large congregation.

An acceptable supplement to bells, organ and hymns was a carol sung from the chancel step after the signing of the register, by a friend of the family, Miss Daveen Playle. Friends of the bridegroom made an archway of agricultural implements and golf-clubs outside the church porch for the bridal party to pass beneath as they left for the reception at West Mead. Doubtless that great old-fashioned farmer and churchwarden the late Mr. Eli Lenthall would have had something pithy to say about the combination of golf-clubs and farm-tools if he were proposing the health of the grandson who is so like him physically.

February 1971

Church mice

Church mice are supposed to be poor, but the Dottery mice know how to be poor and well-preserved, even fat. They are developing a taste for the altar hangings. These are costly, so the economical churchwardens get them on to cheese, and literally hooked. Now it is not the sermon that is assessed after service, but the state of the war on the mice. Ten have been accounted for so far. The Askerswell churchmice incline to a little of the organ bellows when they fancy something nice. Both churchwardens at Askerswell are ex-submarine commanders. The mice play with these in a way Hitler couldn't.

April 1971

Easter gardens

'Martha had a garden,
And she tended it with care.
She took a pail and watered it,
Each slug or snail she slaughtered it.
There were no greenfly there.
She scratched and scraped it with a hoe,
There were no seeds she did not sow,
And yet her garden wouldn't grow.

Mary has a garden which is full of happy flowers.
She doesn't do a thing in it,
But walk about and sing in it,
For hours and hours and hours.
She never weeds and never hoes,
And yet her garden always grows –
Because she loves it, I suppose.'

So writes that keen countryman, Mr. Reginald Arkell. At our Agricultural Discussion Club Dinner another countryman gave another theory of gardens. He told how a rather pedantic vicar congratulated a parishioner on co-operating with the Almighty in making such a splendid garden. 'Yes,' conceded the gardener, 'it's all right now, but you should have zeed it when t'Almighty had it to Hisself'.

Each to his own theory. The fact remains that primroses are showing on sheltered banks, nettles are establishing their stranglehold on ditches, rooks are nesting, and Spring's new surge of life has started. We have to be up and doing, and in the world of the spirit, too, for both worlds, having the same creator, are in accord. Spring is also Easter.

April 1971

Sheep abroad

Our Missionary link, Miss Carol Harper, writes cheerfully from her post in Tanzania. She wishes us a good day for the fête, and laments the passing of Mr. Fred Vacher. 'We have just been presented with a sheep's tail,' she says. 'It is long and gristly, and we are not quite sure what to do with it. Fortunately, this is not an Arab country. I would never be able to swallow the sheep's eye . . .'

July 1971

Agricultural accidents

The feelings of Loders people have never been more deeply stirred than they were by the appalling accident at *Boarsbarrow Farm*, which robbed the village of one of its brightest and most likeable young men, Alec Norris, and Roberta, his wife-of-two-years, of a husband. He was drawn into a silage machine he was servicing, and killed.

The funeral was at his home village of Symondsbury. So crowded was the church that people were standing at the west end of the nave and in the transepts. His workmates formed an escort for the coffin, and the lesson was read by the farm-manager of *Boarsbarrow*, Mr. Rob Wrixon. He is not used to jobs of this kind, and he must have been under great emotional strain, but he did it as to the manner born, reading slowly, distinctly and feelingly.

To Commander John Streatfeild fell the difficult task of taking up position by the coffin and making the funeral oration. He confined himself to saying how Streatfeild Hood and Co. had found Alec as an employee, and what sort of a boy he had been in Symondsbury. The speech was short and simple, and seemed to fit the occasion exactly. Alec's connection with Loders is not altogether ended, for his widow hopes to continue living in the farm cottage for a while.

* * * * *

Mrs. Miller and family, formerly of Askerswell, have sent a cheque for £32 towards the repair of the Askerswell church roof, in memory of 'Tink', Mrs. Miller's son who was killed in a tractor accident three years ago. The terrible accidents that can happen in farm work are much on our minds at present. That one whose memory is still an open wound to those most concerned should assist so materially in a good work on the church will stir the hearts of Askerswell people very deeply. It is splendid of the Millers to sink their gift in a common fund where it is really needed, rather than to present some memorial object that could be done without.

August 1971

Mrs. Mabel Crabb

The Loders scene has lost one of its most colourful and pleasant characters by the death of Mrs. Mabel Crabb, mother of Raymond, of *Bell Farm*, and Clive. In 1945 she was left to bring up her sons alone, her husband having been gored by a cow. She overcame this with her customary fortitude, and found comfort in the services of Loders Church, which she loved. When she was absent from her seat in the Lady Chapel one could be sure there was a good reason. At one time she was church organist of West Milton, and she often played for our Mothers' Union services. At her funeral, the Mothers' Union banner was draped with black crêpe, and a pitcher of magnificent chrysanthemums at its base bore tribute to her memory.

October 1971

Accidents on road and farm

Congratulations to Mr. Geoffrey Randall and Mr. Dick Deacon on coming lightly out of potentially serious accidents. Mr. Randall's tractor and baler turned over in a hollow while he was operating on Eggardon, but he escaped with damage to shoulder and arm. Mr. Deacon's and another car were in collision one night at the bottom of Mill Hill, Loders. He received no bodily injury, and his car, unlike the other, was not much damaged, but he is suffering from shock.

October 1971

Two ways of looking at it

A recent visitor to Loders noticed on an afternoon's walk through the village that a small farm had a card sticking out of the wall with AI on it. Down the road he saw a bit of slate stuck into another wall with AI on it. Further along he met a third card on a gate saying AI. 'Well,' said he, 'how truly splendid this is.

The spirit of Churchill lingers on. These farmers take the power cuts and all the inconvenience in their stride, and instead of giving the V sign, put up these little notices to say they are A One'. (The Milk Marketing Board's Artificial Inseminator on his daily round reads the notices less romantically.)

March 1972

Cows in the barley, mother in hospital

Dottery people were perturbed to learn that their much loved Mrs. Bagwell, who prepares the church for services, was in Bridport Hospital with heart trouble. Though short of breath, she had walked from her cottage down to Higher Pymore to warn Mr. Cecil Marsh that one of his cows was in the barley. Then she went to the doctor. He sounded the alarm and whisked her into hospital, thereby averting a breakdown, we trust.

Hospitals always find her buxom motherliness and cheerfulness excellent for the other patients. We can see the hospital holding on to her until the women's ward are all better.

July 1972

Harvest

It took a farmer's eye to note that the ladies had used a few wild oats in their decorative scheme, but it was none the worse for that. The harvest supper in the village hall was the perfect end to the festivities. 'Eats' were marvellous, as always, and delicately served. The entertainment that followed was also home-made. But why the sigh of relief at the Rector having to depart before it came on? Ex-Army chaplains are not that squeamish. A jug of water that now appears beside the wheaten sheaf at Askerswell is proof that somebody once listened to a sermon in which our dependence on water was mentioned.

A lump or two of coal among the exotic show of flowers and fruits at Dottery proved that somebody there was listening too. The Dottery congregations were large, and the collections a record. A point about one of the collections was that it included an offering from a widow of 99, who, in her childhood lived next door to the church, saw it built, and saw the roof blown off in a gale before the church was completed. She is Mrs. Chard, who now lives in Bradpole, but keeps in touch with Dottery through Mrs. Cecil Marsh.

At Loders, congregations that filled the church twice in one day trooped through a porch whose flowers not only delighted the eye but dilated the nostrils with a delicious scent of lilies, and were a foretaste of the decorations within. Singing was thoroughly congregational and robust, with the choir offering an anthem that was light and joyous. The singing of *The Loders Hymn* (p. 222) showed that the congregation has now taken it to heart.

November 1972

'It must be the plough'

Our Dottery organist, Mrs. Sylvia Johnston, is the only member of her family not to have been gloriously in the news, or even at all. Her menfolk appear to have won all the top prizes in husbandry that local shows have to offer. Her husband came first in the Melplash hedging and ditching; her eldest son Raymond took first for ploughing in the Young Farmers' section, then beat all the firsts in the local and open sections to become champion ploughman. Her second son David came first in ploughing in the Young Farmer's section at Sherborne.

Possibly in the eyes of the Lord the most meritorious was her youngest son Brian. Inspired by his brothers, he learnt to plough in a week, and took first prize for novices at Sherborne. With a humility eloquent of the teaching received in Dottery Church, they all say, 'It must be the plough.' Whether the plough was at any time blest by the Reverend Doctor Omand, of Chideock, we cannot say, but it was certainly borrowed from Mr. John Marsh, from whom it may have acquired a knack or two.

November 1972

Feathered comfort

Our part of the world was spared the bad weather that the rest of the country had, but the Black Angel has been unusually busy among us, and the undertakers (of whom one prefers to be called 'a forwarding agent to the Lord') have found the days not long enough for their work, one having been asked to conduct seven funerals on the same day.

There are many mournful hearts among the friends of Loders Church. Lieut. Colonel Arthur Shirley, perhaps the best-liked member of the congregation, and churchwarden of less than a year, had a stroke in his sleep and died without really recovering consciousness, at the age of 74. His devotion, and that of his wife, to Loders Church, had its counterpart in their work, through the Chantry House Charity, for the lonely old people of Bridport. To his own and everybody else's amusement, the latest of the old people's comforts he had managed to secure was four budgerigars, each in a cage with a pound of bird seed, and these arrived on the day of his death.

March 1973

Death of a countryman

The death of Mr. Eddie Greening, of Loders, was a sad loss to the little corps of native countrymen in the village which has been much eroded of late. He was raised in all the skills of hedging, ditching, shepherding and the like, and was a good gardener, which so often a good farmer is not. Living close to nature, and taking a delight in it, he would remark to anybody who came his way on whether the ash had burgeoned before the oak, or the promise of a fine summer in the rooks nesting high. He had a reverent regard for the moon, and sowed his seeds by what he called her rise and fall.

In all this he was a kindred spirit of his ancient father-in-law, Shepherd George Crabb, who could tell unerringly what the weather would be by feeling the bit of iron nearest to hand, and could tell the time of day by the sun's shadows. An instinct of machine-age man is to take leave of his work when he may, and not return to it till he must, but Eddie Greening, having worked in the fields of his employer all the week, would walk his daughters on Sundays to see how the fields of the other farmers were doing. He was certain that work done on Sunday never prospered. He was a ringer, and liked attending evensong till hearing and sight began to fail. He knew his good fortune in having a wife who was a ministering angel, and made bold to tell the various hospitals he made the acquaintance of that, kind as they were, he would be much better off at home.

July 1974

The archway of pitchforks

The archway of pitchforks, hold by white-smocked Young Farmers over Mr. Raymond Johnston and his bride Miss Christine Rich as they blossomed out of their wedding in Yarcombe Church, was never better deserved. The local papers were proclaiming the prowess of Raymond and his brother David in the ploughing matches, and of their father in the hedging and ditching competitions. What is news is not that they do it every year, but that they go from glory to glory, and Dottery, their home, is kept well and truly on the map by them.

The photographers had a field day. Never were a couple more diligently snapped in every posture during the service, and in the churchyard before the long trek to the wedding feast in the Victory Hall at Stockland. The speeches were earthy and appetising, fertilised by the natural genius of a best man for teasing a brother of a bridegroom.

November 1974

The April wasp

Mr. Cecil Marsh missed the Easter Vestry for the first time that anybody could remember. It was feared that he must be ill indeed. The meeting heard to their surprise that he was suffering from a wasp sting. Interest switched at once to the wasp. What manner of wasp was this, to be about in early April, and an April when there was snow on Eggardon?

May 1975

Inflated dandelions

How refreshing to be reminded by our perspicacious Mr. Robert Ward that inflation is not our only nightmare! There are dandelions, two, but he has devised a way of putting paid to them. In a letter to the Vicar dated 'Monday, 1.30 am, in bed,' he writes: 'Dandelions in Loders churchyard: I noticed how very thick these are after matins yesterday, and would gladly supply half a dozen Touchweeder which is/are like to shaving stick, though dark brown, inside a green plastic case, with a rod lid. They are held in one's hand, and you dab the end on to the centre of the dandelion plant, and in due course the same withers, rots and disappears.

Marvellous! I wondered whether gentlemen and maybe ladies from the matins congregation might volunteer to spend fifteen to thirty minutes after service to *commence* the elimination? Small sections of the turf could be marked out with the aid of two moat skewers (apply Robin Wells) joined together by, say, three yards of string, each line spaced about one foot parallel to the other, beginning, say, opposite the porch path and gradually working eastwards. If volunteers increase, the grass next the south aisle could be set upon.

I believe there are some ancient disused kneelers below the back pew in the south aisle. These could be used to speed up the process and lessen the wear on the men's trouser knees, especially if the turf becomes damp again. Though I daresay you are fully occupied with the fête, perhaps the idea could be mulled upon ... The elimination may take a year or more, as seeding continuously takes place, but I have succeeded here in my small rear garden.'

All volunteers to contact Mr. Ward direct. And they had better screw their courage to the sticking place. He is a perfectionist. After the dandelions the plantains. After the plantains the buttercups.

August 1975

Son of the soil

A sizeable congregation gathered in Loders Church to pay their respects at the funeral of the late Mr. Charlie Symes of Well Plot. He was 80 and was buried at the cemetery in the grave of his wife, who had died long before, in 1942. He was a native of Misterton. After working on farms in that area and serving in the Great War, he came to Loders where successive employers, Mr. Harold Bishop, Mr. Raymond Crabb and Mr. Newberry, soon discovered his sterling qualities.

In the funeral oration the Vicar regretted that the conservation of the environment and characteristic buildings of villages like Loders could not include 'old-timers' like Charlie Symes, for they were irreplaceable. He was a true son of the soil, who loved it and served it and when he was at work on the Bell

Hills, seemed to grow out of it as naturally as the hedge he was laying. Like the others of his kind, leisure was no problem to him, for most of his pleasure arose from the consciousness of congenial work well done. A capacity for hard work went with an impish sense of fun, and the little hills of Dorset gave him a clear view of world affairs and what should be done to put them right. He was fortunate to have children who gave him a happy home life to the end.

December 1975

Of farmers and their wives

Cows have to be milked on Easter day as on any other, and the bulk of the little community at Dottery are working farmers, but they 'made it' to church for the nine o'clock communion. What they thought of the decorations was on their faces as they looked wonderingly about them at a bevy of flowers ranging from the humble primrose to the lordly lily. To them, fairies were more likely than their substantial wives to have contrived it all.

May 1976

June is the month for lupins

Those that border the approach to Loders Church are coming into their glory. We are not alone in thinking that they grace an already beautiful church. The Blandford Press has lately published *The parish churches of England in colour*, by Mervyn Blatch and it includes a fine picture of Loders church at lupin time.

According to the author there are ten thousand medieval churches in England. He chooses only one hundred and five of them to illustrate the beauty characteristic of the various styles, and Loders is one of the hundred and five. Winterbourne Tomson is the only other Dorset church to be shown. There are two in Cornwall, five in Devon, three in Somerset and one in Wiltshire.

June 1976

Drought

The villagers of Askerswell are opening their gardens to the public on Sunday 18th July. Last year when they did this visitors came from far and near, and enjoyed the cream teas on offer as well as the gardens. The present lack of rain is hindering the working up of the gardens to a July peak of perfection. Some gardeners are irrigating theirs from the River Asker if they happen to be near it. The not-so-fortunate are enlisting the bath-water, and even the washing-up water.

* * * * *

Nothing can better illustrate the dryness of these parts than something that happened in the orchard of Knowle Farm, Uploders. It borders the River Asker. It is perilous to mow at any time, but deadly in time of drought. Frantic from the heat – obviously – the motor-mower that Mr. Maurice Lawson was driving plunged into the river and submerged. It is not his nature to let go of anything, so he didn't. He hung on and submerged with it. When it decided to come out, he, still hanging on, came out too, and it mowed all the better for its bath. Possibly his natural modesty prevented Mr. Lawson from telling us, Parochial Information Officer though he be. The intelligence was communicated by his friend and admirer, Mr. Harry Crabb.

* * * * *

The continuing drought has evoked requests to parson to pray for rain. This is unusual. Nine times out of ten it is fine days for May fairs and the like that he is asked for. A neighbouring squire is alleged to have told his parson it was high time he prayed for rain, and the parson to have confessed a fear that if he started the rain it might not stop. Your parson, less confident of his standing with the Almighty, has already prayed the Rogationtide prayer to 'grant such seasonable weather that we may gather in the fruits of the earth.' The fruits of the earth are more important than the weather, and they are appearing in their season. New English potatoes are down to sevenpence a pound, and our farmers are garnering fine hay while hay lies rotting in the rain-soaked fields of the north.

So your parson lets well alone. And he hopes his clerical neighbours may not give way to his squire before 18th July,

which is Gardens Sunday in Askerswell. It would be cruel for
the gardeners to have nursed their gardens so laboriously
through the drought and then to see them washed away on the
great day.

June–July 1976

Comfortable Lettuces

The sympathy of every nice person would have been with the
devoted housewife of Purbeck Close who looked out of her
kitchen window and saw her husband lying prone, that is, face-
downwards, on the garden. His sobriety, like his maturity, was
never in doubt, so inevitably she had visions of nasty things like
coronaries and strokes as she rushed to the rescue. Our readers
would have rejoiced with her to find that he was only weeding the
lettuce in the posture he considered the least uncomfortable.

July 1976

Urban pansies

When it comes to decorating Askerswell Church for the carol
service, the ladies annually thank providence that the wooden
candlesticks which lighted the pews in pre-electric days were
consigned to the parish chest instead of the bonfire. For the
service is by candle-light, and what candles lack in power they
make up for in beauty when dotted among the holly and the
ivy. Their flickering played tricks with the faces of the congregation (which filled the church), so that the native farmers
could be looking like urban pansies and the former urban
pansies like buttercups.

Any doubts as to who was who were dispelled when some
of each came up to read the lessons. They were a delightful
blend of Dorset and Standard English. The eight songsters of
the local Women's Institute who came to the fore and sang a
carol had about them a touch of television efficiency that was
not at all out of place. They woke up the Rector to the fact that
here under his wing he had an embryonic church choir, and
what was he doing about it?

January 1977

Red, white and blue

The fear of our church decorators that the primroses and the daffodils might be over before Easter were not well founded. They were in good supply, and were used to fine effect in the company of abundant garden flowers, and those hot house beauties the madonna and arum lilies and carnations. Jubilee had imparted a red, white and blue motif to the borders leading up to Loders church, and they were in their prime on Easter day. Easter is a time for Communion.

May 1977

English oaks

Mr. George Hyde, of Uploders, is offering the parish a couple of seven-year-old English oaks for Jubilee planting. He grew them from acorns, to his complete satisfaction.

May 1977

Sprucing up the village for the Silver Jubilee

Council workmen have been smartening up the village with their sickles: County Hall reacted with usual vigour to the horrid possibility of invading cars coming to grief in the luxuriant vegetation of the lanes.

July 1977

Of missing tortoises

Some visitors to Loders who were exploring New Street Lane met a tortoise, and took him to *Mudlark*, Mr. John Hyde's cottage, supposing he had strayed from there. The owner can have him on application, but proof of ownership may be difficult. The look on Julie Hyde's face when the tortoise is mentioned shows that she for one hopes the owner will not turn up.

August 1977

Sermons in stone

This growing season is drawing to a close. It has been different in almost every way from the hot and continuous sunshine of last year, and yet it has produced a more abundant harvest. This should not be wondered at, seeing that flowers, fruit, vegetables and cereals, like the animate creation, consist mostly of water.

All is as good as safely gathered in, despite the fickle weather, so the singing of Harvest Home at the Uploders Chapel, by a large congregation, which had giant potatoes and beans in the windows to inspire them, was uninhibited, and even boisterous.

A thoughtful and sometimes humorous address was given by the Reverend David Bumphrey, of Sidmouth. Incidentally, it might be inferred from the Chapel notice-board that the congregation enjoy a rough ride, or being bullied, or being put to sleep, or being fleeced. If memory serves us right, Mr. Bumphrey's name has been preceded by Mr. Batteram's, Mr. Boreham's and Mr. Skinner's. The congregation lay no claim to being tough. They have long known that these reverend gentlemen quite belie their names, and can be sat under with pleasure and profit.

October 1977

Apple holes

A light moving on the side of a hill overlooking Loders School on a dark night would not excite the curiosity of a local passer-by unduly. He would say to himself, 'Dear old Raymond Crabb, steering in a newly calved cow.' But a light that stays put for a long time is mysterious.

Had anybody climbed Waddon the other night to investigate they would have found a resident retired captain of industry, Mr. Nick Balfour, camped beside a badger-hole. It was not a passion for badger ham, or a belief in the healing power of badger grease, or a preference for the badger bristle shaving brush that kept him there. He was waiting for his Dachschund Apple, who had gone down, to come up. This, Apple did after a couple of hours, none the worse. It seems that this badger-hound enjoys the company of badgers. He likes to go down every hole he meets.

January 1978

Captain Lumby's steer

Captain Lumby's steer was one of a bunch which he keeps well away from home. When he finally succeeded in fighting his way through to their habitat in Broadwater, he counted the bunch and found one missing. How he located the missing steer is still the wonder of Askerswell. A submariner's instinct perhaps?

The snow was higher than the hedge. The steer had walked over the hedge and sank nine foot into the ditch beneath the hedge. The snow had closed over him. When the captain uncovered his head, he was alive, but seemingly only just, having been there a day and a half. The captain extricated himself, got through the drifts into the village, raised the alarm, and ere long a dozen anxious faces were looking down on the steer in its snowy grave.

Then they got to work. With help, the steer, who was a plucky one, was on his feet, albeit unsteadily. Like Uncle Tom Cobleigh's mare, he was pulled from the head and pushed at the tail to safety. Quite soon he was eating heartily, and now seems none the worse for his adventure. Saved from the snow – for the butcher eventually.

March 1978

Seeing things

Seeing things was what the Vicar thought he was doing when passing *Lower Ash Farm*, Dottery, on a recent dark night. There, in a patch of bright light on the hillside, was a gaggle of men, roped together and swaying about like slave-workers at their last gasp in a Russian labour camp. But Mrs. Sylvia Johnston, the farmer's wife, was not at all perturbed: it was only the Marshwood Vale Young Farmers' tug-o'-war team practising. Incidentally, the people who put on that hilarious hockey match at Yondover on Boxing Day are switching their talent to a male versus female tug-o'-war across the River Asker on Saturday July 1st.

April 1978

Buzzards overhead

Two hundred and ten adults paid for admission to the annual Maypole Dancing on the School Field at Loders. Many of these brought children who were not required to pay, so, with the pupils, they made a large company that the surrounding little hills of Dorset embosomed with tenderness.

In his speech of welcome to the crowner (and her consort) of the May Queen, the headmaster was apprehensive of a black cloud in the background, which only joined in the applause with a low growl of thunder, and, mercifully, shed no tears. An amiable business executive, looking up at the thunder, saw six of the local birds of prey, the buzzard, hovering overhead, and feared they were a sign of the premature promotion to glory of his kind. Luckily, he has faith in the Vicar, who was standing next him, and who convinced him that it was the Vicar they were orbiting.

June 1978

Foxy solutions

Foxes have been busy in Loders. One managed to get into Mr. Henry Tucker's supposedly impregnable hen run and kill eleven good layers. Henry had the wry satisfaction of finding that the fox, unable to get the hens as well as himself back through the defences, had left them all. He has scruples about eating hens killed irregularly. Not so Mr. Anthony Sanctuary and some of the neighbours. They were happy to have free meat for several days.

In Lower Loders Mr. Raymond Crabb has been losing hens to foxes in broad daylight – no less than fifteen on one occasion. As he is a tender-hearted man, and the vixens had cubs at the time, he changed the family motto from, 'Live and let live' to 'Live and let die'.

September 1978

Of Old Man's Beard and falling hymn-boards

The Askerswell decorations were done to an overall design, with manifest art, and were rewarding in quiet contemplation rather than in first impression. At the font the trimming of Old Man's Beard was remarkable this year. It had been fetched all the way from a spot between Dorchester and Blandford because the local specimens were not up to standard. Congregations both morning and evening were very good, and the singing spirited. When the vendors of the harvest produce came into church next day, they found that the heavy oak hymn-board over the pulpit was on the stone floor of the nave, broken. Not vandals this time, but a rusted screen. Had the fall occurred in the sermon, the Rector's ideas might have been shaken up.

November 1978

Of chrysanthemums and church cleaning

The *Bridport News* front page was lately graced by a good photograph of Mr. Clifford Harris, of Uploders, holding two silver cups won by the chrysanthemums at his elbow. It may be true that a good farmer makes a bad gardener, but not when the farmer retires. Some of his blooms adorn Loders Church for most of the year, and here we would like to acknowledge our debt to the ladies who keep our three churches looking homely and loved, with flowers, throughout the year. At Dottery these ladies clean the church when they do the flowers. No verger up there.

November 1978

Of fungi

His old friends in Loders were sad indeed to hear of the death at Emsworth of Geoffrey Beavan, and felt deeply for his widow, Nosta. He had been a model church-warden at Loders, and a bit of the best of old England. Oddly, he had been an authority on fungi. He ate without ill effect 'mushrooms' that the locals swore were deadly.

November 1978

Saving the barn owl

The 'Reels on Wheels' drew another good attendance to Askerswell village hall for the film *Whisky Galore*. On Friday, December 8th at 7.30 pm there will be a slide show and talk by Colin Varndell on the wild birds of West Dorset. Admission will be free, but patrons will be invited to give to the campaign for saving the barn-owl.

December 1978

Of barn fires

Group Captain Deric Newall has been much condoled with over the vicious fire at South Eggardon Farm which destroyed two thousand bales of hay and but for the efforts of three fire brigades might have enveloped the whole farming complex. There had been no sign of anything wrong when he and his wife passed the buildings on their way home half an hour before the fire broke out.

December 1978

The true countryman's respect

Dottery church was not built for a numerous congregation, nor the approaches to it with the parking of cars in mind. The late Mr. Stanley Smith of *New Close Farm* was popular, and a much loved family man, so some of his funeral congregation had to stand. The positioning of all the cars called for a marshalling genius, but the undertaker managed without losing 'his cool'. In the address the Vicar said that his own long tenure of office had allowed him to savour Stanley Smith's qualities to the full. A love of horses was his prevailing passion, but he also had the true countryman's respect for the things of God.

April 1979

Of butchers and cowsmaids

Weddings are rare red letter days of Askerswell. Because the village wanted to be in on it as well as the very numerous guests, they could have done with a bigger church. The bride was Miss Faith Marsh, of East Hembury Farm, known over a wide area through the Hereford herd for which her father is famous, and the bridegroom Mr. Keith Brown, a butcher, of Wool. The little bridesmaids evoked almost as much admiration as the bride. They wore milking-caps and carried bunches of cowslips. The ringers were in dual capacity. Between ringing the bride in and out of church, they stood in a bunch beneath their ropes and made a good impromptu choir.

The reception was in the ballroom of the Askers motel. An advantage of this was that all the presents could be spread out on the stage, at the feet of the bridal party, who sat feasting behind the three-tiered cake. The bride's grandmother was present, but not her grandfather, regrettably. Never at a loss for the right word, he describes himself as 'allergic to transportation' (which means apt to be sick when in motion).

June 1979

Of badgers and men

In the latest bungalow to be finished at Home Farm Close, Uploders, are Mr. Edward Church and his wife Florence. They are much travelled, he having been a personnel manager in transport, retiring twenty-three years ago from the National Freight Corporation. They find the 'true-fixed and resting quality' of Uploders enchanting after all their moves. They propose calling their bungalow *Badgers* because they find their dustbin ransacked and tipped over. A badger might well be the culprit. One seemingly injured has been active in the vicinity. The Parochial Information Officer, Mr. Maurice Lawson, had a dossier on him that reads like *Tarka the Otter*.

June 1979

The rain it raineth

The two inches of rain that fell on this district in four hours on May 30th produced flooding, and landslides on to the road, which our native inhabitants could not recall the like of. Dwellings in the lower roaches of Bradpole, Bridport and Allington were hardest hit, but none worse, perhaps, than Hole Farm, the *Old Mill* and *Sunnyside* in Loders; and *Garden Cottage*, *Knight's Pightle* and *Brook Barton* in Uploders. In Askerswell the mill at *Hembury* and the mill stream dwellings off The Square had traumatic experiences, as did *Lynch House* at West Milton, but not as much damage.

A mercy it all came in the noon day: the terror by night is worse. Misfortune usually brings out the best in people. Our victims cannot praise too highly the neighbours who came to their rescue. And fortunately all the victims here seem to be covered by insurance.

The flood did some funny things, which are still being

chortled over. An antique chamber-pot survived the rapids of the River Asker and landed in perfect condition at *Knowle Farm* where, apparently, it now graces the nether regions of the Parochial Information Officer's pallet. The illustrious inhabitants of the *Mews* at *Uploders House* are bewailing the loss of a pram. In the context of their well-known allergy to infants, it is surprising that they should have had a pram.

The smallest cottage in the parish, a detached one-up-and-one-down establishment in Uploders, is the home of a bachelor girl who likes her own company. It is called *Knight's Pightle*. When the rain descended and the flood took possession of the lower floor she adjourned to the upper. To ward off would-be rescuers, she hung a notice out of the bedroom window – 'Have Food, Can Swim', but this only inflamed the knightly instinct of the landlord of the nearby *Crown*, who got in, and removed the flood water with the bilge pump from his boat. She was not at all ungrateful to him. Indeed, she praised him warmly to the Vicar.

* * * * *

The day after the flood was that of the Archdeacon's Visitation in Sherborne Abbey. The Vicar was ushered to a spot to robe in where he found himself staring at an old plaque on the wall, which told how, on May 16th, 1709, a hailstorm between one and four in the afternoon caused a flood which burst open the north door of the Abbey and left through the south door, carrying with it 222 foot of the pavement. That took some doing, seeing that abbey pavements were not jerry-built.

July 1979

Church martins

'O how amiable are Thy dwellings,' says Psalm 84 –
'The sparrow hath found her an house, and the swallow a nest where she may lay her young.' At Askerswell, cock and hen house-martins have been sitting together on a nest above the church door, taking no notice of the worshippers passing in and out three feet beneath. The latter are careful to avoid the mat the verger put under the nest for the birds' convenience.

August 1979

Country life

An outsize slated shelter of triangular shape with an Alsatian in it in the yard of the *Loders Arms* puzzled passers-by for some days. Could it be the landlord's defence against intruders? It turned out to be the roof of 'The Loders Arms 1900' on a float for the Bridport Carnival. The float was very well done. It showed the bar, with a cauldron on the fire, swinging oil lamps, bread and cheese on the table, fresh-killed rabbits and pigeons with now forbidden gins and a gun on the floor. It even had that necessary (to some) little place at the back called the 'Yer 'Tis'.

Major Harris was eyeing the spectacle with an air of military calm and detachment. 'Is that little place at the back real?' asked the Vicar. 'It is fully operational' said the Major solemnly – 'It has to be: the bar is fully operational and the personnel will have to be there for anything up to five or six hours'. The personnel were as good a gaggle of maltworms as could be found anywhere and were in the dress of the period.

September 1979

Country missiles

Mr. Geoffrey Randall takes unusual experiences in his stride, but one at Medway Farm, Askerswell, at the beginning of harvest was almost too much for him. He was working on top of an old corn bin made of hardboard when without warning it burst with a bang, and he found himself mixed up with 45 tons of barley responding to the pull of gravity. One would have expected him to have felt like Blondin falling from his tight-rope into Niagara, but he said he thought a jet aircraft had hit him. Or perhaps a straggling bit of the burnt out America space laboratory? He was none the worse, and the grain was later sucked on to a lorry and re-housed in a bin at Court Farm.

October 1979

Mr. Samuel Fry and a hard-working fox

Congratulations to Mr. Samuel Fry on reaching the ninetieth anniversary of his birthday on November 23rd. He is a hale and hearty widower. When the Rector called on him at his cottage off The Square, Askerswell, he was cleaning the floor of his living room. Asked if he had any message for the younger generation, he said 'Yes,' emphatically. 'Tell 'em I begun milkin' at ten years old, and hard work never hurt nobody'.

* * * * *

With respect to Samuel, the most interesting inhabitant of Askerswell at present is a tame fox. It sauntered into Miss Thwaites' kitchen, and pretending to be one of her several cats, did justice to their breakfast. At the post office it cleared the scraps Mrs. Savage had put out for the birds, and she noted that there was a white tip to its tail. From the post office she saw it proceeding up the middle of Mr. Webb's drive to his bungalow. Mrs. Lewis has lost some hens, and Mrs. Neville a tame rabbit, but one is reluctant to think that so civilised a fox could have a stooped to this.

December 1979

The winds of change

This issue was begun to be written on Thursday, December 27th, the feast of St. John the Evangelist, and the writer was thanking providence that the tempest then blowing over the west country had not come on Christmas day. Rain was lashing the south wall of the vicarage, having brought down a heap of external plaster and tiles. A post inside the french window of the study only just managed to keep the window from caving in. On the church tower the flag of St George had been blown off its perch and was clinging miserably to the spout of a gargoyle.

In the churchyard the marble tombstone that had been leaning for months at an angle of a hundred and sixty degrees was still leaning at the same angle, while one of inferior stuff that had stood stiffly to attention was flat on the grass, face downwards, and shattered, never to stand again. The river was over its banks, and the victims of the earlier flooding were getting nervous. But what of the dustmen trying to empty dust-bins into their juggernaut on the highly exposed road up to

Colfox? And having to retrieve the contents of some bins from the road before they could be got into the grinder?

January 1980

One of Nature's gentlemen

The day following Mr. Clifford's funeral saw the nave of Askerswell Church full for the funeral of the oldest inhabitant, Mr. Samuel Fry, who had died in the Sidney Gale home after a brief sojourn there, at the age of ninety. His wife had predeceased him by six years.

Like other patriarchs before him, Samuel had begun life in delicate health. He could not get through his 'medical' for the Great War. Fifty-three years ago he moved from his farm at Sixpenny Handley to the remotest farm in Askerswell, *Nallers*, isolated enough to have inspired Hardy's *Far from the madding crowd*. Later he was joined by his cousin Sidney. There the two families lived for years under the same roof and brought up their children. *Nallers* used to go public for its Boxing Day shoot: the sight of the table awaiting the return of the hunters and their lucky guests lingers still in many memories. When one of the two cottages fell vacant above *The Square*, which the hub of Askerswell is strangely called, Sidney and his wife left *Nallers* and took it.

Looking down on life in central Askerswell was a new experience for Sidney. His ruminant nature found much food for thought, some pearls of which he secreted with the Rector – too choice for a publication like this. When the other cottage fell vacant, Samuel and his wife came to live again next door to Sidney. *Nallers* knew them no more, but life in Askerswell was richer for the nearer presence of Samuel and Sidney. It was horse's work ever to get Samuel to church, but he had the countryman's innate respect for the things of God, and was one of nature's gentlemen.

His burial was interesting. The bearers were lowering the coffin on to Samuel's wife's when agitation, urgent whispering, and pointing at the wife's tombstone, erupted around Sidney. It occurred to the Rector that he might be burying Samuel in the wrong grave: such things are not unknown. So he went over to Sidney and found what was the matter before doing the committal. And the matter was that the inscription said that Samuel's wife had died on 23rd May. Was not Samuel being buried on 23rd May? Sidney was always a one for omens, prodigies and portents.

Samuel's death was the fourth in Askerswell in two months. The average for the ten years leading up to this was one a year. Samuel's death greatly affected the parish philosopher. He was moved to remark, 'We are dying like flies.' The combined age of the four was 314 years.

June 1980

Dorset in eclipse

The Dorset Cream Tea at Askerswell House took place in a curious half light that prompted some people to ring up the weather office and ask if there were an unpublicised eclipse of the sun. Askerswell escaped the bad weather that accompanied the bad light elsewhere. Tea was served at tables each under a gay umbrella. So unobtrusive were the cake and produce stalls and so inviting the lawn that a stranger might have wondered whether he had gatecrashed a rectory tea-party in the time of Queen Victoria.

September 1980

Christmas treat

By custom the sheaves of corn that adorn Loders Harvest Festival are given to Mrs. Jude Greening, the widowed daughter of that magnificent Dorset character the late Shepherd George Crabb. How exactly she disposes of the corn came to our ears by accident. She keeps it till Christmas, which she spends with her daughters.

The Newberrys, of *Cloverleaf Farm*, see to her hens as well as her few sheep while she is away. On Christmas Day, on her strict instructions, they put the sheaves in the hen house for the hens to scratch about in. 'They be God's creatures just as we be, so why shouldn't they have a little Christmas treat?' demands Jude in that tone of voice that nips any contradiction in the bud.

Bonfire night for dogs

A bitterly cold wind cut the attendance at Askerswell Bonfire Night, but those who turned out found the wind cancelled by the exterior warmth of the fire, and the interior activity of coffee, soup and hot-dogs. The firework display came out of Hall funds, assisted by donations. In Yondover, Loders and Uploders there were good fires, but not many bangs, for which the canine creation must have been thankful.

December 1980

Snail mail

The old letter-box in Colonel Stack's wall in Uploders was already notable for bearing the monogram of Queen Victoria and having too small a mouth for many of today's letters, when a local wit was said to be stuffing it with anti-snail pellets in protest against the slowness and costliness of today's mail. Alas, there is not that amount of wit in that vicinity. The amiable postmaster of Bridport, who lives nearby, tells us that it was a postman who put in the pellets. For snails it is a routine exercise to get into rural letter boxes and eat the letters, and for postmen to take counter-measures.

December 1980

A gardening farmer

All Askerswell seemed to be in mourning for one of its best-liked characters, Sidney Fry, who died at *Knapp Cottage* overlooking The Square after several weeks' illness. He was 79 against his cousin Sam's 90. In his address the rector cited Sidney as a contradiction of the proverb that good farmers make bad gardeners. He was good at both. He prided himself on the earliness of his spring crops, and usually insisted on giving the prime specimens to visitors who did a tour of the garden with him.

Sitting by his window in summer observing any sign of life that occurred in The Square, and beside the fire in winter, he felt he had 'done his bit' in his time, but he and his wife were more than ever the centre of unity of a numerous family.

Anything that makes for stability in these days of appalling family disruption is precious indeed.

March 1981

The Stoke Poges tabby-cat

A party of motorists returning from somewhere to their home of Gray's *Elegy* fame, alighted for refreshment at *The Travellers Rest*, on the border of Loders and Askerswell. Getting back into the car to resume the journey, they found that their beloved tabby cat, travelling with them, had alighted too, and was nowhere to be found. The gallant Major Hall, who resides near *The Travellers*, and occasionally graces the serving-side of the bar, assured the distressed travellers when they had to call off their search that he would make enquiries and keep in touch.

So he raised the alarm in Askerswell, where a tabby cat, he learned, had been seen. The alertest gentleman in Askerswell found a tabby cat with no right to be there in his garden – the gentleman, of course, being Nick Nicholson. He first ascertained that the tabby had the identity mark of a nick in its ear, then phoned the gallant major, who collected it, and rang Stoke Poges, who were soon en route to the major. Askerswell people had thought it 'positively intriguing' to have a Stoke Poges tabby on the loose in the village, and Nick enjoyed people looking at his halo.

But not for long. He received a visitation from the lady wife of Colonel Lewis at *Askerswell House*. In an icy voice that was hotter than hell she told him he had kidnapped her mother's cat (the mother also lives at the *House*). There was a conference over the tabby at Major Hall's. As the Stoke Poges people could not be sure whether the tabby was theirs, and Mrs. Lewis was dead sure it was her mother's, the Stoke Poges party wearily wended their homeward way, empty-handed.

The excitement in the village died down. Then somebody spotted a small notice on the board in The Square that had not long been there, and spread the news – 'Found, a tabby cat, Apply Miss Thwaites', or something like that. Now Miss Thwaites enjoys her own company, and that of a regiment of stray cats on her ration strength. She cherishes every one, and it must have cost her dear to part with the Stoke Poges tabby, whose joyful owners came again to Askerswell.

So all's well that ends well.

March 1981

The farmer calls on the Treasurer

What the butler saw when he peeped is not generally known: what the Treasurer of Askerswell church saw when he peeped he had told in the hope that Askerswell may follow the good example of one of their number. It was on a recent summery morning. The treasury front door was open. The treasurer was about to step into his bath. A voice of somebody who had appeared in the doorway called for attention. The bathroom door in this bungalow is precisely opposite the front door. Through the bathroom door the treasurer explained his predicament – all his covering was in an adjoining bedroom. The caller, a farmer, apologised and said he would call again. Not so, said the Treasurer. At his direction the farmer fetched a gown from the bedroom and with averted eyes slipped it through the slight opening that had now appeared in the bathroom door.

An obliging Treasurer? Not wholly. The Treasurer had done a peep without the farmer knowing, and had seen in the latter's hand a form of covenant needing the Treasurer's signature. Covenanted giving to the church attracts a tax refund making it about a third more valuable than straight giving.

August 1981

Rugged farmers

Newspaper pictures are often not up to the aesthetic qualities of their subjects, but this cannot be said of the treatment accorded lately by the *Bridport News* to prominent parishioners of Dottery and Askerswell. Churchwarden Harry Johnston receiving the Melplash trophy for the champion local ploughman from the glamorous Maureen Curran, had a rugged film-star masculinity not at all apparent from the pulpit at sermon time in Dottery. His son Brian, last year's local champion, appeared winning the vintage tractor and plough class with the verve of the young pianist winning the championship at Leeds town hall with his Rachmaninov *Concerto*.

Tom Marsh, of Askerswell, his wife Kit, daughter Faith, were shown beside their magnificent Hereford bull, which had been judged breed champion at the Dorchester show. Press photographers are merciless, as the Prince & Princess of Wales know. It was tough on Tom & Co. to be shown as a family group with the champion when Beauty was also the Beast.

October 1981

Miss Pam Pocket

The death of Miss Pam Pocket at the age of 57 cast a shadow over Uploders, where she was an essential part of the local scene, and far beyond. After a spell under observation in Dorchester Hospital, she was on her way to her 82-years-old mother's at Storrington, Sussex, when she was taken ill and died in a Midhurst hospital. Her funeral was at a local crematorium.

It is hard to visualise a more public-spirited soul than she. Her cottage window could not fulfil its proper function of admitting light because of the notices of deserving causes always on display there, and she did not leave her charitable activity at that and depend on others to do the giving of time and money. The daily exercise of her dogs made her easily accessible to anybody seeking her help. She used to say she loved animals more than humans – but she did not discriminate between them.

October 1981

Of footpaths and rights of way

Jessica Dunn, footpath officer for Loders Parish Council, writes, 'Although there is no legal right to walk along the old railway line, someone in Loders does not agree with this fact. He goes out with a pair of heavy-duty wire-cutters and cuts holes in the wire fencing erected by the present owners of the railway line. The Parish Council deplores this action and would be glad if this misguided person would stop this practice. Not only is he liable to prosecution if caught, but he is jeopardising the good relations regarding footpaths and rights of way that exist between the Crutchley estate and the parish'.

November 1981

Snowbound

Our day and age prides itself on its mobility and quick communication. The January blizzards over Europe and North America were a salutary reminder that man is not the absolute master of mobility and communication. The gentle snowflakes like to waltzer down from heaven like falling feathers, but when fierce winds blow them into huge drifts, and Jack Frost turns these into icebergs, our vaunted technological civilisation is reduced to a snail's pace.

Living now in the country lanes instead of on the main road, the Vicar had his admiration for the family farmers on either side of him well and truly kindled by the weather. The snowbound fields confined all their animals to the cramped area of the farm buildings; water could not stop freezing; milk had to be got through blocked lanes to the collecting depot; dung had to be got back on to the fields; and to crown all, the ewes were lambing. One of the farms is run by Steve and Harry Newberry, and the son of each; the other by Raymond Crabb and his four daughters. The Vicar is still a firm believer in the natural dominance of the male, but he marvelled to see the girls measuring up to the emergency.

February 1982

Of farming service and military service

Gill Evans, the chairperson of Askerswell parish assembly, tells us that at a recent meeting of Parish Council officials Mr. Bugler of Beaminster said farmers deserved rates relief if only for having saved the country in the two World Wars. The speaker, Colonel Woodward, was quick to add that by the same token so did all who served in the armed forces of the Crown.

February 1982

Of farmyard smells and parakeets

Dottery's Mr. Sidney Morris died suddenly last month, and was cremated in Yeovil at a sung service conducted by the vicar and attended by a full muster of the family. He was 81. His working life had been spent in the electrical business. He, his wife and a married son with family came to Dottery from Croydon eight years ago, and being of a nice neighbourly disposition soon found a niche there. They brought a whiff of the great metropolis to our farmyard smells. The son is a dealer in exotic birds. A discreet notice outside the cottage invited inquiries within for love-birds, parakeets and the like.

Master of all the arts of agriculture

The memorial service at Askerswell for the late Fred Marsh on the evening of the third Sunday in February drew a congregation of harvest festival proportions, and at the family's request included the hymn, *We plough the fields and scatter*. The service was timed to suit one son, Peter, who farms in Canada, and he and his family 'made it'. Another son, Alan, of Corscombe, read one of the lessons.

In the address the rector traced Fred's career, from birth on the family farm at Bradpole eighty-nine years ago to his death on the farm at Askerswell of his son Tom, now famous for its Hereford herd. Fred started farming on his own account at *Meons*, Uploders. After four years there, he put in twelve years at Milborne St. Andrew, followed by twenty at Sidling St. Nicholas. A move to Leigh near Sherborne was shortlived. It dawned even on him that at eighty-one he could not do what he did at twenty-one, so he moved finally into the bungalow at *Hembury* that he called his 'layby'.

Fred was a master of all the arts of agriculture, and could be frighteningly self-sufficient. Once when a reaping machine failed to appear he took a scythe and cut an eight-acre field of corn alone. Farming is a vocation, and in Minnie he found himself married to the right wife for fifty-five strenuous but happy years. So united a family were they that all their five children took to the land for a living, and made a success of it. The features of *East Hembury Farm* might well be the prize bulls in the estimation of Farmer Tom, but in the rector's it was the prize character of the late Fred and his widow Minnie.

March 1982

The language of farmers

Higher Pymore Farm, Dottery, had an unusual experience one evening in April. The two big downstair rooms of the old farmhouse were full of people, young and not so young. Tables laden with a luscious variety of food, and a look of giving rather than getting on everybody's face, was a sign that churchwarden John Marsh and his wife Brenda were not in process of selling the home of his ancestors. And the central figures, the Vicar and Mrs. Willmott, were the focus of a reverent attention not often bestowed on auctioneers.

The flock that he had tended for thirty-five years were giving a party to mark his retirement. One of the joys for him of this flock was its marked identity with the flock he had inherited. Natural wasteage had robbed it of its elders, but their children and children's children were there. The Dottery population is not as fluid as those of Loders and Askerswell. By the look of all the food provided, the company expected to be there a week, but all was over in two hours – alas!

Churchwarden Henry Johnston made a speech. The flock are not naturally articulate, and he is one who can be understood when he is, so this function usually falls to him. With him brevity is the soul of wit. Before the vicar knew it he was holding a magnum of sherry, and an envelope that Henry called 'the change', and a bottle of vintage port from Philip Smith (there is much to be said for a flock being as knowledgeable of its pastor as he of them). This was followed by a framed sketch of Dottery church by Angela Johnston, and a long-handled basket with Madagascar jasmine climbing up it for Mrs. Willmott, which delighted her because it matched her Ascensiontide hat, and looked as if its perfumed flowers would be in full bloom by then. Later that night, when she was not about, the Vicar investigated Henry's packet of 'change'. It was £164, and in banknotes, in which farmers always seem to do their really important transactions.

May 1982

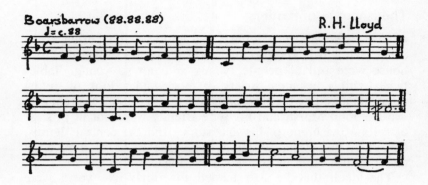

The Loders Hymn

Boarsbarrow (88.88.88)
♩=c.88   R.H. Lloyd

I

The seasons pass, the fields remain
To take the blessing of the sun,
The midnight frost, the morning rain,
Until their harvesting is done,
And day by day beneath these skies
We catch a glimpse of Paradise.

II

And when across our ancient hills
The gathering storms of winter roll,
It is Thine hand which soothes and stills
The tempest in each fearful soul
And gives our troubled minds release,
And all the beauty of Thy peace.

III

Though leaves shall fall, and grasses fade
Our country ways shall stay secure,
No truth denied, no love betrayed,
Our faith in thee, serene and sure,
Thy plan for us revealed at last
When all our travelling days are passed.

IV

We offer then, ourselves to Thee,
Whose radiance is the springtime air,
The whisper of the summer sea,
The answer to our every prayer,
And sounds afar, or silence near,
It is Thy voice, O Lord, we hear.

Leonard Clark

CHAPTER 7

Change and decay?

A village is like the seashore – it always feels the same, with the sound of the wind and the gentle thrash of its country waves. Pebbles move, flotsam and jetsam get thrown up, lasting cliffs fall and disintegrate, new life washes in, old washes away. Treasures are discovered; wrecks are dismantled. Paradoxically, it always has a new face, where you can read the tide-lines of its past. It's organic.

There was one hymn that Rev. Willmott was singularly disenamoured of, and that was *Abide with me*. When asked closely for an explanation of this 'foible', it was found not to be a foible, but to spring from deeply-seated religious and secular convictions. He himself had been chaplain to the Totnes Football Team just before the Second World War, and had no snobbery about the Wembley National anthem. He would have been inspired by some of the most memorable lines:

> 'What but Thy grace can foil the tempter's power?'
> 'Hold Thou Thy Cross before my closing eyes.'

He took issue with the line—

> 'Help of the helpless, O abide with me.'

and from his own experience rejected the sentiment:

> 'Change and decay in all around I see.'

The religious passivity and sentimental relapsing upon God was seen by him to be weak. The secular assumption that everything is going to the dogs annoyed a man who energetically encouraged new enterprises: 'The new Methodist minister in Bridport, and the lay preacher in Bradpole, who is chief assistant in the enterprise, are advocates of anything but a defeatist policy, and feel that a shut-up place of worship is a reproach. They are bolder spirits than the previous Minister. Our own sympathies lie with the bolder spirits. We wish them good luck in the name of the Lord.' (*Yours Reverently* p. 77)

Between 1948 and 1982 the parishes of Loders, Dottery and Askerswell enjoyed a unique period of stability, when community meant all, old traditions were kept alive, and new ones set up. There was a healthy marriage between the old and the new. The last phase of *The Parish Notes* contained sadness, and bitterness, about the way that old country vicarages were being sold off recklessly to make short-term financial gains at Diocesan Headquarters. Team Ministries were not seen as the only viable country way, but as the wilful destruction of the idea of the parson, or 'person' for the village (*Yours Reverently* pps. 200–1).

Nevertheless, new ventures that made English country life richer were actively encouraged. There was change, but not decay – just the natural death of defunct customs and activities. Surprisingly, perhaps, the Vicar was on the side of the innovationary activists. Squirearchy took a back seat; supermarket shopping and T.V. took over; the little hills of Dorset winced, but carried on the same as ever. The Village Hall Committee undertook the creation and maintenance of rural energy. The Vicar could still report in February 1983, 'Mercifully, there is no segregation of age-groups in any of our three parishes.' A nice touch (from an ex-Army chaplain) is the welcome given to in-coming German families in *Yours Reverently* (p. 33 Foreign Visitors), and the welcome of Mrs. Margaret Millard in this chapter (p. 240) as 'a German with winning English ways'.

Distances were being pruned drastically by the private 'motor-car'. Vandals broke into churches in broad daylight (p. 14). Farmers' cottages became retirement homes. Mrs. May Osborne became the exception rather than the rule (p. 234): 'In this age of mobility and tinned entertainment, she still found most pleasure in the simple village activities of Mothers' Union,

Women's Institute socials and fêtes, and by participating as a worker.' (October 1972) Women took a more noticed part in public affairs. T.V. started to dominate the timetable.

Perhaps the real victim was active Christianity, which faded in importance. For one reason or another, the Parish Church ceased to be the hub of communal life:

The Canon Rev. Gregory Page-Turner retired to Beaminster in May 2001. He was the last incumbent Vicar of Loders (1989–2001).

Canon Nerissa Jones is residing at Loders New Vicarage. She is non-stipendiary.

Loders School is still on its original site as built in 1869 by the Nepean family as a Church School. It has 74 pupils, has plans for extension, and has enough land available from *The Barn-House* to enable the Maypole dancing to take place (though not enough for a football pitch). It was acclaimed by Ofsted in 1999: 'The school's ethos is very good and there are good links with the community.' It is on the Internet @ loders.dorset.sch.uk

The site for new Loders Village Hall was provided by the Hoods of Loders Court. It gained a Lottery Grant of £86,000 in 1997.

Diana, Viscountess Hood opened the Hall in November, 1999.

The Hood family are still in residence at the Court.

In the 1960s myxomatosis decimated the rabbit population of West Dorset. In 2001 foot-and-mouth concentrated on Devon, leaving Dorset surprisingly free. Nevertheless, the traditional Loders Fête at Loders Court was cancelled because of transport restrictions.

For a short interregnum Christopher Miles collated *The Parish Notes*. They were replaced in 1982 by *The Eggardon View* under the guidance of the Rev. Gregory Page-Turner and the chairmanship of Martin Evans. As a magazine it is thriving under the

Chairmanship of Bill Budden (p. 119 'Peppered with Buddens') and the Editor, Derek Burbidge. It is on the Internet @www.poortonpress.co.uk/eview

Loders was the 'Small Village Winner' in the 2000 Best Community Village Contest.

A correspondent who wishes to remain anonymous in case his/her property is inflamed has stated that 'Loders now suffers from city affluence. There are twelve holiday homes between the church and the school.'

Sic transit gloria mundi.

The end of coppers and threepenny pieces

History was made one Sunday in November in Loders Church when the churchwardens were counting the collection after matins. The congregation had been large, and the collection likewise, and for the first time anybody remembers, the collection did not contain a single copper, nor even a threepenny piece.

It could, of course, have been by chance. The faithful might not have been able to lay their hands on any before taking off to church. We hope the reason was that it is coming to be realised that inflation has rendered coppers and threepenny pieces almost valueless. Whereas a penny would once buy a newspaper, it now takes people nearly all of sixpence. Church collections should be stepped up to counter money's loss of value.

December 1968

Changing Lent

Lent begins on Ash Wednesday, February 19th. The report of a liturgical commission on the Calendar proposes to eliminate the Sundays in Lent and to call them instead the Sundays before Easter. It also proposes to substitute nine Sundays before Christmas for the four Sundays in Advent. What will those who are bent on streamlining the Church think up next?

If they get their way the Church will be unrecognisable. Lent may not be 'with it', but the trend of present events cries aloud for more of its 'godly discipline'.

February 1969

Death of an air-raid warden

The death of Mrs. Norman Adams of Askerswell had not been unexpected. In her latter years she was a great sufferer, and one of the rare souls whose character was enriched by it. Like Mrs. Sanders she had a devoted husband to look after her and also a daughter and a sister. It was hard to realise that she had once been perhaps the most active woman in the parish. In the last war she was air-raid warden, billeting officer for evacuees and rationing officer and she put her skill with the needle into the work of the Red Cross. Her needle was also much employed for the church.

March 1969

Drainage for Loders and Askerswell

Mr. Lucas and Group-Captain Newall, our representatives on the Rural District Council, have both given assurances to public meetings that the sewer will be begun in 1970, if not in the autumn of this year. Connecting up should impose no great financial burden on any householder.

April 1969

Very conservative

The congregation of Dottery have been stimulated by something or other to new forms of activity. Things get done without any deliberation that the Vicar is aware of, and to him this is a welcome change. In the vestry one Sunday he noted that a smart curtain was now concealing his old cassock and surplice hanging on the wall. Two chairs with foamy seats and a new window curtain seemed slightly suggestive of a bathroom, and new shelf coverings in the cupboard drove home the lesson that cleanliness is next to godliness.

As he threaded his way out of church after service, it was

pointed out to him that one of the three lampshades was ridiculously unmatched with the other two, which themselves were not beautiful, and there were to be three new ones, if he did not object. He could safely say he did not object. The natural posture of his eyes in divine service is heavenwards, and therefore lampwards. If for twenty-two years he had not noticed the ugly shades, he was not likely to be troubled by the beautiful ones.

The church treasurer told him the names of kind people who had made donations to the outside painting of the church. These he remembers with gratitude. Then he was invited to a little sale for the same object which two valiant ladies of the congregation were holding in their home. Here he found a crush of ladies and one gentleman buying, selling, and drinking tea, and enjoying themselves. The passing of money the hostesses obviously considered indecent, like Victorian chairlegs, and in need of concealing, so he did not see much of that, but he will be surprised if the painting fund does not get a fillip.

The final evidence of something stirring at Dottery was an advertisement proclaiming that Dottery Church would be holding a Christmas whist drive in Salwayash schoolroom on December 8th. If he had any fears of revolutionary tendencies in his flock they were allayed by the price of admission, a pre-war two-and-sixpence: very conservative.

December 1969

Forewarned is forearmed

The people who seek to make Jesus fit the contemporary scene are certainly enterprising. Not long ago a scholar of standing suggested in no less a place than the pulpit of the University Church in Cambridge that Jesus might have been a homosexual. Now a lecturer in Old Testament studies in the University of Manchester insists that if Jesus was not actually a drug-addict himself, he had his roots in a community of drug-addicts who once lived in the wilderness round the Dead Sea.

The lecturer is Dr. John Allegro. He has written a book on this theme. Excerpts from it will be published at Easter by a popular newspaper trying to step up its circulation, and he will expound his thesis on television. He is one of the many scholars who have been studying the *Dead Sea Scrolls* discovered in a cave by a shepherd boy in 1947. In case any of our readers fear what John Allegro may do to their faith, let it be said that nearly all the eminent scholars who have studied the Scrolls dismiss the Allegro thesis as flamboyant nonsense. His previous book on the *Scrolls* was repudiated by the six greatest authorities on the subject in a letter to *The Times*.

The Scrolls were a tremendous discovery. Your Editor has browsed through the translations of them, and been mightily impressed by the way in which they confirm what was already known about this Dead Sea community on the evidence of Josephus, Philo and Pliny. Until the discovery of The *Scrolls* our earliest manuscript of the Old Testament was 9th century AD. Among *The Scrolls* is a manuscript copy of Isaiah nearly a thousand years earlier. But here is the vital point, *The Scrolls* text of Isaiah is virtually the same as the later one, and the same as in our English bible. If you hear John Allegro on television, ask yourself why he differs from the other authorities on The *Dead Sea Scrolls*. You may not be far wrong if you sense a financial motive. His first eccentric book on The *Scrolls* sold a quarter of a million copies. His publishers have sold the serialisation rights for this second book for £90,000, and there will be other cash to come. Shocking the public is an easy way to big money in this year of grace. One hesitates to say who is more to blame for this, the shockers or the shocked.

The times of our Holy Week and Easter services need not be given at this point, for they are in the table at the end. We can answer the Allegros and the Furiosos by turning out in strength to celebrate the Resurrection on Easter Day.

March 1970

Making a will

Time was when properly disposed people kept at bay the thought of making a will until they were within striking distance of kingdom come, and if they had to utter the awful word, did so under their breath. Our Women's Institute showed how progressive they are by getting a local lawyer to give them

a talk on the making of wills and on legal aid. They even
followed it up with a competition to see who could draw up
the most humorous will. This was won by Mrs. Morris. Her
will was cleverly done, on good old-fashioned parchment, and
the ladies found it highly entertaining.

But ancient superstitions are not so easily eradicated.
Unease lurked in the depth of some earthly Dorset hearts. If
Mrs. Morris were shortly to be summoned to Higher Service
the forces of Progress in Loders would suffer a reverse from
which they might never recover.

March 1970

The old police station

The police station at Well Plot, although a newish building, is
now officially described as *The Old Police Station*, because
Loders comes under an area police service operated from
Beaminster and no longer has a police officer of its own. Having
had good reason in the past to value its policemen, Loders is
pleased that one of the team policemen is occupying *The Old
Police Station*. He is Constable Brian Tufnail, from Poole, and
he has a wife and two young children. A warm welcome to them.

February 1971

Deaconesses

The bring and buy stall which the Mothers' Union had at their
February meeting made nearly £5 for their funds. Mrs.
Willmott gave the talk. She had in mind the then impending
debate in the General Synod on church services which might
fittingly be taken by deaconesses. She fully agreed with the
contention that women as a whole did more for the Church
than men as a whole, recollected the value our Lord himself
put on the ministrations of women, and pointed out that yet of
his several eligible women disciples he did not appoint one to
the apostolate or indeed to any ministerial function. The
feeling was that the physical constitution of a woman militated
against her being say, a good surgeon, and also against her
being an efficient priest or bishop.

March 1971

Rights of Way

A party of ramblers came to matins at Loders one Sunday in May. On their way out they asked the whereabouts of various rights of way with the intention of walking them ('To keep them open', they said). The Chairman of the Parish Council, Mr. Lucas, assures us that now that rights of way have been plotted on a definitive map it will not be necessary to walk them to keep them open. Relevant sections of the new map, giving rights of way and bridle paths, have been framed by the clerk, Mr. Brown, and put in the church porch. Mr. Small, licensee of *The Crown*, is arranging to have another copy in or near his establishment.

July 1971

The Village Hall Committee at the Fête

Stop press. We have just been told that a suggestion has been agreed to that Loders Village Hall Committee should have a sideshow at the Church Fête at Loders Court on July 31st to finance a plan for helping the Hall to stand on its own feet in meeting its running expenses. We hope the sideshow will do well.

July 1971

The last forger and the last miller

Loders lost the only remaining one of its many forgers when the late Mr. Charlie Gale retired from work. It now looks to have lost its only working mill by the death of Mr. Hamilton Barnes, of *Loders Mill*.

In literature, millers appear as a race apart. Readers may remember the one on the River Dee who sang,

'I live by my mill, she is to me like parent, child and wife;
I would not change my low degree for any other in life
... and I care for nobody, no, not I;
if nobody cares for me.'

Hamil, in his forty one years at the *Mill*, seemed to grow attached to it as by an umbilical cord. The lures of the outside world, and even poor health could not wean him from his work, in which he was a great believer.

Occasionally his powers of expression exceeded his powers of thought – and that was the time to be listening – but he had a philosophy of life to work by, which made him a rare and colourful bird in times like these. Devoted wife and four daughters saw to it that they were not suburban to The Mill in his affections. They will leave us pleasant memories of times shared in Sunday School and in their family occasions at church, else the tantalising thought that had Derek, the only son not died in all the promise of his young manhood, the Mill might not now be phasing out of Loders life.

February 1972

A nostalgic excursion

That children can tire of sophisticated outings and long for the simpler forms of yester-year had been shown by Loders Sunday School. On Whit Monday they used to take tea to the old cricket ground on Welcome Hill and play games. But the custom died. This year, however, the children asked to take tea again to Welcome Hill, and they did. The older ones walked, and Mr. and Mrs. John Hyde (the genies of the lamp to all the children they know) took the tiny tots in their car. Up on the hill the bracing air energised the games of rounders and pig-in-the-middle, and ensured that there were no crusts left over from tea.

Rover, the Vicarage Labrador, who attends Sunday School, and is a great pet of the children, was easily the most efficient fielder for the rounders, but was not as good at disgorging the ball. Now the field at Welcome Hill is for a few weeks at the mercy of the oil-explorers. A crane and mounds of earth indent the skyline, which salves the Sunday School conscience in forgetting to ask Admiral Sir Victor Crutchley's permission to use the field, for if he does not mind the crane and the excavators he cannot have minded them.

July 1972

The continuing fête

The season of fêtes is now well past its zenith. Perceptive readers of the local press will have noted that Loders fête took more than any other church fête within range – £669.72. They will also have noted that although Askerswell was easily the smallest of the parishes holding a church festival of flowers, at £255, it beat all the others in its takings. The fête was for the repair fund of Loders and Dottery churches and the flower festival for the re-roofing of Askerswell church. The success of both supports the contention that if parishioners and parson are resolved to keep their church, nobody can declare it redundant.

Loders and Dottery have held a fête for church repairs every year since 1947, twenty-six in all. These fêtes could have been strangled by their own success. Parishioners might have fallen one after another into a habit of saying: 'The fête always does so well that my little offering won't be missed.' But they didn't.

When the collector comes round, the vast majority are ready with an offering in cash or in kind. Sometimes it is those who are sparing in their use of the church who are remarkably generous. Those who are not ready when the collector calls, and say they will send something along, usually keep their promise. It is this giving beforehand and the kindness of distant friends, that is the foundation of the fête's continued success. This year, for instance, £193.20 was given in cash, and the gifts in kind brought in around £350 from stall, refreshments and competitions. But the giving would not be as fruitful if the general public did not flock to the fête, and for this we thank the unfailing attraction of Loders Court, and the constant co-operation of the clerk of the weather.

September 1972

Retirement homes

Mr. and Mrs. L. W. Clifford will doubtless overlook the belatedness of our welcome to them to *Paddock House*, Askerswell. Houses hereabouts change hands so frequently and quietly that the pastor, knocking on a door, often has it opened to him by somebody who has become his parishioner without his

knowing it. Most of the newcomers are amiable and inclined
to be interested in village activities, and Mr. and Mrs. Clifford
are no exception. They responded to the jumble sale appeal,
and look forward to the harvest supper. As one would expect,
they are retired.

October 1972

Mrs. May Osborne

Uploders and Loders are not often plunged into a gloom like
that occasioned by the unexpected death of Mrs. May Osborne.
She was the personification of public-spiritedness, which is not
attractive in itself, but was made so by the union of good looks
and a sweet nature in her. Few were aware, as she delivered
these *Parish Notes*, or collected for good causes, that she was
battling with chronic physical disabilities. It took a lot to keep
her from her place at service in Loders Church, or from
supporting at evening service the faithful little band that maintain the Uploders Chapel. To miss a meeting of the Church
Council, as she sometimes had to, or of the Deanery Synod,
or of the old Diocesan Conference, was to her something of a
criminal offence. In this age of mobility and tinned entertainment, she still found most pleasure in the simple village
activities of Mothers' Union, Women's Institute socials and
fêtes, and by participating as a worker.

She died at the General Hospital, Poole, only a few hours
after her husband and daughter had spent a cheerful time with
her, in which she had dictated a letter to the Vicar asking who
had sent 'the beautiful talc, and soap by Yardley, wrapped in
gold paper', as her husband had forgotten; and ended, 'Please
give my regards to all my friends in the village.'

Her funeral cortège set out from her cottage in Uploders
where she was born, and where her body had lain overnight.
The bells were ringing muffled as it went down the path into
a church full of friends. Mrs. Tiltman, who as Vera Knight of
The Old Forge had been a girlhood friend, was at the organ.
The burial was in the grave of her parents under the yew tree
near the south porch.

[Near to the (later) grave of Rev. Willmott – p. 263]

October 1972

Route Seven

Loders Parish Council are being 'slated' by some people for supporting the notorious 'Route Seven'. But at least the Council is reasonable, which is more than can be said of some of the opposition. Bridport has clamoured for years for relief from its summer traffic congestion; and Route Seven is, of all the schemes, the one causing least hardship. It also would eliminate the traffic dangers at Loders Cross and Viney Cross, for which the Parish Council has been clamouring. Hearts ache for the four parishioner householders who would lose their homes. The Council are concentrating on trying to obtain for these not merely the full value of their homes, but new homes comparable with those sacrificed.

February 1973

St. Mary Magdalene's Day

St. Mary Magdalene's day 22nd July, falls on a Sunday this year. It is the Dedication Festival of Loders Church. The ladies who decorate the church never fail to respond. It could be wished that the parish in general would also respond by treating it as a festival, but new ideas are slow in taking root here.

July 1973

Askerswell Fête

The Fête left the Rector pondering over God's mysterious ways. It seemed a shame that the great Christmas congregation should buckle the church floor to the tune of £650 and make necessary a fête. Yet the work put into the fête had greatly helped to weave the new inhabitants with the old into one community. Indeed, a comparative newcomer, Mr. Brook, as chairman, had been on the bridge. With engaging modesty he passes all the credit to 'the splendid team down in the engine-room'.

August 1973

Conservation area

A recent parish meeting agreed with the proposal to make Lower Loders a conservation area, and extracted from the planning people a promise to make Uploders one also. A benefit of conservation would be to have the mess of overhead wires put out of sight. It is a pity that conservation comes too late to preserve the distinguishing characteristic of Loders. It was not anciently called Long Lother for nothing. It was more or less one street, stretching for two miles from *Hole Farm* to *Matravers*, with no development in depth. To preserve this, the council houses at Well Plot should have been continued along the road from Shatcombe, which was the first site suggested for them.

February 1975

Dottery defies the Exodus

Dottery congregation are lamenting the departure of their faithful Mrs. Bagwell to a home, she hopes to find more convenient, in Bradpole. She is emphatic that she remains of Dottery, if not in it. Alone of our three parishes, Dottery has lost a big percentage of its population, which was only tiny to begin with. At present three houses are unoccupied and three others have been demolished and turned into a car park.

Fortunately for the church, some of the re-housed inhabitants are tenacious of their connection with it and still attend service. Some of the remaining population, notably the farming families, are also zealous in attendance, in spite of farming being a seven-day occupation. So, reduced though the congregation is, if its size proportionate to the population were uniform throughout England, the churches would not be able to contain all the worshippers.

December 1975

Sharing the fortunes of change

It is one of life's established maxims that we tend to destroy the things we enjoy. The internal combustion engine has put the countryside and the beach within reach of everybody, so that we get more and more engines and people every time we visit them, and less and less countryside and beach. If we take off to the mountains of Peru in an exasperated search for the unspoilt, we may find the natives trying to sustain it by offering Teas Without Hovis. When piped water came to our villages in the valley of the Asker, and drainage, dethroning the bucket, it was inevitable that lovers of the unspoilt should come and build their habitations here. New habitations change the character of a place, and when the character of a place changes the character of the inhabitants seems to change as well. Those who got in first, exuding the milk of human kindness at finding a place exactly to their liking, let the milk go sour when others come in and following their example alter the place still more.

Villages so abundantly beautiful as Loders and Askerswell can sacrifice some of their pristine beauty without becoming less easy on the eye, and the small sacrifice is a large moral duty when it enables others to share our good fortune. Without going into the vexed question of who exactly are the new-comers – and to the hard core of locals fifty years do extinguish the foreign taint – it may be said that most of them are nice worthy people who have assimilated themselves into the community, and perhaps saved us from degenerating into a jungle clearing where elephants come to die. 'The city shall be full of boys and girls playing in the streets thereof,' said the prophet Zechariah.

Our school is bursting at the seams, the churches are filling, and the pubs have nothing to regret. The Vicar is wallowing in smug satisfaction as he writes this. The Vicarage has not been spared the inconvenience of these changes. It was had to put up with more than most. Over a period of twelve years demolition and building have been going on to the west, north and east of it. The neighbours can see what goes on in our yard now, which may improve our deportment, and we can hardly avoid seeing a windmill clothes-line that revolves five yards from the kitchen window. But all in a good cause.

July 1976

Past Times

An old photograph belonging to Mr. Bill Tiltman shows a crowd
of locals in festive attire outside Loders Church gate. He thinks
they were celebrating St. Mary Magdalene in the fair that used
to mark her feastday, 22nd July. And he may well be right.
Incidentally, the late Martha Crabb, who died in 1960 at the ripe
age of ninety, was fond of showing her visitors little chimney
ornaments that had come from the cheapjacks' stand at Loders
Feast; and Mr. Balfour has preserved in the floor of the upper
storey of the former *Farmer's Arms* the stone on which the
fiddler played for the dancing.

But the puzzling point about Mr. Tiltman's picture is the sheet
two men are holding high on poles saying 'Welcome.' The
assembly might be something to do with a former squire, Sir
Molyneaux Nepean, whom the said Martha Crabb referred to
reverently as 'Sir Molly Noakes.' His were the days before the
Welfare state, and his annual provision of beef and coals for the
poor were reckoned by Martha to have bankrupted him. She said
that once when he arrived at Bridport station from a holiday in
Scotland the men of Loders unhorsed his carriage and themselves pulled it to The Court.

Whether the photograph is a relic of this rather than of the
patron saint of Loders' Feast, goodness knows, but we shall be
marking her day with a Communion Service on 22nd July, and
thanking God for the church dedicated in her name on the
Sunday in the Octave, the 25th.

July 1976

Keeping the lamp of God alight

'The hardest festival' is what a wag calls this year's Harvest
Festival because, says he, it will be hard to thank God for the
shortages from the severe drought. But there was no such difficulty, restraining the crowd at the Uploders chapel harvest. The
Reverend Norman Skinner pointed to the splendid sheaf of corn
lording it over an equally splendid array of flowers, fruit and
vegetables out of neighbouring gardens, and said he for one did
not recall a better harvest exhibition. The congregation
expressed their approval in a vigorous rendering of the hymns,

one of which was led by Mr. Skinner on his accordion, and the rest by the veteran Miss Daisy Boxall at the harmonium; ladies and gentlemen dividing in some of the verses, and coming gloriously together for the choruses. It was a happy, exhilarating occasion. The faces of the chapel stewards, Mr. and Mrs. Morris, exuded deep satisfaction. They are well regarded for their devotion to keeping the lamp of God alight in the Chapel.

October 1976

Continuing Remembrance Sunday

The common excuses for not attending a Remembrance Sunday service are: 'I was not in either of the World Wars,' or, 'I have nothing to remember, because I had not been born then,' or 'The Wars are best forgotten.' The first two excuses are selfish, because we still have with us the parents of relatives of many who gave their lives, and not to join with them in the observance of their most poignant day of the year is brutish. The third excuse is stupid, because salutary lessons learnt at such awful cost should not be forgotten. Further, the day is the zenith of the British Legion's yearly effort to show practical gratitude by relieving the needs of the wounded.

November 1977

Standards at Loders School

The children of Loders School gave the Lord Jesus a Christmas present after His own heart. Their concert and mission sale made £83, and the collection at their carol service in church for the children of soldiers killed in Ulster brought the total of their offering to nearly £100. Had the Prime Minister heard their reading of the lessons in church, he would have known that he had no need to be worried about the standard of eduction in Loders school.

January 1977

Pubs

A writer of *The Guardian* says: 'A pub is the social and convivial centre of a community. The closing of its only pub can kill a village and turn it into an unorganic huddle of dwellings'. Whether this will be true of Dottery remains to be seen. Its only pub, *The Blue Ball*, has closed, and will be for sale. Mr. and Mrs. Roger Hill, the last incumbents, took only fourteen months to discover that it is not a viable pursuit, as it seems to have been when the old thatched pub was burnt down in 1951 and the present one built. The good old malt-worms who used to patronise it have gone the way of all flesh or to new dwellings in Bridport, and one of its best ornaments, Mr. Stanley Smith, is permanently 'On the shelf' at his home in New Close, lucky to have survived an illness that would have extinguished ten teetotallers. We suspect that a feeling that it was he who punctured *The Blue Ball* is now soothing the frustration of his enforced inactivity.

February 1977

The old originals

The death of Mr. Sidney Hansford, of Uploders, at the age of 76, reduced the 'old originals' of the parish of Loders to eight, according to the Vicar's reckoning, but fourteen according to Mrs. Lizzie Crabb's. Let us hope she is right, for the 'old originals' had qualities that the new world is not producing. The Hansfords go back to the church register of Charles the First's reign. After a sung service in Loders Church Sidney was buried in the grave of his late wife at the cemetery.

January 1978

Ring in the new

Complaints against the ringing of bells erupt from time to time in towns, and are suppressed in the countryside which is more sympathetic, even when the bells are a cause of discomfort. Messages of appreciation of ringing are few and far between. So Askerswell ringers were delighted to receive a letter from a family fairly new to the parish saying how much they enjoyed the ringing at the passage of New Year's Eve into New Year's Day. And this year several villagers came to church to watch the ceremony.

February 1978

Family continuity

Candidates for the Bishop of Sherborne's [John Kirkham] confirmation in Loders church on Palm Sunday are meeting as a whole at the vicarage on Wednesdays at 7.30 p m. There are other arrangements for those who find this time unsuitable. It is still not too late to enrol. Family continuity is a nice feature of Loders confirmations. Some mothers who were themselves confirmed here and now live away are taking the trouble to bring their children to the classes. One is bringing her son from Ferndown!

February 1978

The English and the Germans

The *Loders Arms* seems to have settled contentedly under the wing of its new landlord, Mr. John Millard, who had been managing a hostelry in Weymouth, and his wife Margaret, who is a German, with winning English ways.

February 1978

The vortex of change

Old friends departing, and new potential friends arriving, seems to be the way of life in Loders at present, with Purbeck Close the vortex of change. Four houses next to each other have lost, or are about to lose us, valued parishioners. At High Acres there is also some going. There seems to be a demand for houses on this estate. All have been sold, and four more are being built. Michael Malyon and his wife Tessa, newly married, and he ex-the Army and now a farm student, are at Court cottages. They replace the Trebbicks, who leave in the summer, and who again were exceedingly nice neighbours whom we shall miss.

May 1978

High Acres Arts

Mrs. Jennie Glyde packed over forty people into her home at High Acres for the first social event on the new estate, and served them with refreshments. The meeting was to interest parents in forming a club for children between four and nine. Its base would be the Arts Centre in Bridport, where any talent they might have for music, poetry, acting, painting, fossils, photographs, etc. could be encouraged. A Steering Committee was formed, and operations begin Sept 9th.

May 1978

New growth at *High Acres*

High Acres is the name of the new housing estate above Loders school. Our vigilant look-out at the crow's nest end of the estate told us that five new families had moved in. The vicar called to welcome them. Nobody was at home because most of the wives are out at work as well as the husbands. He plucked up courage to call towards seven on a Friday evening.

Courage seemed to be called for, because he thought he would not be a welcome diversion from 'the box'. Further, being used to the seclusion of the Vicarage, entering the estate was to him like blundering on to a stage before a crowded auditorium, or going down the gullet of that beast 'full of eyes within' in the Book of Revelation.

The estate must have been amused at his efforts to get into the homes of the newcomers. Each house seemed full of doors. The family within would see him arrive, point excitedly to one door, and open another where he was not. Every house exuded a good smell, for every family was either dining or cooking something. If they disliked the intrusion, they imparted an air of spontaneous welcome, and the Vicar was glad he had ventured forth. One family began to make room for him at their table.

May 1978

Breaking the habit of a century

For the first time in its century and a half of existence a wedding will take place in the Uploders Chapel. A licence to solemnise marriages there has been obtained from the Registrar General, and next month Mr. Tom Wall, and Mrs. Barbara Boyle, both of Bradpole, will be married by the area superintendent of the Methodist Church, in the absence in Germany of the Minister, the Rev. Norman Skinner. The licence cost £20. Our friend Mr. Joe Morris, the devoted custodian of the Chapel, is trusting he has not been reckless with Chapel funds. He may have made an excellent investment. Jesus Christ's 'Till death us do part' is not the fashion today.

Into the nineties

Mrs. Bertha Johnson, of Uploders, crossed the Rubicon on July 9th, when she and a large family gathering at *Knowle Farm* celebrated the ninetieth anniversary of her birthday. She is the mother of Mrs. Dick Wood, and a monument to the diligence of Mr. Maurice Lawson, her Grannysitter-In-Ordinary, who is relieved by Captain Harry Crabb whenever Granny's pulse calls for a little medicinal brandy.

Mrs. Frances Barnes kept her ninetieth birthday down in the secluded dale of Bilshay at Dottery some time last November. We have only lately heard about it. More of our senior citizens are nearing ninety, and they are less shy then Mrs. Barnes.

July –August 1978

Faces sorely missed

On the day after Harvest, Loders Church had parties in early taking photographs in fear that the decorations were to be dismantled immediately. They were relieved to find that in Loders this is done slowly, beginning with the corn, fruit and vegetables, so that some of the harvest glory lingers on the succeeding Sunday. But done slowly, it seemed still a crime to destroy anything so beautiful. Congregations both morning and evening were very good, and the choir's anthem about the valleys laughing and singing was well received.

After evensong somebody said how nice it was to be rung out of church as well as in. Several faces lost in the past year by death and removal were sorely missed, but there were new ones to compensate.

November 1978

Versions old and new

At the time of writing, it is nearly November, but the autumn weather has been highly congenial for weeks on end, and we seem to be still in the afterglow of a memorable harvest festival. Several of the parents were new to the children's harvest in Loders school, and were loud in praise of it. The west end of the big room was like a greengrocer's window in London's west end. In front of this, the children who are now a young lot, led the singing and the prayers and read the lessons.

Judged purely as a performance, the best item was their antiphonal chanting of the great nature psalm, which is not easily done well. They were splendid, doing it in the Authorised Version, which is less poetic, and therefore harder to recite, than Coverdale's version in the Prayer Book.

November 1978

T.V. Time

New arrivals in Loders are numerous, and more than we have been able to catch at home outside television time. (Our tact will not be lost on them, we hope).

November 1978

Reels on Wheels

'Reels on Wheels', an experiment in rural cinema at Askerswell Village Hall, started well, with the hall comfortably full for a showing of *It shouldn't happen to a vet*. Patrons to arrive early noted that males were shown to their seats by an usherette, and females by an usher, but this nice touch was lost when the trickle of arrivals became a flood.

November 1978

More in the village

December is socially the busiest month of the year for Loders, if not for Askerswell. On the first there is a social in Loders Village Hall at 7.30 pm in aid of hall funds. On the tenth the carol service at the Chapel at 6.30 pm. On the fifteenth at 5.45

p.m. the School Christmas Concert followed immediately by the Mission Sale. On the nineteenth the School Carol Service in Loders Church at 3 p.m. On the twentieth the School Party at 4 p.m. Also on the twentieth, the Carol Party Singing in Uploders and collecting for the Children's Society, beginning at 6.30 p.m. On the twenty-second the Carol Party Singing in Loders for the same object, beginning at 7 p.m. On Christmas Eve the usual Sunday services plus 'The Midnight' at church beginning at 11.45 p.m. On Christmas Day the Family Service with carols and Christmas tree at 11 a.m. On Boxing Day the Comic Hockey Match at the Well Plot Playing Field at 11 a.m., followed by hot punch at *The Crown*.

It had just occurred to the Vicar that he must give accurate notice of all these coming events in the *Parish Notes* when he saw tucked beneath the handbill at the vicarage door a folded paper, which began, 'Dear Resident, Do you ever wish that there was more going on in the village? Would you like to join a gardening club, or a country dance club, or an afternoon club? Or how about a drama or pantomime group, or a cricket club? Would you like to have regular bingo sessions or jumble sales or whilst drive or dancers?' The letter was from the energetic and public-spirited wife of the landlord of *The Crown*.

It was some relief to the Vicar to find that the letter was not personal to him. A copy was to be delivered to every house in the village, inviting residents to a meeting in the Village Hall on November 24th. 'I have been asked by the Loders Village Hall Committee to form a separate and independent social and entertainments committee,' wrote Mrs. Upton, 'and in order to do the job properly, I need to know what your wishes are.'

* * * * *

Mrs. Shelley Upton's meeting referred to in our opening paragraph drew a large attendance by Loders standards – twenty-five, with many apologies and offers of help. Her strong feeling that the village should be rescued from being a place where people come to die was shared by the meeting, and a committee chosen, to meet at *The Crown* on December 5th. Incidentally, Mrs. Upton had herself scrubbed the hall for the occasion.

December 1978

New as well as old

If the corpses in Loders churchyard could come to life and read the handsome posters advertising our Country Fayre (on Saturday, June 30th) they would be surprised to see that we had acquired a Village Green at long last. This is what our Entertainments Committee call the new playing field tucked away behind the council houses at Well Plot. Wishful thinking on their part, but good endeavours deserve to succeed.

Village Greens are still the focus in summer of the social life of virile villages, and our Committee have done all they can to make our Green just that on June 30th. Programmes are circulating, so there is no need to itemise the attractions here. Suffice it to say that the art exhibition in the village hall will include the 8ft. by 4ft. bird's-eye view of the Lyme Bay Deanery, which was part of the pilgrim '79 exhibition in Salisbury Cathedral, and was much admired. John Whyte, of the old school house, painted it, proving that a house-decorator may be a painter in both senses of the word. The perpetual trophy for the tug-o'-war between Loders and Uploders comes from Michael Wood's *Mickkimug* pottery at Matravers, and is a good example of his craftsmanship. The dance at the hall in the evening will be new time as well as old.

July 1979

Village Appraisal

Earlier in the year the 360 people on the Loders voters' list each received a sizeable form with questions for them to answer on matters vital to the village. Form-filling is so rampant nowadays that the recipients might well have said 'Enough is enough' and put the forms in the fire. But they did not: no less than 325 of them did as they were bid. Their answers are presented in an attractive report, now on sale at 50p. It makes fascinating reading, whether or not its aim is achieved of steering Loders into the 21st century according to the ideas of 1979. Hats off to the public-spirited parishioners who did the Appraisal at no charge to the parish.

Space confines our observations to just a few of the questions:- Do you read the Vicar's *Parish Notes*? Yes 271, No 23, No answer 31 (our total circulation is 350 copies per month). Do you read the *Parish Information Sheet* as well? Yes 171, No 101, No answer 53. The Entertainment Committee are planning more activity in the Village Hall; do you approve? Yes 225, No 48, No answer 52. Are you likely to take part? Yes 109, No 146, No answer 70. Are Loders' three pubs an asset to the community? Yes 270, No 14, No answer 41.

Is the Parish Church a valuable asset to the village? Yes 288, No 6, No answer 31. Is the Chapel an additional asset? Yes 257, No 17, No answer 41. Is it important to have a resident parson? Yes 245, No 39, No answer 41. Are there any village eyesores which could reasonably be altered? Yes 120, No 93, No answer 112. (High Acres housing estate and the Village Hall were among several 'eyesores' named.)

The young people's response to the questionnaire was disappointing. Only 24 replied, and one said, 'Less time should be spent on old people and more consideration given to the young. By old, I mean anybody over the age of 25'.

December 1979

Change for the better

The arrival of piped water and drainage in our district several years ago wrought a great change in Askerswell and Loders. New houses sprang up, including a housing estate in Uploders and another in Loders. Old cottages were sold at prices that would have stricken their former present owners dumb with disbelief. In their resurrected form they are mostly holiday homes, some with the retirement of their new owners as the chief end in view. On the whole the change has been for the better. Our derelict buildings have vanished and we have acquired nice new parishioners whose community spirit is often more robust than that of the 'old originals'.

Change has come at last to Loders Vicarage. A small and more convenient vicarage is to be built on the kitchen garden opposite the front door of the present Vicarage, and the latter with the remainder of its curtilage sold as soon as possible. It turned out that the south wall of the dining-room was not in imminent danger of collapse, as the Archdeacon's architect had supposed. The Vicar called in a firm of structural engineers, the burden of whose report was that the rebuilding of the wall was a counsel of perfection rather than of present necessity.

The West Dorset District Council architect, who was also called in, said that any application to demolish the Vicarage would be rejected in no uncertain terms – the whole building, and not the fifteenth century part only, was protected, and it graced that part of the parish which was a conservation area. The WDDC architect bore out the finding of the engineers that the building as a whole was in good condition. He said that if the house were his, he would put a buttress to the leaning wall, which has been leaning a long time, and be happy to sleep for the next fifty years in the Vicar's four-poster, which is kept poised between heaven and earth by the said wall.

So the Vicar's removal to *Bell* with be a dignified and orderly retreat, not a rout. The transition from gracious living in a baby manor-house to cottage life will be traumatic at first, but he hopes to learn, like St. Paul, to be content with whatsoever state in which he finds himself. How are the mighty fallen! For three centuries his spiritual forebear, the Prior of Loders, was effectual owner of the whole village.

The new Vicar will be sitting on all that is left of this, a tenement on the old Vicarage cabbage-patch, warming himself with calor gas, perhaps, while a lay magnate sits before the great fireplace where the Vicars sat for nearly five centuries. 'Money is the root of all evil' is the apposite text here. The stipend of Dr. Edersheim who was Vicar in the 1880's was £300. That was then about ten times the wage of a cowman. Now a vicar's stipend falls short of a cowman's. Hence the shortage of clergy and the lumping together of parishes. The next Vicar of Loders-cum-Powerstock and Rector of Askerswell will have five churches to look after. So he can well do without a manor-sized house and garden.

March 1980

On the periphery

People who say that life at *Bell*, on the periphery of the parish, must be lonesome compared with the old Vicarage, in the heart of Loders, forget that the old Vicarage was moated by a yard from the village street, whereas *Bell* has only a few posts and a chain between it and a busy farm road.

At the old Vicarage a nourishing whiff of pig slurry every now and then was the only conscious contact with agriculture: at Bell one cannot avoid becoming honorary members of the Crabb and Newberry families who farm all round it, and this is a delightful fellowship to be in. Friesian cows seem immense as they mouch past the kitchen window to and from milking; each one looks like a map of Europe going by. It is a pleasant little game to guess which of Farmer Raymond's four lovely milkmaids is bringing up the rear of one procession. The cows know and behave accordingly. There is no guesswork about David Newberry's other procession. His moves fast like a phalanx of buffalo, quite defeating the efforts to get through them of the *Marquis of Lorne* car, which is in a mighty hurry always.

September 1980

Village entertainment

Loders Women's Institute gave their neighbours a pleasant evening of a different kind and in the process added £70 to their village hall improvement fund. The main item was a play in a relaxed Victorian atmosphere so well done that it might have come straight from the BBC's *Ripping Yarns*.

The theme was the attempted murder in an old ladies' home of the oldest inmate by another inmate. We saw our Nan Balfour, the ninety-seven-year-old victim, making a speech after a severe throttling by Valerie Nash, the would-be murderess. All the speeches were clearly spoken and near word perfect. The other performers were Mrs. Pilford, Mrs. Brill and Mrs. Taylor. Mrs. Bowden, the W.I. President was producer. We could do with more of this sort of entertainment.

September 1980

A proliferation of clubs

The flower show, the second organised by the Loders Entertainment Committee, enticed many admiring spectators away from Saturday afternoon television to the Village Hall. The quality of the 250 entries was high, and the handicraft sections revealed much unsuspected talent.

But why the talk of starting a gardeners' club when the competitors had done so well without one? True, there is usually room for improvement even in the best, but a proliferation of clubs may dissipate rather than strengthen the life of a village community.

October 1980

Modern Entertainment

The usual meticulous planning of Askerswell Harvest Supper was not thwarted by an explosion in the electric pay-as-you-use

meter as the guests were about to arrive at the Village Hall.
Somebody remembered that the dustbin was full of empty
wine-bottles from a Golden Wedding Party. Candles were stuck
in these. Some of the guests thought the committee had 'seen
the light' in that they had been converted to dining by candle.
The pre-prandial sherry tasted as good as it looked. The soup
was hot, and the jacketed potatoes that went with the beef,
ham and salad were likewise, as if the electric cooker were still
working. In the flickering shadows the beer and cider still
landed safely in the glasses, and plates of apple tart and cream
between the appropriate fork and spoon.

While the coffee was being contentedly gossiped over, two
mechanics from Southern Electricity were doing a sort of open
heart surgery on the meter. They extracted a vein of wire from
somewhere and bypassed the offending meter. Their ingenuity
elicited cries of dismay from the diners instead of clapping. In
the sudden, civilising glare of the electric lights the diners had
suddenly to get respectable. This was obviously not easy, but the
throb-songs of a party of Bridport Dramatic Society entertainers,
which wound up the proceedings, made the transition tolerable.

November 1980

The survival of the W.I.

We hear that Eileen Bryan, in her capacity as emissary of the
Dorset County W.I. handled the meeting at which Loders W.I.
had to decide whether to die or live with a delicacy and charm
which were a revelation to any misguided person who might
have thought she was an apostle of the letter of the W.I. constitution rather than its spirit.

Mrs. Holmes, a comparative newcomer to Uploders, accepted
the presidency, and began by presiding so graciously over a
dinner celebrating the victory of the will to live that there are
now no qualms about the future of Loders W.I. Husbands of
Askerswell W.I. who thought they were doing their wives a
favour by being their guests at the Christmas dinner at *Spyway*
did themselves a greater service, much to their surprise. The
dinner was terrific. Next time the wives will not need to put on
their siren act to wean the husbands from the fireside or the box.

January 1981

Embracing the whole church

The New Year was welcomed in Loders Tower by the Ringers – alone, as usual. At Askerswell the Ringers were watched by quite a number of parishioners, which is possible there because ringing is not only on the ground floor but open to the church. The spectators had among them jars of red and white wine and glasses, with which they toasted each other and the new year. Then they joined hands and sang *Auld lang syne*. All quite natural and pleasant and not irreverent: one felt that the Lord was enjoying it too. And, who knows, it may grow sufficiently for parishioners to embrace the whole church from the outside, as the custom of a few parishes still is?

February 1981

Askerswell Church

CHAPTER 8
The legacy
cx/cx/cx/

'The wheel has come full circle'

At the start of *Yours Reverently (1948–1953)* I set myself, and the readership, the question: 'Do the *Parish Notes* present a pastoral idyll, or a rural backwater, or the quiet murmur of country repose, or what?' Elsewhere in the trilogy I have declared, 'Let the man speak'. Now, I have decided to speak myself, and to try to answer the question.

In *The Parson Knows* (p. xi) I mentioned the Welsh poetess Gillian Clarke who informed me that there is quite a tradition in Wales of sons of the clergy writing a *cofiante*, or tribute, to their father, as a minister of the church. It would consist in the main of examples of the sermons he preached. In this trilogy there are no sermons, largely because he did not write them down. But a student from St. James' Secretarial College, Bradpole, Felicity (now) Burge had an interest in testing out her shorthand skills, so she has preserved a sermon pretty well intact (p. 266). It demonstrates the art of combining the deepest of scripture and belief in a contemporary, local medium which is challenging and yet eminently accessible – and concise.

In the *Parish Notes* there are short exhortations about Lent, Easter, Remembrance Sunday, Christmas, etc. There are exhortations about a number of secular matters, like getting your children to bed on time, or how best to dispose of your jumble, or the effects of television on the social life of common mortals.

The time has come for me to say what I think the *Parish Notes* are. Although critics have jumped to Parson Woodforde and Francis Kilvert to find precedents, and a corpus of English reverent writing, they have in fact been misleading. If Parson Woodforde and Francis Kilvert were taken as stalwarts of Anglican-Christian pastoral life, somebody, somewhere, would be being seriously misled. They both make excellent coffee-table reading. Each was writing under different circumstances, but always with the motive of private diary uppermost, and Christianity and their community at some distance. They are both delightful in terms of English prose, and the observations made, and the historical commentary exposed by accident. Parson Woodforde is interested in how much he paid the ostler yesterday morning. Francis Kilvert is interested in walks, and archery, and local views (particularly of local farmers' daughters).

The Parish Notes had their most pertinent criticism from *The Catholic Herald*. Brian Brindley recognised that, 'Criticism is almost impossible, for this work is *sui generis*.' [of its own kind] His article was entitled, challengingly, *More gossip, vicar?* and subtitled ... *on the musings of an indiscreet country parson*. But the Vicar was discreet, with the added ability to apologise when he had made a mistake. 'The better part of valour is discretion.'

They are a single-minded endeavour to hold the whole of a small community together under a broadly Christian umbrella. The driving force behind them was, in the first instance, the mind of a journalist. I don't believe that many who read the *Parish Notes* knew that Rev. Oliver Willmott had learnt his trade on the *Somerset Standard*. Few people know that Winston Churchill set off on a journalist's career as a London correspondent during the Boer War. That fact helps to put *his* powers of oratory into perspective. Both journalists enjoyed collecting juicy, readable stories: it was their first job in life, and a life-long hobby. My father liked to be funny, and had to be concise. He expected to shock, and take the consequences. He always carried a tiny notebook for statistics and quotes.

The result of his work is a unique English document, covering 34 years of English life, month by month. Social historians will be

Loders Church

delighted by the factual evidence of when fridges, and sewage systems, and supermarkets began to affect local life, and how British Rail axed the country lines. Family historians will be fascinated to find whole families chronicled from the font to the grave – via some very funny weddings, and other incidents. (The Somerset and Dorset History Society have a complete set.) Christians, looking for fundamental encouragement, will be inspired. People who love the English language will revel in the pithy use of it.

In studying Jonathan Swift I learnt from a critic about an intellectual habit called the desire for *'superbia'* – which means supremacy in argument. In *The Parish Notes*, this trait is demonstrated in a number of ways. There was no right of reply, unless permission were granted. The Vicar was editor-in-chief, correspondents few, critics none (in print). Then, he used words wonderfully, to pin down events, characters, opinions, moral attitudes, the Church, Society and England. He needed to win, to prove Loders best, to prove his *Parish Notes* 'meatier than most'. (p. 15) He wanted to exercise his mind, to push Christ gently forward. In the meantime, some sensitivities were ridden somewhat roughshod over.

Even now, the juxtaposition of certain paragraphs, veering between the ludicrous and the deeply sincere, can stretch the critical appreciation of the most avid supporter. But his cultivated practice made people want to read.

An important critic, who eventually lost in a libel case brought by the Vicar to defend his accounting of a five-pound note claimed: 'In my opinion, these *Parish Notes* should be closer to the Church than they are. For instance, we don't get any Salisbury Diocesan news at all. These *Notes* seem to be making fun of people – they are more like comic cuts.' He had half a point, because the *Parish Notes* were Loders-centred, and Vicar-centred, and the Vicar enjoyed a laugh. (The critic, who was Chairman of the Parish Council, did not attend church.)

In that débâcle, the *Bridport News* reported that, 'Even the Vicar would prefer that the *Notes* were for local consumption only.' *That* was only half a truth, because the Vicar loved the feedback from readers far afield, and I know he had an instinct, as he wrote, that these 'notes' were for posterity, as well as the present. Otherwise, he wouldn't have handed them on to me.

But in the main, the Vicar's Call brought joy, particularly in words, and the fellowship that they bring. Someone has said somewhere – and if they haven't, they ought to have done – 'words are the glue of society'. *The Parish Notes* are first and foremost a celebration of the English language in action, welding a community. He had a mission. He wanted to be heard. A psychiatrist might say they were his obsession: a gentler friend would know they were his love.

In his defence in the libel action about the missing £5 in 1969, the Vicar said: 'I write the *Notes* in the only way I know how – and they are very popular with most people here. I have never had any complaints from those I have written about.' He used them in whatever way he felt fit, even to save sending thank-you letters. 'Before some of us have got used to writing 1977 on cheques and letters it is 1978. We offer the warmest seasonal greetings to our readers, especially those who regularly send us Christmas cards and never get one in return.' (January 1978)

These are also the village annals of Loders, Dottery and Askerswell. Village annals are in danger of being boring. Because of his journalist's training he had inbred the criterion of newsworthiness. If there was nothing to say, he didn't say it – and I haven't included mere records in this trilogy. Anyone can find out how much the Tombola took in the 1954 fête by going to the Bridport or the British Museum, or Dorchester Archives, and seeing for themselves: he didn't miss a statistic, or a house-move. He was the complete Registrar for Births, Deaths and Marriages (and home-visiting gave him a privileged entrée into wonderful local gossip).

In no way are *The Parish Notes* autobiographical. But the Vicar's private thoughts and anxieties as well as his enthusiasms inevitably seep through. In the last phase there was a danger of being bitter and retrospective, and certainly a few discords can be heard. He got tired of taking funerals of close friends and parishioners, and trekking to Yeovil and Weymouth crematoria, though he kept up his hospital visits to Port Bredy in Bridport and Dorchester. He died in Dorchester Hospital with his family assembled in the last peaceful hours. (On his last night in Dorchester Hospital he mistook his bed for the couch at *Bell Cottage*, and gently said good-night to his wife – 'You go on upstairs now.' Another of his last lines was, 'The wheel has come full circle.')

He would be proud to know that his words from the *Parish Notes* were first broadcast on that Hospital Radio quite soon after his death. He would be bemused to know that his books were on sale on the Internet – he would assume divine intervention. (Seriously, he did think that the thunderbolt which hit York Cathedral in 1984 was divinely inspired because of some of the wrong words emanating from the Church in England.)

His epitaph was suitably cryptic, but generous, and outward-looking: '*Be ye thankful.*' He loved most Dorset people, and all of the Dorset countryside, with the changing of the seasons. Somebody said he was part of the landscape, with his dogs.

So, here are some final words, from a man of whom Prebendary Brook Lunn in the *Catholic Messenger* said:

'You can't pigeon-hole someone like this.'

'Let the words of our mouths, and the meditations of our

hearts, be always acceptable in Thy sight, O Lord, our strength, and our redeemer.' (Psalm 19, vs 14–15, said before every sermon – there must have been 5,000 at least in the combined parishes of Loders, and heaps before, and elsewhere.) He changed the pronouns to the plural to be inclusive.

'Loders Church is a great heritage from the past that our duty is to pass on intact.' July 1977

'A church so well cared for must be a good advertisement for God.' [Askwerswell Church]

August 1977

A missionary activity

Loders Fête has long been known as one of the happiest and most profitable in West Dorset. Its very reputation is its danger. The sturdy giving of its parishioners of all sorts and conditions is the basis of the profit. If because it does so well, everybody should have left the giving to everybody else, it could end up like that apocryphal collection in a synagogue for a deceased Jew's widow, which produced nothing, because everybody put only his hand in the bag, confident that his kind neighbours would do the necessary in so deserving a cause. To pass on to future generations in good condition the church we have inherited is more than a moral obligation in the cause of conservation. It is a missionary activity, for the church speaks of God to those who go into it, as no person could.

So . . . from now onwards, be thinking of what you will give the Vicar when he does his house-to-house collecting of things to sell, in the week before the fête. Discarding something useless is not giving. He is not a dustbin – yet.

July 1976

Reducing the rate

The Carol Service at the Uploders Chapel was one of the events the Vicar had to miss. By chance their organist Miss Daisy Boxall was also away at a funeral. The versatile and Reverend Norman Skinner played his electronic organ and conducted the service, which was well attended. Members of his Bridport Youth Orchestra augmented the organ.

He thanked the wife of the chairman of the parish council, Dora Hyde, for helping with the decorations in the continued absence through illness of the chapel steward's wife, Florence Morris. George Hyde, as chief citizen of Loders, was prevailed upon to read a lesson. Now that he has achieved a longstanding ambition to reduce the Loders rate – and at a time when all other rates are rising – he feels it not unfitting that he should lift up his head in public.

January 1981

Looping the loop

The family service at Loders was enlivened by a little lady in the congregation whose *Away in a manger* went into orbit round the rest and held the limelight. The vocal loop-the-loop she did in the Creed was unintentional – she had touched a hot pipe under the seat.

January 1978

Respect for the old

When the late Mrs. Bertha Johnson was remembered among the faithful departed in Loders church, some of the congregation wondered who she might be. And well they might, for nobody in the parish was living a more secluded life. She was the ninety-one-year-old mother of Mrs. Dick Wood, of Knowle Farm, an invalid for some years, and requiring much attention.

For something like thirty years Mrs. Wood's household dutifully and not unlovingly revolved round her. The families were present in strength at her funeral in Yeovil crematorium, knowing that had they been Chinese ancestor worshippers they could not have done more for their matriarch's happiness.

December 1979

Fête jottings

Little girl, announcing the arrival of the Vicar on his mission of fête collecting: 'Mummy, God has come.'

Little boy, asked by the roulette lady how he managed to win every time: 'I pray to God, keep my fingers crossed, and turn my toes in.'

September 1980

Forgive us our Christmases

'Forgive us our Christmases' was what a boy at school was once found to be saying in the Lord's Prayer, and Christmases need forgiving, if they omit Him whom Christmas is all about.

December 1979

Making your will

Illness caused the veteran churchwarden of Dottery, Mr. Cecil Marsh, to miss the Melplash Show for the first time in fifty years, but he made a marvellous recovery, and got to the ploughing match as usual. There is nothing like making your will to give you a new lease of life.

October 1978

[The Vicar would have admired the Vicar of Beaminster, Dorset, who has come up with a blockbuster title – '*Churchwardens I have buried*' – not for the sentiment, but for the title.]

The dangers of hard work

Congratulations to Mr. Samuel Fry on reaching the ninetieth anniversary of his birthday on November 23rd (1979). He is a hale and hearty widower. When the Rector called on him at his cottage off The Square, Askerswell, he was cleaning the floor of his living-room. Asked if he had any message for the younger generation, he said, 'Yes,' emphatically. 'Tell 'em I begun milkin' at ten years old, and hard work never hurt nobody.'

December 1979

The need for clarity

Mrs. Lowle had a story for these *Notes* showing the need for public speakers to be distinct. A Mothers' Union speaker finished her address, and proceeded thus to the Lord's Prayer: 'Let us now close with the prayer He taught us.' As the members were departing, a little girl who was hanging back asked her mother: 'But where is the PRAIRIE TORTOISE?'

November 1979

Commander John Streatfeild

Boarsbarrow Farm has lately had the melancholy experience of seeing two of its members buried with exceptional honours. First, at Loders, Mr. Joe Legg, a skilled hedger and stockman, and a true countryman, who died in his car after a life free of illness. Four workmates carried his coffin, and the church was so full that people were standing.

Then, at Symondsbury, there were more people in the churchyard than in the church for a memorial service for Commander John Streatfield. Invalided out of the Navy in 1949, he made a brilliant career in agriculture, mastered a pack of foxhounds, chaired the local magistrates, served as Deputy Lieutenant, and best of all, never lost the common touch. Throughout this time he was battling with a malignant disease, that was getting him bit by bit, though he died from heart attacks. Looking at him, who could deny that basic principle of Christianity – No cross, no crown?

May 1977

REVEREND
OLIVER LEONARD
WILLMOTT
1910 — 1996
VICAR OF
LODERS & DOTTERY
1947 — 1982
RECTOR OF
ASKERSWELL
1952 — 1982
BE YE THANKFUL
7ᵀᴴ MAY 1996

Postlude

Finally, two quotes from a scrap of paper, with quotations from a book by John Whale (Head of BBC TV Religion), with heavy exclamation marks to show Rev. Oliver Willmott's disapproval:

> 'By accommodating diversity of belief, the Church of England accepts that uncertainty is unavoidable.'

> 'Believers must do what their consciences bid them.'

With his logical brain and his religious conviction, he could not stand flabbiness of this nature. At Kelham, he didn't eventually become a monk because of disagreements with the absolutist Abbot. Instead of becoming a monk, he entered the Anglican Church, because it was the broadest umbrella under which to place his convictions.

His Christian belief was rock-hard, and he wouldn't wish to be remembered as a village entertainer (though he would have enjoyed the fact.) In his retirement he had time to read, and in his scraps of paper has appeared a testimony, which is peculiar from a backwater, 'parochial' parson.

A dream of a Tory country parson.

'In the *Daily Telegraph* of 26th March, 1990, I read the notice of Dr. Runcie's impending resignation as Archbishop of Canterbury, and studied the photographs of the eight bishops in the running to succeed him. Later I dreamt, as follows:–

I advised Mrs. Thatcher to ignore all the bishops and advise the Queen to nominate the Reverend John Polkinghorne, Doctor of Science and Fellow of the Royal Society, as next Archbishop of Canterbury. This delighted Mrs. Thatcher – not famed for her devotion to bishops, and appealed to Her Majesty, who, as a true sport, had not begrudged a hundred-to-one outsider's victory over Desert Orchid in the Cheltenham Gold Cup. Very, very reluctantly, Doctor Polkinghorne accepted. The country was startled, and half-drowned by the enthusiastic effervescence of the media. Tory fortunes revived, and the Church of England lived happily ever after.

In cold daylight the dream seemed less fantastic. Consideration of the poor showing religion makes in popular esteem against the mighty achievements of science convinced me that religion would revive under an Archbishop of Canterbury who bridged the gulf between science and religion.

Dr. Polkinghorne was elected to the Royal Society for his contribution to Physics. In 1979 he resigned as Professor of Mathematics and Physics at Cambridge, to study theology. He had always been a practising Christian. He was ordained priest in 1982, served as a curate in Bristol, then as Vicar of Blean in Kent. He was recalled to Cambridge as Dean of Trinity Hall, and has lately been appointed President of Queen's College, Cambridge. A stream of theological books has issued from his pen, and his recent religious broadcasts are being well received. He finds the new Quantum Physics in which he specialises to buttress his belief in the Christian Creed. Unlike some present bishops, he has no difficulty in accepting literally the virginal conception of Our Lord, His miracles, and His bodily resurrection.

On another scrap of paper he noted the unresearched statistic that more than 50% of scientists are Christians. It was much harder for an atheist to be an atheist than a Christian a Christian, given that so many random chances would have had to coincide to make a miraculously ordered universe.

His cell-mate at Kelham College was Leslie Grover, who after Kelham became an avowed atheist. He wrote in 1999 – 'Although Oliver and myself had a lot in common, we must have had very different views on many things – I am a republican and cannot stand the "royal" family and the rest of the aristocracy, and Oliver was royalist and traditional. I suppose I am also a bit of an iconoclast – I would ban foxhunting, but I could never be an activist. Nevertheless, we never argued; I am only sorry that we did not keep in touch.'

On the wall of their cell was a Latin tag that both absorbed daily – '*Sine metu, quaerire veritatem*' – 'Without fear, seek the truth.' It was literally a 'cell', for when family or friends came to visit over the six-year training period they had to speak through a grille, as for prisoners.

Rev. Oliver Willmott left some strong statements that he lived his life by: 'We are all for unity, as opposed to uniformity' (March 1975). And he left another Latin tag – '*Solvitur ambulandum*' – which implies that if you walk around all will be solved. This was not an advocacy of *laissez-faire*: he walked deliberately, and composed sermons, and inclusions for *The Parish Notes* – and solved most things. A close friend, Dr. Maxwell Jones, whose medicinal sermon was mentioned in *Yours Reverently* (p. 67) said recently: 'He's another example of the heroes in faith in Hebrews 11, who like Abel, "Being dead, yet speaketh".' Robert Burns might add: 'He was a man for a' that.'

In *The Parson Knows* p. 135–6 Rev. Willmott claimed, 'Quite apart from the helpful things Dr. Maxwell Jones said, it was good to have a doctor in the pulpit, shewing that religion and science are not mutually exclusive, as some people imagine they are.' He has already offered his universal apology (in *The Parson Knows* p. 233–4): 'May we plunge into 1958 proclaiming with Peter Quince that, "If we offend, it is with our good will?"'

His two favourite quotations from the *Bible* were Isaiah Chapter 48 verse 31, 'But they that wait upon the Lord shall renew their strength: they shall mount up with wings as eagles; they shall run, and not be weary; and they shall walk, and not faint.' From Job Chapter 28 verse 7: 'There is a path that the wild fowl knoweth not, and the eye of the vulture hath not seen.'

He made a proclamation in *Yours Reverently* (p. 55): 'It is good for parsons to have their sermons pulled to bits and chewed over. Besides, any shred of evidence that somebody was awake and listening, is to be hailed with delight.'

Let him speak on.

Sermon Given by Rev. Oliver Willmott on May 3rd 1964

I was in Bridport hospital yesterday afternoon, in the Women's Ward, and a man came in and talked to one of the patients, and then he moved along to all the other beds and had a word with the other patients – mostly jokes – and he went out. When he had gone out one patient said to the Staff Nurse who happened to be there, 'Who was that nice man?' and the Staff Nurse said that he was Mr. Hannah, the Surgeon. 'He is a very, very clever man, strings of letters after his name and a very nice man too.'

There was quite a buzz of talk after that, and the conversation that arose was that Surgeons were very wonderful men indeed. 'Twas a job that nobody would like to do, but was a very worthwhile and very wonderful job, and they were some of the cleverest men in the world, and we could not do without them. Well, those are sentiments that everybody would share, I think. We have a tremendous respect for the medical position and especially for the Surgeons and for the wonderful things that they can do. That series on television *Your Life in their Hands* has brought home to people their amazing skill, and the incredible things that they can do nowadays. Operations on moving hearts, grafting kidneys out of one person into another, all these incredible things, and there is no profession, I think, that has more regard from the general population than the medical, and particularly the Surgeons.

And yet, you know, this is an odd thing. Not so very long ago, the Surgeons of the United States, having done much investigation into the subject, put out a proclamation that smoking is the cause of lung cancer, and our own medical profession in England, they followed it up with a similar proclamation, and there have been pronouncements like it on the Continent. The medical profession have warned us that smoking is one of the causes of lung cancer, and Doctors everywhere have stopped smoking to show that they practise what they preach. Notices have gone up in hospitals and in factories and in public places and on boards that smoking is dangerous to health.

You think to yourself, that with the Surgeons and the medical profession generally standing so high with the public, the public would take notice of what they are saying and that smoking would cease. But what do you find? That when the figures of tobacco consumption came out the other day, since all these warnings, smoking has increased considerably. It really is an amazing thing, and you wonder how it should happen when those people are so regarded by mankind in general, and yet when with all the authority that they can muster they say this thing is dangerous – stop it – nobody takes much notice, and as a matter of fact they do more of it than they did before.

It is an amazing thing: it makes you realise what religion is up against. If the medical profession with all their authority and with all the regard that the public holds them in, if they cannot stop people from doing what they are sure is dangerous to health, how do you think the poor old Church is going to make people do things for their spiritual health and for their everlasting salvation?

This Sunday, Rogation Sunday, is the one on which we are supposed to fix our attention on the importance of prayer. Prayer Sunday, and our Lord leaves no doubt about it that prayer is absolutely vital to the Christian life. He says over and over again what that hymn says: 'We perish if we cease from prayer.' Prayer may be defined as conscious contact with God. It is the life blood flowing between God and us. If we do not pray we are like a limb with no blood coming into it, and it is bound to perish. We perish if we cease from prayer. Prayer is absolutely essential to our spiritual health, absolutely essential really to the well-being of the Nation, and our Eternal life, as well as this life, depends on it. And yet how are we going to make people understand that and take the right action?

With the medical profession with all their esteem that they are held in by the public, if they cannot get the public to do what they want the public to do, how on earth is the Church going to get people to do a much harder thing? No Paul Report with all its suggestions for the deployment of clergy and the grouping of patients is going to meet the situation – nothing. I wonder what the answer really is? Well, there again perhaps the doctors have suggested a solution. Last week a health Congress was meeting and one of the doctors who was present had said (they were talking about smoking and lung cancer by the way) the way to get people to be aware of the dangers of smoking and to give it up would be to enlist the Beatles on their side! You know last week the Beatles appeared in Madame Tussauds for the first time, their wax models had been done and the Beatles went to Madame Tussauds to see them and the national papers showed a photograph of one putting a cigarette into the mouth of his waxen brother. Apparently the Beatles are smokers. This doctor said, if only the Beatles could be encouraged to give up smoking, to lead a crusade against it, then the young people especially, and perhaps the whole nation and finally the whole world might be induced to do what the doctors wanted them to do. They as doctors could do nothing, but probably the Beatles could do it. Well, I expect that is true, you know, I expect that if the Beatles did go out and lead a campaign, people would take notice, and then it would be catching.

What I am coming to is this. Here is a doctor saying we cannot do this by argument, but if you can get someone with an enormous public following to do it, something may happen, which brings me to the only solution to the problem of prayer. You will never argue people into prayer. Dr. Johnson rightly said, 'Sir, there is no argument for prayer.' You cannot argue people into praying, but if you make the person of Jesus Christ real to them, prayer will automatically follow. If Jesus Christ becomes real to us then prayer will automatically follow. We shall want to talk to Him. We shall want to share our troubles with Him, and we shall want to share our joys with Him. He will become the most important thing to us. The worship of Him, the thanking of Him for all He gives us will become one of life's necessities. Once He becomes real, prayer will follow automatically. You cannot argue people into prayer, yet that doctor, I think, was very right in imagining that if we can enlist persons like the Beatles then there will be less smoking, and if we become attached to the person of Jesus Christ, prayer will automatically follow. It can only arise out of the love for Him. Once again you find somebody who is no professional expert of the Bible catching the sayings of the truth: Tennyson. He said: 'He prayeth best who loveth best.' If we love Jesus Christ, prayer will follow.

Historical background
(1968–1982)

THE ROYAL FAMILY

1972   Duke of Windsor dies
1974   Marriage of Princess Anne and Mark Phillips
1978   Street parties in towns and villages celebrating the Silver Jubilee of the
        Queen's Coronation (p. 24)
1979   Earl Mountbatten killed by Irish Republican Army bomb off
        Mullaghmore in Sligo, Eire
1981   Marriage of Prince Charles of Wales and Lady Diana Spencer (pp. 36;
        104)
1982   Birth of Prince William

BRITISH POLITICS

1970   Voting age lowered to 18
        Conservatives win the General Election: Edward Heath Prime
        Minister (p. 9 Heath, take note)
1971   Internment in Northern Ireland (p. 9 Enemies in Northern Ireland)
1972   Direct Rule over Ulster
1973   UK joins the EEC (p. 12 The Commonmarket and Whitsun)
        Value Added Tax introduced in the UK (p. 15)
1974   Harold Wilson forms minority Labour Government.
        TUC agree on 'Social Contract'
        Labour wins second General Election of the year
1975   Margaret Thatcher elected new leader of Conservative Party
        Majority vote stay in European Economic Union in UK referendum
        British MP John Stonehouse arrested in Australia
1976   Prime Minister Harold Wilson announces retirement
        James Callaghan becomes PM
1979   Airey Neave killed by Irish Republican Army bomb at the House of
        Commons
        General Election – Margaret Thatcher becomes first woman Prime
        Minister in the United Kingdom
1981   Formation of the Social Democratic Party by 'The Gang of Four'
        Race riots in Brixton
        Hunger striker Bobby Sands dies in prison in Belfast

1982   Unemployment tops 3 million
        Argentina seizes the Falklands
        Argentinians surrender in the Falklands
        IRA bombs kill 11 and injure 50 in London parks

NATIONAL AND INTERNATIONAL EVENTS

1968   Ronan Point disaster
        Martin Luther King assassinated
        First decimal coins (p. 226 The end of coppers)
        Soviet attack on Czechoslovakia
        Richard Nixon elected President of the US
1969   Open University begins courses
        Woodstock Pop Festival
        Belfast to London Civil Rights March ends in violence
        Arafat new PLO leader
        President de Gaulle resigns
        QE2 leaves on maiden voyage
        Neil Armstrong first man on the moon
        British troops deployed in Belfast (p. 18 St. Albans Remembrance)
1970   Court-martial of Lt. Colley for My Lai massacre
1971   Chay Blyth sails round the world
1972   Bangladesh becomes independent state
        President Amin plans to expel 50,000 Asians
        Yom Kippur War as Egypt and Syria attack Israel
        Oil prices rise by 70%
        Ceasefire in Middle East following Israeli advances
1974   US spacecraft *Mariner* photographs Mercury
        Earthquake in China kills 20,000 people
        India tests nuclear bomb
        Peron dies in Argentina
        Nixon resigns as US President after Watergate; Gerald Ford takes over
1975   Nixon aides sentenced for Watergate cover-up (p. 21 Watergate)
        Saigon falls to the North Vietnamese
        Suez Canal reopens after 8 years
        Franco dies: Juan Carlos becomes King of Spain
1976   Concorde makes first commercial transatlantic flight (p. 20 'Our supersonic lady')
        176 people killed following rioting in the South African township of Soweto
        Olympic Games open in Montreal, Canada
        US spacecraft *Viking* lands on Mars and sends first pictures
        British Ambassador in Dublin killed by a car bomb
        Chinese leader Mao Tse-tung dies
        Jimmy Carter elected President of the USA
        Drought in the UK – driest since records began in 1727 (p. 58)
1977   Oil 'blow-out' on the North Sea Bravo platform
        US Space Shuttle makes first test flight
        Death of Steve Biko in custody in South Africa

President Sadat of Egypt addresses Israeli Parliament
1977   Ayatollah Khomeini's supporters set up government in Iran (p. 77
        Ayatollah Khomeini's appearance at Well Plot)
        USA and USSR sign SALT II Treaty
        Soviet troops invade Afghanistan
1979   Famine in Cambodia (p. 33)
1980   State visit to Tunisia (p. 35)
1981   Robert Mugabe elected Prime Minister of independent Zimbabwe
        President Tito of Yugoslavia dies
        Special Air Service squad ends hostage crisis in the Iranian Embassy in
        London
        Olympic Games open in Moscow despite boycotts
        Polish workers strike – birth of *Solidarity*
        Ronald Reagan wins United States Presidential Election
1981   Greece joins the European Community
        'The Yorkshire Ripper' murderer arrested
        President Reagan shot
        Pope John Paul II shot in Rome
        Martial Law imposed in Poland
1982   Pope John Paul II visits Britain
        Princess Grace of Monaco killed in car crash
        Soviety leader Breznev dies

PEOPLE

Richard Lloyd Beeching 1913–1985 Chairman of the British Railways Board 1963–1965. Devised the now notorious Beeching Plan which resulted in a substantial contraction of the U.K. railway network (p. 16 The Maiden Newton Line)

Jacques Cousteau b.1910 French naval officer. Invented the Aqualung diving apparatus in 1943, and a process of underwater television (p. 25 Miss Bowyer and Jacques Cousteau)

Adge Cutler and the Wurzels (p. 8). Real name Alan John, born in Portishead, Somerset b.1930, road manager for Acker Bilk 1960, died in a road accident at a roundabout near the Severn Bridge in 1974. 'I thought a good roaring local pub song, that's what they want.' Bristol City Football Club adopted *Drink Up Thy Zider*, self-penned in 1966.

Germaine Greer b.1939 – Australian feminist, author and lecturer. 1970 *The Female Eunuch* (p. 18 Women's Lib.)

Parson Hawker of Morwenstowe in the eighteenth century invented Harvest Festival, buried Christian shipwrecked mariners in Christian fashion, and buried sinners under the church path to ensure they were perpetually trodden on, and echoed church design in his multiple chimneys. (Morwenna was the name given to the first Willmott daughter p. 68)

Ted Heath (wartime Commanding Officer over Army Chaplain Rev. Willmott) b.1916 One of R. A. Butler's 'One Nation' new Tory intellectuals. Chief negotiator for Britain's entry into the Common Market. Since 1979 he has become an increasingly outspoken critic of what he has regarded as the extreme policies of 'Thatcherism' (p. 9 Ted Heath and inflation)

Dame Barbara Hepworth 1903–1975 – 'one of the foremost nonfigurative sculptors of her time' (p. 31)

Francis Kilvert 1840–1879 English clergyman and diarist. Curate at Clyro in Radnorshire, and Vicar of Bredwardine on the River Wye. His diary of 1870–1879 was discovered in 1937 (pp. 42; 253)

Blaise Pascall, French mathematician, physicist, theologian and man-of-letters. By 11 he had worked out for himself the first 23 propositions of Euclid. 1669 *Pensées*: 'a casebook of Christian truths' (p. 10)

Egon Ronay. Before writing his first guidebook in 1956, Egon Ronay managed several prestigious London restaurants and wrote a weekly dining column in the *Daily Telegraph*. As his guidebook series expanded, Ronay also wrote a weekly column for the *London Evening News*, and in 1979 became the only non-French member of the Academie des Gastronomes. (p. 30 Of Snowdrops and Egon Ronay)

James Woodforde 1740–1803 Diarist. For 45 years Rector of Weston Longville, Norfolk. 'He concentrates on the daily minutiae of domestic and parish life. The diaries reflect no intellectual interests.' (pp. 38; 253)

ENTERTAINMENT

1968   Lionel Bart's film *Oliver*
1969   *Monty Python* first broadcast
        Midnight Cowboy
1970   Ted Hughes' poem *Crow*
        Butch Cassidy and the Sundance Kid
        Jimi Hendrix dies (p. 11 drug dealers and the fowl-house)
1971   Andy Warhol Exhibition at the Tate
        Kubrick *A Clockwork Orange*
1972   Lloyd Webber's musical *Jesus Christ, Superstar*
        Francis Ford Coppola's *The Godfather*
1973   Peter Shaffer's play *Equus*
        Deaths of W. H. Auden and Picasso
1974   Nobel Prizewinner Alexander Solzhenitsyn exiled from USSR
        David Hockney exhibition in Paris
1975   Charlie Chaplin dies
        Steven Spielberg's film *Jaws*
1976   National Theatre opens
        Deaths of Agatha Christie, Benjamin Britten and Paul Robeson
1977   Deaths of Bing Crosby (aged 70) and Elvis Presley (aged 42)
        George Lucas' film *Star Wars*

1978   Christopher Reeve in *Superman*
        John Travolta in *Grease*
1979   August 6th Death of Gracie Fields
        June 11th Death of John Wayne
        Peter Shaffer's film *Amadeus*
        Francis Ford Coppola's film *Apocalypse Now*
1981   Hugh Hudson's film *Chariots of Fire*
        Andrew Lloyd Webber's musical *Cats*
1982   Richard Attenborough's film *Gandhi*
        Steven Spielberg's film *ET*

THE CLERGY

1876–1883   Dr. Edersheim, Vicar of Loders – wrote erudite theological books about the Jews, and a forerunner of the *Parish Notes* (p. 42)
1905–1975   Cardinal Heenan The 'Radio Priest' on the BBC during the Second World War – a convinced ecumenical.
1961–1974   Arthur Ramsey, Archbishop of Canterbury
1974–1980   Frederick Donald Coggan, Archbishop of Canterbury
1980–1990   Robert Runcie, Archbishop of Canterury
1963–1972   Joseph Edward Fison, Bishop of Salisbury
1972–1981   George Edward Reindorp, Bishop of Salisbury
1960–1976   Victor Joseph Pike, Bishop of Sherborne
1976–   John Dudley Galtrey Kirkham, Bishop of Sherborne
1977   Archbishop of Uganda murdered by troops of Idi Amin
1978   August 6th Death of Pope Paul VI
             September 29th Death of Pope John Paul I